Under African Sun

Under African Sun

Marianne Alverson

The University of Chicago Press
Chicago and London

The University of Chicago Press, Chicago 60637
The University of Chicago Press, Ltd., London

© 1987 by The University of Chicago
All rights reserved. Published 1987
Paperback edition 1989
Printed in the United States of America

98 97 96 95 94 93 92 91 90 89   6 5 4 3 2

Library of Congress Cataloging in Publication Data

Alverson, Marianne.
  Under African sun.

  1. Tswana (African people)   2. Alverson, Hoyt,
1942–   3. Anthropologists—Biography.
4. Alverson, Marianne.   5. Anthropologists' wives—
Biography.   6. Botswana—Description and travel.
DT797.A45   1987   968.1'1   86-16474
ISBN 0–226–01623–4 (cloth)
ISBN 0–226–01624–2 (paper)

This book is dedicated to you, Keith and Brian,
that you may remember and live again
Tswana time and wisdom.

I returned and saw under the sun
that the race is not to the swift,
nor the battle to the strong,
neither yet bread to the wise,
nor riches to men of understanding
nor yet favour to men of skill;
but time and chance happeneth to
them all.

Ecclesiastes 9:11

Contents

Acknowledgments

Brenda Cooper, after reading several pages of my memoirs urged me to write a book. Her enthusiasm gave me the courage to pursue her suggestion. Three friends, Anna Penner, Debbie Hodges, and Kathy Swift, carefully read and commented on the entire first draft, and my friend, Keitumetse Matsewane, advised me on certain points of Setswana usage. John Hunter of New Brunswick, Canada, contributed his wit and wisdom to this book. Farmer, author, and Dartmouth English Professor Noel Perrin inspirited my enterprise. Professor Louise Kidder of Temple University gave me invaluable advice. Noel, Louise, as well as Professors John Middleton of Yale University and Michael Dorris of Dartmouth College encouraged me to seek publication. My work received a warm endorsement from Professor of Anthropology James Fernandez. My manuscript received sensitive, critical readings which strengthened it. I am very grateful to these friends and professionals.

My family was supportive of this project. My husband, Hoyt, helped me with the Glossary, the Note on the Setswana Language, and aspects of Setswana throughout the book. My son, Brian, created the kinship and homestead diagrams and map and consistently and calmly came to the rescue whenever, in the final stage of manuscript preparation, the computer had me tied up and screaming. My son, Keith, and my mother, Karin Melchior (Muschka), inspired me with their optimism.

I am thankful to our Tswana friends and neighbors including Beverly and Ellwyn Miller, now of Vernon, Vermont. *Ke a leboga, ke a leboga thata, bomma le borra* to Maria and Iphapeng Mosou, to

Miriam, Moremi, Phakalane, Polwane, Kgotlaitsile, and Thilinkane, to Lucy Botshomanyane and her family, and to Kireleng and Herbie Moloantoa. In the text, most names were changed to protect anonymity, but the name, Gustav Ernst Segatlhe, is authentic, and he remains our Tswana father and *madala*.

Village People,
Homesteads, and Map

Village People

Homestead 1

Rre Gustav Ernst Segatlhe   host and Tswana father of the Alverson family

Modise (Hoyt) ▲ ┬ ● MaoKeef (Marianne)

Tsotsi (Keith) ▲ ─────── ▲ Madala (Brian)

● MaMoremi   Rre Segatlhe's servant
▲ Moremi   Rre Segatlhe's goatherd and shepherd
● Morwadi   MaMoremi's married, 16-year-old daughter
▲ Deêpe   Morwadi's infant son
● Mpho   MaMoremi's 10-year-old daughter
● Leraka   MaMoremi's 8-year-old daughter
● Elina   MaMoremi's 4-year-old daughter
● The Old Woman   MaMoremi's mother
▲ Manaka   Re Segatlhe's goatherd and shepherd

Homestead 2

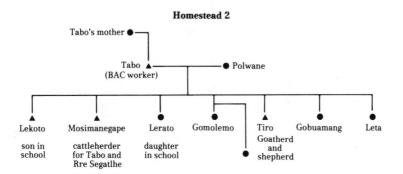

Tabo's mother ●

Tabo ▲ ────────── ● Polwane
(BAC worker)

▲ Lekoto	▲ Mosimanegape	● Lerato	● Gomolemo	▲ Tiro	● Gobuamang	● Leta
son in school	cattleherder for Tabo and Rre Segatlhe	daughter in school		● Goatherd and shepherd		

Homestead 3

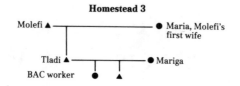

Molefi ▲ ———————————— ● Maria, Molefi's
                                    first wife

Tladi ▲ ——————— ● Mariga
BAC worker ● ▲

Homestead 4

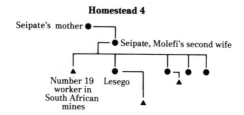

Seipate's mother ● ———
                      ● Seipate, Molefi's second wife

▲   ●   ● ▲ ●
Number 19   Lesego   ▲
worker in
South African
mines

Homestead 5

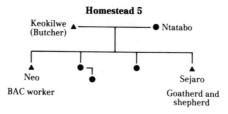

Keokilwe ▲ ———————————— ● Ntatabo
(Butcher)

▲   ● ▲   ●   ▲
Neo   ●   Sejaro

BAC worker   Goatherd and
                    shepherd

Homestead 6

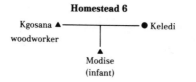

Kgosana ▲ ———————————— ● Keledi
woodworker
                   ▲
                Modise
                (infant)

People from Other Homesteads

Kabo and son	roof thatchers
Kerileng	Rre Segatlhe's niece from Johannesburg, South Africa
Mrs. Lydia Kgosietsile	Mochudi school teacher
Mother of Mrs. Kgosietsile	potter
Naledi	15-year-old daughter of Mrs. Kgosietsile
Maria Maloma	student in Maokeef's "bush school"
Molema	friend of Number 19, fellow mine worker
Montsho	sewer of hides, independent spirited artist and entertainer
Moses	cattleherder, boyfriend of Lesego
Joseph Pulanka	Tsotsi's schoolmate at the village school
Raus	adolescent street boy in Gaborone

Close-up of a Typical Homestead

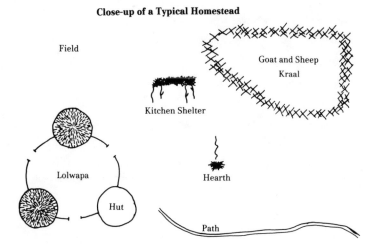

Crossroads and Sandpaths

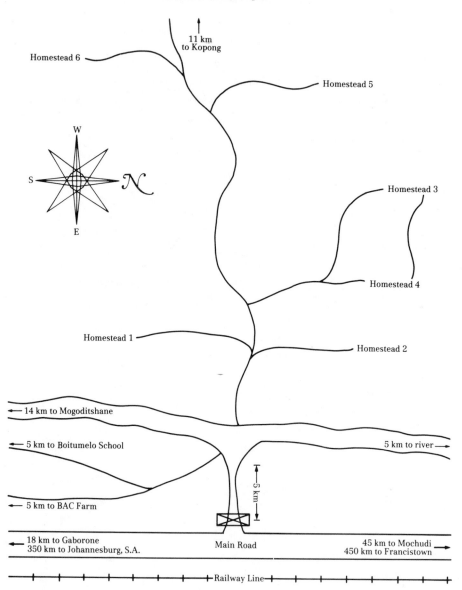

Under African Sun

"... but little is known or said about your Botswana." (Our hut in the left foreground, men sitting in the lolwapa, and Modise's bicycle leaning against our water supply.)

1

In the Iron Snake

Montsho, you would be impressed: I am not clutching a strap, nor am I squeezed and rocked on a wooden bench between the sweat and sound of others, I am alone on a cushioned seat taking tea at a table with white linen, a basket of breakfast buns, and shiny, little envelopes of sweet jelly. I am traveling in the iron snake, riding not to the bowels of the earth in South Africa, like Seipate's son, Number 19, but from one American city to another.

Look out the window, Montsho, and you see my America. Trees, higher than any giraffe, stand together so close that the ground is black in shadow. Here there are no sand paths to collect the sun, burn your feet, and lead you to your neighbors. Fields of firm, tall grasses blow idly in the breeze. Where are the women to pick the stalks and weave them into baskets? Where are the girls to chase birds from the grain? By the rail bed, you see clay holding yesterday's rain. What a rain! But look closely at the pool of water, Montsho: no animal tracks, no footprints encircle the edge of this dark liquid, where fat for cars paints blue rainbows on its surface. We pass many kinds of water. The gods are generous here. The iron snake crosses over water so abundant you need not pray for more.

The waiter comes to pour more tea and passes me little plastic cups filled with cream. If I use two of these cups, they will color my tea as did the drops we pumped out of Rre Segatlhe's reluctant goat. Montsho, you are probably sitting with Rre Segatlhe right now—that is, if the old man is still alive. Surely, the two of you are there on "the lands." Rain or no rain, nothing would entice you to leave. You are as much a part of Botswana's countryside as the acacia tree.

I picture the two of you seated by the hearth in the shade of the kitchen shelter, looking past the thorn bushes to the plowed field which is dry and wanting for rain. What would you say, were you here with me in this train approaching "a place of numbers," where hard, black roads connect houses, row after row, known only by the number at the doors? Rre Segatlhe knows the cities, he would not change expression. But you, Montsho, would look for the hearth in the yard of every house and wonder at the smoke and flames coming out of the uneven, concrete skyline. Rre Segatlhe would not exclaim or wonder in silence but would instruct us both, as is expected of an elder.

"Those people on the platform stand shoulder to shoulder, not face to face. When one joins the group, he does not greet the others, for they are something to walk around, like a post or trash can."

Trash cans are brimful with refuse, and still more goods are thrown by the wayside. The waiter brings my bill. He moves around my table to the next and folds the corners of the tablecloth up over plates of uneaten food and breakfast bun baskets: a feast for you, Montsho, to be swallowed by plastic garbage bags, which are twisted, tied, and tossed at the next station.

If at the next station, you were to enter this iron snake, following the right arm that leads you to your meals, you would join me here at the table. But would you recognize me, Montsho? Wearing suit and toting briefcase, I look like any other white one, "a *lekgoa* riding on her bottom to get from place to place." Look closely, Montsho, and you will recognize my face and grey-blue eyes, twelve years older.

Twelve years ago we met under African sun.

"Lekgoa with the long yellow hair, why are you here on the lands at Segatlhe's place?"

"I'm with my husband—whom you call *Modise*." In America, where we come from, he is a teacher, and we have come here as a family with our two small sons to learn from the people of Botswana about how it is to live here."

"Truly! You come from America. But you are living here at Segatlhe's place! You are not like the American *mavoluntiri* [Peace Corps Volunteers] I have seen on the roadside who carry their

4

clothes, like a baby, tied to their backs. You live here in the *lolwapa* like one of us, speak Setswana, and learn Tswana wisdoms from Segatlhe."

"And from you, Montsho."

"Ow! It is a very long way for a foot to travel to gather bits of wisdom. Did you cross the sea in the thing that flies?"

"No, we traveled slowly, by ship and then by train."

"Ow! You rode to Botswana in the iron snake from the sea through the place of the Boers to Botswana."

"*Ee*, through South Africa."

"South Africa is the place of the Boers and apartheid. This apartheid is a poisonous animal with skin pulled over its eyes so tightly that it cannot see Tswana wisdom. It's a good thing you have only passed through it and have come to Botswana where we do not separate people by color, where people are people. . . . The Tswana people across the border in South Africa are trapped in the hole of the Boers. They may see the rain fall on the field, but it is a field only for the lekgoa to eat from. In Botswana everyone drinks from the same puddle. You have come to the right place to find Tswana wisdom."

"*Ee*, Montsho."

"What do you hear about Botswana in your America?"

"Nothing."

"Nothing? Nothing at all?"

In the following moment of silence, my mind flashed to the "nothing." Maps of Africa remained in the closet of my schoolroom. As a youth my exposure to Africa was limited to fiction: Tarzan comics or stories of the fated hero rushing hopelessly across Sahara sands to collapse in a mirage. Films of famine and news reports from South Africa struck my consciousness, yet I continued to conceive of Africa distantly.

"It is good then," Montsho jolted me out of reverie, "you live here, collect our wisdoms, and when you go back to your America, tell them of our Tswana ways!"

Many years have passed since my husband, Hoyt, your *Modise*, the anthropologist has written the book on his fieldwork in Botswana. There is much talk of the poisonous animal living next door to you, but little is known or said about *your* Botswana. There is a great distance between us, and time speeds like the iron snake. But to you, Montsho, I am still *Maokeef* and my

5

teenage sons, Keith and Brian, are an eight-year-old *Tsotsi* and a three-year-old *Madala*. From this train window I see a vine and think of Maria's bougainvillea flowering scarlet in the sand and sharing dishwater with the pig. I am reminded of our arrival twelve years ago.

"Boloko is a treasured word."

2

The Lolwapa

Between the setting sun and a rising full moon, we ended our long journey to Botswana. After driving our loaded truck down the last narrow, winding, dirt road, we came to a *lolwapa:* three huts in a circle surrounded by a cracked, mud wall. A tree and some tall, spiny cacti bordering the goat *kraal* and fields rose above the straw rooftops to the sunset sky. The truck stopped. The dust settled. Except for a few birds, there was an immense silence as Hoyt and I and Keith and Brian walked through the mud walls into the courtyard. A man approached. His straw hat was the same shape and color as the thatched roofs of the huts. Over a white shirt suspenders stretched to hold up a pair of large, wool trousers. He walked straight and slowly toward us, his polished, worn, hobnailed boots thumping on the courtyard floor.

"*Dumela, Rra, o tlhotse jang?*" I heard Hoyt say. The Tswana handshake followed. The old man turned to me. I repeated my rehearsed Setswana greeting. To my surprise, he answered in English: "I am Gustav Ernst Segatlhe." He pulled up hand-hewn stools and chairs with seats of sparsely woven leather strips. In the twilight, the children and I listened to a mixture of Setswana and English as Hoyt and Rra Segatlhe exchanged bits of family histories.

Darkness never came. The brilliant moon, casting our shadows across the courtyard floor, shone on the old man's brown face. A small nose framed by wide eyes set far apart above his high cheekbones revealed his handsome youth. But for the few wrinkles that smiled with his eyes, his smooth, clear skin showed no signs of aging. It was his lack of teeth—or shall I say the few stumps remaining—which first indicated that he was a man of some years: a "*monna mogolo*," as the Tswana would say. It was the well-maintained, sparse, white beard on his chin that expressed the authority and wisdom of a true "monna mogolo."

"Courtyard—*lolwapa*," he said. "You must call it lolwapa and care for it well."

"*Ee*, Rra Segatlhe," I replied.

"*Rra* is for other men," he corrected. "You will be my children. I will be *your* father. You must say *Rre* Segatlhe to me. I am your Rre Segatlhe," he emphasized.

"*Rre* Segatlhe," we repeated in unison.

Silence; an immense nighttime sky; a moon fuller than I ever knew it could be—I was overwhelmed with a sense of peace. We took only blankets off the truck that night. There would be time tomorrow to unpack and organize.

Even though I heard the roosters crow, I rolled over to sleep again. It was a different sound that woke us for the day: a din of human voices. Curious to know the source of the apparent commotion, Hoyt, the boys, and I dressed hurriedly and stumbled out into the sunlight of the lolwapa. A crowd of stares met my glances. Hoyt stepped forward to a gathering of men, greeting them and shaking hands. Brian, lured by what was probably the sandbox of his dreams, toddled off past the women to the dust outside the lolwapa walls. Bare-legged, barefoot boys with shirts and shorts that hung like rags moved in around Keith until he disappeared from my sight. I stood there, blinded by the sun and bewildered. We were on display. Facing me, a crowd of women tittered, laughed, and gawked.

I could just stand there and wait for them to go; or I could try the Setswana greeting—but to whom should I go first? Frantically, I groped around for some sort of strategy, all the while feeling I was the butt of each cackle, every glare, and every pointed finger. "Hoyt should help," I thought. "He got me into this. He is the anthropologist. He must know what all this means. He should have warned me . . . explained this." The should-haves led me nowhere. I couldn't appeal to him for help. He did not look particularly comfortable either there amidst the men pouring and passing a gourd filled with a seemingly coveted brown liquid. He took his turn, but his grin was obviously one more of relief than of pleasure.

"And where is my newly adopted, calm, kind father? This Rre Segatlhe? He knows English. . . . Why doesn't he help me?"

I spotted him at the far end of the lolwapa sitting on the same seats we had sat on the previous night, but this time, he was with a small group of elders passing and drinking that same brown liquid out of an old mayonnaise jar.

"Should I smile? That's safe." I smiled.

Gathering from all areas of the lolwapa and crowding closer together, the women surged toward me. I tried to turn myself into a spectator. I could be removed, merely watching this strange, exotic, African ballet.

Long skirts caught the dust raised by stomping bare feet. With their arms held high beside their heads, the women clapped left then right. From their swaying unison, an old woman stepped out. The ankle-length skirt matched her wrapped, blue, head scarf. Suddenly she raised her arms. She darted straight toward me, shaking her open hands back and forth. Her fingers fluttered wildly; her pink tongue rolled furiously, ululating a piercing trill. She charged aggressively into my space. A breath away, her shrieking tongue and flapping hands blurred my vision and deafened my ears. I stood there, stupefied, as she circled me again and again like a vulture. I froze in terror until, to my great relief, she retreated to her group. The dance wound down. The clapping chorus faded.

To smile after a perceived assault is difficult. My efforts surely were not convincing. Enough. I could not cope. The women settled down on the lolwapa floor, and I stepped away from them. I withdrew to what little of my own world was left and mechanically took to the task of unloading the truck to set up our "home."

This task could hardly render consolation. The straw mattresses which we had tied on top of the truck were covered with fine, red dust. The plastic sheets we had used to cover them were thoroughly ripped. Three of the metal bedframes set up easily, but the fourth was badly rusted and hopelessly stuck. I unpacked the box of used camping gear which had been loaned to us by the Anthropology Department at the University of Witwatersrand in South Africa: aluminum pots which rocked on any surface, candleholders with globs of wax drippings, scratched plastic plates, and enamelware mugs stained with years of coffee. I set up the small metal folding table inside the hut and rummaged desperately through the disarray of boxes to find a cloth for it. A cloth on the table and four chairs around it: that would be home! The floor was just dried mud; I would deal with that later. I carried the clutter from the truck into the hut. No closets, of course; the suitcases would hold the clothes and, at the same time, support the sagging bedframes. I tried it out by shoving my suitcase under a bed and sitting down.

Keith and Brian rushed in to remind me that they were hungry. The people had left, they said, and "Daddy said we could eat now." Hoyt filled the one-burner stove with kerosene. He looked as lost as I felt. We didn't admit anything to each other. "This brass Primus stove actually has some shine to it," Hoyt said. "Big deal," I thought, but opened the can in silence. Hoyt worked on the rusted bedframe.

"What's for dinner?" Keith didn't wait for a response. He rushed right on with exuberance. "This is really going to be fun!" "Join the Boy Scouts," I thought while stirring the beans.

"Sure it is," I answered. What was I doing here? I wanted to cry, and Hoyt, I'm sure, had his misgivings. The glowing moon and stars and the silence of the night soothed us, but the chaos of our leap from twentieth-century urban life to rural Tswana existence whirled restlessly in my dreams that night.

The next morning, she—the vulture—returned. Rre Segatlhe announced her arrival. "It is Maria Mosou," he said to me. She followed a few paces behind her husband as they entered our lolwapa. I recognized her blue scarf and faded skirt. She had seemed to tower over me the day before, but now I noticed that she was actually a small woman, so slender and so old that bones protruded from her joints and deep-set wrinkles framed her eyes. Rre Segatlhe greeted her husband, Molefi, but Maria headed straight for me. I felt her eyes, and although this time she moved slowly, I stiffened, anticipating some strange encounter. She approached me with a red hen in her arms, and just as she passed it on into mine, Rre Segatlhe stood by me explaining *"ke mpho"* [It is a gift].

I could have feasted on her smile, but the warm body and feathers now wriggling in my arms sought escape. As I wrestled to clutch it tighter, Rre Segatlhe grabbed its feet. Slinging the bird upside down, he carried it to the hearth outside the lolwapa. In a quick circular motion, he swept the hen's beak in the cool ashes and threw the bird in a nearby tree.

"It must sleep in the tree to be safe at night," Rre Segatlhe explained.

"The center of home is the ashes of your cooking fire. That is for the hen to know," he said, all the while staring straight at me.

Thus, my hen found its roosting place, and I, full of gratitude, asked Maria and Molefi to share our midday meal. We sat eating every morsel of cherished food. It was clear to me now that the day before had been a public welcome and Maria's dance its most powerful display. Her rolling tongue was a ululation of joy. Determined to make up for my perplexed, unresponsive presence of yesterday, I now repeatedly broke the silence with my Setswana thanks, *"ke itumetse thata. Ke itumetse thata."*

By the end of the day the little table in our hut displayed the gifts brought one by one by our neighbors and visitors: a clay pot, painted red; a handmade wire basket; a *"motse"* and *"kika"* fashioned out of Morula wood to stomp grain; and fresh eggs.

Rre Segatlhe was careful not only to introduce each woman to me as she arrived but also to point out which sandpath led to her lolwapa.

"Take the sandpath toward the sunset, and in front of Maria's hut, take the path *moja*, at your eating hand [the right]; go to the first path *molema*, at your plowing hand [the left], and you will find her lolwapa."

Since my introductions to the men were more perfunctory, I sensed that my relationships with the women would somehow be significant.

"*Ke* [Here is] Ntatabo," Rre Segatlhe announced as I watched another woman saunter down the sandpath to our place. Her bony feet scraped the lolwapa floor as she approached us. I could smell the sweat that stained the two torn dresses which covered her round body and hung to her thick, scaly ankles. Her handshake, rough and firm, diverted my attention from bloodshot eyes to the heavy jaw and random teeth smiling at me. As I repeatedly shook hands, face to face, my Setswana greeting felt less like abstract sounds and more like meaningful utterances.

Ntatabo triumphantly presented me with a Tswana broom for the lolwapa. She had made it from a bundle of *bojang* [a high, reedlike grass used also for thatching]; it was firmly woven and tied together at the grasping end. She showed me how to sweep by bending at the waist and using a broad, low sweeping motion to take advantage of the full arm-length of the broom. The loose dust flew out of the lolwapa through the closest mud-wall entrance. I had thought three entrances to be ornamental, but now the practical purpose was quite apparent as she swiftly moved from one-third of the floor surface and its entrance to the other. With superbly efficient motions, she finished the job and then straightened up to pass me her gift, my new broom, my *"lefeelo."*

At sunset, Ntatabo, Rre Segatlhe, Hoyt, and I sat passing and sipping *"kadi."* Rre Segatlhe told us how to make it.

Kadi is a homemade brown liquid beer derived from the kadi root. The kadi plant thrives in a desert climate and is, therefore, abundant when nothing else can be harvested. Even though *"bojalwa"* beer is universally preferred, its production is dependent on the sorghum harvest, ever linked to *"pula"* [rainfall] and *"Modimo's"* will. Kadi, however, has the unique status of being the reliable, year-round beer. The large, round kadi root is dug up, broken into many pieces, then dried for several days in the sun on the lolwapa floor. The brittle, bleached pieces are added to a boiling mixture of brown sugar and water to cook. The liquid is poured into a clay pot, covered with burlap, and left to ferment for a few days.

As in our own society, there was pressure to drink at social gatherings. Nevertheless, I could not be optimistic about acquiring a taste for kadi. I took the gourd passed to me, let the rim touch my lips, and swallowed air, all the while trying to beam with satisfaction.

We sat around the hearth to greet visitors one by one: a firm Tswana handshake with a *"Dumela, Rra"* or a *"Dumela, Mma,"* followed by *"O tsogile jang?"* They smiled to hear me say it and repeated the greeting for me again. Rre Segatlhe passed the kadi. My earlier fears and frustrations were gone. At ease among them, their gifts in my lap, I felt accepted. I could now comfortably enjoy the sights and sounds which would become a part of our every day.

Life is simple here. To the east, the rising sun filters through a small forest of moshu trees. Rre Segatlhe rises to start the fire with wood collected the day before. He heats a bit of water to wash and puts a three-legged pot on for tea. Nearby, the cat and a stray dog lie lethargically, like skeletons, in the sand. While I sweep, the roosters and hens, down from their tree, cluck about the yard and lolwapa, scrounging up a diet of insects and worms. The pig grunts constantly in search of food.

This morning, as Hoyt stooped over the washpan in the lolwapa with his face buried in a washcloth, the pig victoriously took off with a whole cake of soap. Rre Segatlhe laughed as Hoyt took chase, remarking that we needn't worry, for in the end, justice would be done. He showed us long bars of soap he had made of an earlier pig's fat.

Each day defines itself. People come and we go on the winding sandpaths between kraal and field nestled in thorn trees. As the sun lowers and the goats and sheep are returned to their kraal, I know it is time to set the fire to cook. We pause to sit on the wall, still warm from the day's glow and now reflecting the light of the fading sun. We face Rre Segatlhe's field to the west which, along with a single, distant mountain, is our backdrop to each day's end.

Some weeks after our arrival, Rre Segatlhe announced he had hired a woman to make kadi and to plant and harvest beans when it is time. Her son, Moremi, will herd the goats, he said. They are destitute, and since Rre Segatlhe has no wife and family living with him, he must often hire help. In exchange for their labor, he will house and feed them. Keith will be expected to help Moremi with the animals. I certainly look forward to female help and companionship, for I can already detect that "women's work" in Tswana society goes far beyond maintaining the lolwapa. Besides childcare, usually delegated to older siblings, I have seen women sweep and smear floors. Just why or what they smear I do not know. Women build walls, collect firewood and water, cook, wash, and plant and harvest the fields as well.

"What does that leave for men to do?" I ask Rre Segatlhe.

"They send their sons to keep cattle, plow, and of course, 'take the news' over a good, strong sip of kadi!" he replies, tolerantly grinning at my curious presumption of equality.

She, MaMoremi, arrived at midday, her son following closely behind. Tall and straight, she greeted Rre Segatlhe and removed a bundle from her head. The boy looked on, and when Rre Segatlhe turned to him, he extended his hand to the old man, mumbled a greeting, and settled himself in a shaded spot of the lolwapa floor. One bony shoulder protruded from the hole in his shirt. He folded his slender legs to sit small and inconspicuously in the shadow. Rre Segatlhe led her to the hut where they are to sleep. He returned to his chair and did not introduce us until she emerged from the hut without her load.

She has a smooth face; her gaze is distant, her handshake, flaccid. I think she is about my age. She speaks a few solemn words in deep tones and withdraws. I pretend to understand with a casual nod of the head and the usual word for agreement, *"ee."* Quietly she moves about the lolwapa, stacks sticks upon the hearth, and brushes Rre Segatlhe's boots. Here is my closest female companion, MaMoremi.

Poverty surrounds us. We have brought what we considered basic essentials. So as not to be glaringly different, we are restricting ourselves to a minimum of gear. Now unpacked and set up, our *rondavel* hut contains a small red linoleum rug at the entrance, one metal folding table with two one-burner, paraffin campstoves, and another metal table with a set of plastic dishes, enamelware cups, and assorted pots filled with eating and cooking utensils. The bedding and straw mattresses, already shaped to match the contours of our sleep, sag down to the suitcase-wardrobes underneath the bedframes. Lined up along one wall are three rusted Boer War remnants discovered enroute through South Africa in a secondhand shop. They are ammunition boxes now filled with a feast of dried and canned goods. On top of them are a first-aid kit, a sewing box, a paraffin lantern, candles, and two flashlights. On the wall facing the entrance—a wooden, swinging door—I've hung our tablecloth, a piece of Tswana material, for a touch of home.

Outside the hut, under its roof, are three 20-liter plastic water jugs, one paraffin container, and a metal washbasin. In the center of the lolwapa Rre Segatlhe keeps the four kitchen chairs. Their aluminum legs sparkle in the sun, and Rre Segatlhe, although preferring to sit on the hides of his own chairs, will pull up the blue plastic seats for his most honored visitors.

Outside the lolwapa walls, we have one 200-liter water drum, two bicycles, and a small, blue Mazda pickup truck. In the field, a green canvas cloth, supported on either side by poles, hides our chemical toilet. We have brought a minimum of clothing; certainly nothing valuable, and the children have no toys other than a few books, paper, pencils, and scissors.

And, meanwhile, in the rondavel next to ours, MaMoremi and her son, Moremi, sleep on torn burlap bags near the grain that Rre Segatlhe has stored. They have flattened cardboard boxes to use for cover on cold nights. Their possessions, neatly stacked on the dirt floor, include a sweater, a shirt, one cup and plate to share, and an ink bottle with paraffin and wick. Like most of our neighbors, they eat with their hands, and the soles of their feet are like those we see daily shuffling into the lolwapa. With nerves blunted by a lifetime of thorns, the pads are encrusted with dust and callouses.

Rre Segatlhe's and a few other homesteads have beds, a chair or two, iron pots, some dishes, perhaps a pair of shoes and change of clothes, a table, and possibly a radio or a bicycle. But no one owns a car. Our mini-truck Mazda is a sign of wealth, bourgeois town life, and *makgoa* [white] "fat stomachs" (Rre Segatlhe's designation). We are white—the only ones ever to live in this community, and it will be our task to establish an identity as individuals distinct from the stereotype of makgoa.

An old woman, Seipate, visits me often. She comes with a three-inch thorn stuck between her teeth and doesn't remove it when she speaks. Unlike Rre Segatlhe, her speech is quick and clipped. I try to make the most of the few words that come through, and to the rest I utter *"ee"* to appear to understand.

She is content to sit on the lolwapa floor in silence when the conversation wanes. I am not. Scraping her teeth with her "toothpick," she looks out to the horizon, squinting her small eyes in the sunlight. I try again to engage her with a phrase Rre Segatlhe taught me the night before. She looks at me, cocks her head, and screws up her wrinkled face. She shakes her head and returns to her teeth, rolling the toothpick about with her tongue. I still have the attention of her eyes until she claps her hands and shrugs her shoulders with a slow, melodic sigh. While I am to sit with her, my elder, and be content, she returns to her far-off gaze.

But tonight after the sigh, her final resignation of our failure to communicate, I left her side to fetch our only bottle of wine. The men were not home. I poured the dark red liquid into two tin cups, and she, watching, smiled so broadly that the toothpick fell out. We applauded with laughter, and I poured on.

Together we polished off the bottle. Although somewhat slurred, Seipate's speech slowed down, and I, relaxed and reeling, did not notice until later that I had participated in my first, fluent Setswana conversation! It's too bad that I cannot abide the taste of kadi.

"Seipate," Hoyt tells me, means "don't hide yourself." Often names recall events or conditions that occurred near the time of birth. In Seipate's case, her father disappeared just before her birth. She is also called MaLesego after her daughter, Lesego. Just as men can be called by the name of their first son, women are often called by the name of their first daughter. There are times, however, when women take the name of their son. Since MaMoremi only has her son, Moremi, living here, she has taken

17

his name instead of her daughter's, and I, who have no daughter, am Maokeef (they do not pronounce the "th" in Keith). Hoyt, also RaoKeef, has taken on a Tswana name, Modise, which means shepherd. Many names have meaning: Moremi—hewer of wood; Kerileng—what I said; Lekoto—leg or wheel; Mosimanegape—another boy; Tiro—work; Polwane—mud wall; Montsho—black one; Keokilwe—I have been cared for; Tabo—joy; Sejaro—obstinate; Mpho—gift; Ntatabo—their father. Ntatabo is a woman, and a man living nearby has the same name. Although division of labor and social patterns are determined by sex, it is interesting to me that most names have no gender connotation whatsoever.

MaMoremi and I sweep together, and while I cook the morning mealies (a porridge of ground maize), she makes tea and milks a goat. If she is lucky, she can just get enough to color our tea. But this morning she is gone until after breakfast. She returns with a bucket on her head. Leafy branches float on top of the water to minimize splashing as she moves along. I remember spending days of my youth trying to balance books and competing with friends to see who could stack the most. But unlike Tswana girls, we were playing only an occasional game. Here young girls practice balancing things on their heads as soon as they have learned to walk, and certainly, by the time they are five or six years old, they can comfortably carry a bundle of sticks or a sack of mealie.

When MaMoremi sets down her load on the lolwapa floor, I cannot resist lifting it just to feel the weight. She smiles at my grimace as I struggle to lift the bucket up near my head. She reaches for the empty bucket on the stoop nearby and passes it to me. I take up the challenge and fail. She strokes my head and shakes her head. Yes, my slippery strands cannot grip as well as her kinky hair. She gives me a piece of cloth which she has wound to size and sets it upon my head to help support the bucket. This time I am cautious enough to stand still with the bucket well balanced before moving. Slowly, I step out, and after a few steps, while it still looks pretty good, I remove the bucket and place it back on the floor. Applause breaks out. I turn to see Rre Segatlhe and two other men praising my efforts.

"Modise! Modise! they call to Hoyt. *"Ruri, ke mosadi wa Setswana!"* [Truly, she is a Tswana woman!]

Hoyt tells me there are various water sources, but all are far if you consider the weight of a bucket on your head. During the rainy season, from November through April, Mosou's dam, two kilometers away and usually just a sand river, does collect some water. After heavy rains deep puddles accumulate on the dirt roads. Rivers, dams, and puddles are the common sources of water, even though a number of bacteria thrive in them. I do not think people here associate the risks of their water supply with the diseases and deaths they suffer. They take no precautions. Just boiling the water before drinking it could prevent many common and sometimes fatal illnesses: gastroenteritis, dysentery, typhoid, and bilharzia.

The dry season is upon us. People rely on the well of the BAC (Botswana Agricultural College) four kilometers away, or if they can pay the minimal fee, they use the pump at a lekgoa farm just three kilometers north.

I was worried about our dwindling water supply until Hoyt returned home from a trip to town with news. He had met a Vermont farmer!

"How did you know he was from Vermont?"

"He was wearing those green overalls and a Sears & Roebuck shirt. His name is Ellwyn Miller. He and his wife, both in their sixties, are living as Peace Corps volunteers in the BAC. He offered to let us use their water and garden hose to fill up our water drum. But that's not all. He offered to let us use their bathroom for showers!"

Glory! I was ready to go right away and headed for the hut in pursuit of towels when a car drove up.

The sound of a motor is an event: a car, a most significant arrival. We all stopped and turned and looked at the TJ license plate: Transvaal, Johannesburg, South Africa. Rre Segatlhe tucked in his shirt, lifted his suspenders, and rose. Hoyt immediately recognized Kerileng, the woman who tutored him in Setswana during our two-month preparation stay in South Africa. Rre Segatlhe greeted Kerileng, his niece.

It was good, Rre Segatlhe told her, that she had sent the American family to live with him. Yes, Hoyt agreed. Everything had turned out very well. My clipped concurrence lacked enthusiasm. Kerileng looked at my eyes, fixed on her clean summer dress, nylons, and dust-free shoes. She smiled knowingly and unwrapped a parcel of brown paper. She held a dress made of brown Tswana cloth up to my shoulders.

"I hope it fits," she fussed, while Rre Segatlhe expressed his pleasure—"*Oo loo loo!*" It was not exactly what I would define as the height of fashion, yet Rre Segatlhe's continued *"oo loo loo"* and Kerileng's proud confirmation of her selection left me no choice but to be absolutely delighted with my new Tswana dress.

"It has an apron to match," she continued. "You will look like a real Tswana woman," she said.

Indeed, Kerileng was determined to make a Tswana woman out of me.

The next day she had a lesson plan.

"You must learn *go dila boloko*," she insisted.

"What is it?" I asked.

"Do you see that the lolwapa floor is hard like cement? We can just sweep the loose dust and dirt out of the lolwapa walls, and there is a good clean floor!"

"But do you see here," she showed me, "places where the floor is broken up and loose like the sand outside? This happens: children play and dance, chairs scrape, Rre Segatlhe pounds nails into his goat skins. You must fix this floor so it will be smooth and hard again."

"How?" I asked.

"You smear it with a fresh mixture and after it dries in the hot sun, it will be hard."

"How often do I have to smear it?"

"You have many using this lolwapa. Maybe you will have to do it once every month."

"What do I smear it with?"

"With the fresh mixture—come, I'll show you."

She grabbed a bucket and led me to the fields. "There is a very good place down this path—here where Tabo keeps his cattle."

Ugh, I could see it coming. She diligently bent down and scooped up cow dung to throw into the bucket. I stood stiffly at her side, looked into the horizon, and tried to forget where I was.

"This layer here is nice and fresh," she chirped, "and there is plenty for you to use later on. We can go back to the lolwapa to mix."

"Back to the lolwapa—fine!" I replied.

I stood in the lolwapa. Kerileng set the pan of wet cow manure and clay dust at my feet. "Come, let us get started," she commanded.

"Uuh . . . what now?"

She poured water into the manure and mixed it with her

hands. Scooping up a palmful and using circular motions, she quickly spread it and smeared it over an area of the lolwapa floor.

" . . . can't just stand here . . . gotta get down there next to her and get it over with," I thought.

Assuming there would be a stench and distorting my face, I went down on my knees, propped myself up with my left hand, and dove my right into the pan. I threw a blob onto the floor and spread it out. She started to sing.

The hot sun dries it as it spreads, I noticed; better sprinkle water on as I work to keep it smooth . . . and then the sudden recognition: there is no smell!

Relaxed, I worked on. My mixture was too thick.

The trick is to work wet and thin, and in the process of scraping off the last excess layer, make a bold design to dry in place.

She worked fast and left a good design. As I was just beginning to enjoy my quest for a good pattern, for some reason, my mind flashed back to a tennis court: the ladies, in their whites, having finished a set, were just sipping cold lemonade through straws.

"Unbelievable! I am happy here and now smearing shit!"

MaMoremi joined us. I tried to follow their song. MaMoremi asked me in Setswana what we call *boloko* in America.

"Cow manure."

She tried, but couldn't pronounce it. She asked again.

"Dung."

She tried again without success.

"Shit!" I yelled impatiently.

"Shit . . . shit . . . shit," she repeated proudly, for boloko is a treasured word.

I had feared the smell of boloko and found there was none. Was it because of the diet of the cattle or the effects of the hot sun? I did not question my own sense of smell. There were, after all, daily smells difficult to tolerate.

French royalty had their perfumes and powders. At the onset of puberty and through adulthood, we have Madison Avenue working for us. All this is as far away as the tennis courts.

There is a certain strong, acrid smell impossible to ignore. It is by far the worst odor around here: body odor. I think it is caused by sweating into dirty clothes which then absorb the smoke of the evening fire. Nevertheless, we sit close together and pass the kadi, and in the process, we have managed to get used to the smell of human poverty.

Hoyt speculates that this is perhaps because we have not yet had our showers. After his next anthropological rounds, he assures us, we will all grab towels and soap and drive off to the Millers' bathroom at the BAC.

As promised, we drove from the kraal to the suburban community of the BAC. The Botswana Agricultural College is one of many government agencies staffed by foreign "experts" from various Western countries. They have two- to five-year contracts to work within the government and help achieve Botswana's national "progress." Whereas most of the government agencies are centered in the capital, Gaborone, the Agricultural College offices are located outside of town near the experimental fields. Those expatriates working for the College are housed directly on the premises. It is a fenced-in area with two main roads. Each house has its own fence with *Tsaba Ntsha* [Beware of Dog] on almost every gate. It has a driveway and garage, a well-manicured lawn with flowers, servant's quarters, and perhaps a swimming pool.

Even from the front of their house, the Millers' habitation looked unique. The gate was open, the garden overgrown. There were no servants. The Millers were not at home, yet the front door was unlocked. Mr. Miller had assured Hoyt that we could come in to shower any time. We did not hesitate.

Squeaky clean! While waiting for the family, I sat in the sun of the Millers' backyard, looking over the fence at the neighbor. She sat in the shade in a light summer dress, reclining on a lawn chair. On a round table set with ironed linen, the maid set down two glasses of iced drinks. A toddler splashed in a flowered plastic pool on the lawn strewn with plastic toys.

We drove back to Rre Segatlhe.

Brian is playing with sticks in the dust. He is still afraid of the pig, and when it snorts near him, he runs into the lolwapa to grab my knees. Keith and Moremi are just coming back across the field with the goats. The sun is low—my signal to start supper. I am just about to get up when Rre Segatlhe puts his hand on my knee. We sit alone together in the lolwapa.

"*Ke monna mogolo.*" [I am the old man].

"*Ee, Rre Segatlhe. Ke a itse sentle*" [Yes, I know it well].

In Setswana he tells me that he has watched me closely. I cannot get every detail, but understand his message: I work as a Tswana woman, and since he has no wife living with him, I am to be the "*mosadi mogolo*" [old woman].

"*Ke itumetse thata, Rra. Ke mosadi mogolo*" [I am very thankful, sir. I am the old woman].

I am sure this is an honor—just why, I am not yet certain. "*Ke mosadi mogolo.*"

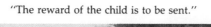
"The reward of the child is to be sent."

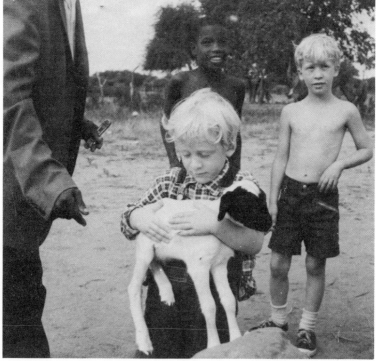

3

Toward Manhood

Keith and Moremi disappear in the late mornings to take the goats and sheep to pasture. Moremi, at thirteen, is small for his age, and the five-year age difference between them is barely visible. Both boys, curious about each other's worlds, are beginning to communicate despite the language barrier.

When Moremi finally got up the courage to stroke Keith's T-shirt and smile, Keith, suddenly aware of the rag on Moremi's shoulders, responded by replacing it with a shirt of his own. Clad in his new T–shirt, Moremi puffed out his chest and spun himself around. Laughing, they ran off to the goat kraal. I could hear their voices above the goats and sheep now maaing and pushing their way through the kraal door for the freedom of the fields. Their voices faded. Sticks in hand, they walked slowly far out into the distance—two boys, one dark, one light; two brightly-striped T-shirts moving within and around the grazing herd.

Convinced that the transition to a different language and culture is less complicated for a child, and also observing, with perhaps some degree of envy, the ease and spontaneity between the boys, I was not prepared for Keith's glum face upon his return. He ate his supper in silence, but just as I came to bid him good-night at his bedside, his eyes filled with tears. Bewildered, I cradled him, while he heaved with sobs and tried to get out the words.

"Moremi is . . . cruel . . . to the goats. He wouldn't let the limping goat stay in the kraal. He pushed it out. He made it go on. I tried to stop him. He laughed. He beat it. He kept the baby goat away from its *own* mother. It wanted to drink. He wouldn't let it. *Why* is he so mean? He never pets them."

As I was just about to launch into a soothing discourse on "let's try to understand Moremi," he interrupted.

"And the goats don't even have names, like in *Heidi*!"

The curtain lifted. *Heidi*! Yes, he had read it and loved it, and here was his chance to love and protect the goats! Amazed, I listened to him tell of the various goat families. He shared the minute details he had so keenly discovered. But before he fell back on his pillow to sleep, I tried to tell him just what I've been trying to tell myself these past days.

"Keith. We're in another place, another time. It is not like home where we have animals as pets to feed and cuddle, to take to the vet or enter in a show. It is not like Heidi's Alps where the goats' creamy milk keeps the children's cheeks rosy. I don't know *why* Moremi acts this way. Stay with him. Watch him. Try not to judge him. See if you can find out why. Maybe there *is* a reason that isn't cruel. And if you learn something new, tell me, because I would like to understand it with you."

He was asleep, and I continued to talk across the dark corner of the hut.

Rre Segatlhe looked rather disgruntled the next morning when MaMoremi's old mother and MaMoremi's three daughters pitched up, blanket roll in hand. They tossed their things in the storage hut, thus indicating that they would sleep in the crowded space already occupied by MaMoremi and Moremi.

There is a family resemblance, although Rre Segatlhe claims to know that each child is of a different father. They are all dark brown, tall, and very slender, and both MaMoremi and her mother have the same stately walk and graceful movements.

MaMoremi told me of her family. Her oldest daughter, six-teen-year-old Morwadi, is married to a man in town with a job. They have an infant son, Deêpe. Three other daughters, Mpho, ten; Leraka, eight; and Elina, four; live with her mother in "Old Naledi," a poor, squatter's section of town. With no husband to help, MaMoremi and her mother must support the growing family. Sources of income are limited, and lacking formal education, they are not employable in town. Since they speak no English, they cannot work as domestic servants. While Ma-Moremi and her only son, Moremi, have hired themselves out to Rre Segatlhe, her mother brews beer for various households in Old Naledi. A jar of kadi is sold for five cents; she receives a small brewing fee per jar sold. Particularly skilled in the art of smearing floors and building decorative walls, she can also earn a certain amount after the rainy season when many households may need help rebuilding.

Upon arrival, the old woman greeted me with a poetic flourish that I could not totally understand. In conclusion, she stated, "I have no gift to give you, woman of America, except the gift of my hands."

She held up her large, knotted hands for me to see. She shook them and stretched them to the sky, and within minutes, she was at our doorstoop with boloko making a beautiful pattern.

Rre Segatlhe, to make sure no one was idle, sent MaMoremi, Mpho, and Leraka to fetch water to brew more kadi. Brian and Elina found each other. Chasing squawking chickens with sticks and squealing with delight, they ran off, and Rre Segatlhe pulled me aside for a serious talk.

He spoke in Setswana, slowly and clearly, repeating words as he studied my face. It was time, he said, to honor our arrival. That night he would choose the goat. The next day it would be slaughtered for a feast. I think he described the details of the coming slaughter to calm my furrowed brow. It, of course, had the opposite effect. My hasty response, which went something like, "Oh, you needn't do *such* a thing for us!" met with his patient smile. The next day would be a day of great honor, a day of great joy, he repeated. I managed to thank him, although I know he read my anxious face with some puzzlement.

Hoyt entered the lolwapa.

"Modise!" Rre Segatlhe called out to him. I rushed over to Hoyt as he headed for the old man.

"Hoyt, he's going to slaughter a goat for us tomorrow. You've got to stop him!" I pleaded. Hoyt, who spent half of his youth on a Virginia farm, was delighted by the news. He went to sit with the old man, and they passed the kadi. Hoyt must have explained my sentiments, for when Rre Segatlhe finally got up from his chair, he came to me. He patted my shoulder and said that if I did not want to watch the slaughter, I could stay in the hut. There would be many other feasts that I would enjoy properly. He assured me that when I cooked the meat and served it and tasted it, I would come to know the honor that he had bestowed on us.

I closed the wooden door and the shutters of the two small windows of our hut. Sunlight streamed in through the cracks anyhow. Brian and I were not huddled in darkness, but in the relief of shade, well isolated from the festivities outside. To three-year-old Brian, it seemed like a good time to play games alone with Mama, but my lack of enterprise and attention surely disappointed him. As he proudly arranged food cans to size and stacked them on the floor, I mechanically acknowledged his efforts while my mind was elsewhere.

Keith had refused to join us. With disbelief, I heard his proud voice tell me that today was the day of slaughter. I did not believe he knew what he was saying!

"Rre Segatlhe says Keokilwe is the best man for slaughter in the whole village, Mom. Rre Segatlhe sent for Keokilwe, and he tapped *me* on the shoulder to help him. He only asked Lekoto, Moremi, and me. Rre Segatlhe says it is a man's job. I am to hold a leg down. Moremi gets to do the other leg and . . ."

Was this the child that cried in my arms?

At this point our neighbors, Tabo, Polwane, and their seven children, entered the lolwapa. They approached me. Moremi stood waiting behind Keith as he urged me to understand. I wanted to be alone with my son. MaMoremi poured kadi for the laughing voices seated by a nearby wall, while from the kraal, Rre Segatlhe and Hoyt walked with Keokilwe as he dragged the goat toward a tree. Our neighbors now faced me: tall Tabo smiling kindly and Polwane, seemingly half his size, shyly at his side. I wanted to be alone with my son.

Keith and Moremi ran toward the men, pulling the goat. Tabo greeted me, as did his eldest son, Lekoto, who announced that he would help with the goat. Tabo smiled proudly, and they left— father and son. His wife, Polwane, greeted me in a voice barely audible, but as she instructed the seven children lined up behind her to step forward, she broke out in a full, rolling Tswana voice.

"Mosimanegape—he is my second son and the herder of our cattle! Lerato—she is my oldest daughter, going to school each morning with Lekoto. And here is Tiro!—you must know him because he herds the goats and sheep with your son and Ntatabo's son, Sejaro, and with Moremi!" The children were quick to disappear after each introduction, and in conclusion, Polwane passed me a melon. Melon had been their food for the last three months, she said, melon and mealie.

"*Gompieno, re tla ja nama!*" [Today we will eat meat!] she exclaimed joyfully.

"*Ee, mma,*" I replied.

More people were coming down the path. I found Brian and

28

led him to the hut. Any minute I thought Keith might barge through the door, and eventually he did. But it was not, as I had expected, the actual slaughter that caused him to seek refuge. He announced that he had done his job. He had held the leg and watched blood drain from the goat's head into a metal pan. Keokilwe had taught him a Tswana proverb, and Hoyt had explained it: "Man is like a sheep; he does not cry out even if he is in pain." "*Monna ke nku ga a lele*," Keith recited. With other children, he had gathered branches to set under the tree to catch the dripping blood as they lifted the goat and hung it by its feet.

Horrified, I listened. What had transpired in these past weeks between Keith and his environment to give him the desire to participate in slaughter? Who spoke with him and when? What did he understand?

"*Monna ke nku ga a llele*," he repeated perfectly. He understood the words. Before me, at that moment, stood a Tswana boy with a Tswana sense of manhood. I could not recognize my son. And yet it was I, not long ago, who pleaded for his tolerance of another culture.

"Why did you come to me now?" I asked.

"Because Keokilwe slit the stomach, and it was awful seeing the guts hang out!"

"They were not guts," I corrected him.

Not knowing what it is to become a man in Tswana society, I could not understand Keith's casual references to the killing. It was the killing itself that posed problems for me. The corpse—as long as I was not party to its death—could, in my mind, be distinguished from the thought of the living animal. At grocery meat counters I had not thought of slaughter. I had dissected animals for science classes without pondering their demise. Once an animal was dead and hanging from a tree, revealing the mysteriously perfect organization of its bodily functions, the zoology lab dissections of my yesteryear triggered an intense desire on my part to pull Keith out of the hut to that hanging corpse for a lesson in anatomy.

Brian, whom I had quite forgotten, ripped me out of my lecture. He stiffly pointed up to the hanging goat and shouted out anxiously. "Why don't it wake up? Wake it! Wake it!"

Back in the hut with Brian, I fried goat livers in onions and spice on my paraffin stove, and together we sang every nursery rhyme in our repertoire. We even sang every verse of his favorite, "Sing a Song of Sixpence," three times over. When we emerged with the plate of meat, I passed it to Rre Segatlhe. He dipped his fingers and passed it on to a waiting hand. Hoyt, as is his fashion, expressed his delight and complimented my cuisine. Keokilwe, stirring the meat-for-all in a very large three-legged black pot, stopped now and then to munch on his reward: the boiled stomach prepared by MaMoremi's mother. Rre Segatlhe, Tabo, and a group of elders, with the cooked head in a pan by their feet, bent over to tear meat off with their fingers.

Rre Segatlhe motioned to me to sit near him and pointing at the goathead explained, "We share the whole of this beautiful goat!"

"This head is for elders," Rre Segatlhe looked proudly at the picked-over skull. "Each part of this goat is for someone, and the skin is for you. Did you see the skin? It is a beautiful one! Someday you will have enough skins to sew together."

"Thank you, Rre Segatlhe," my Setswana voice drifted as I fought to hide my repulsion.

"Mosadi mogolo, Maokeef," he spoke with emphasis, "where you come from in America, do they kill the goat only when it is time? I have seen places in town where they kill and kill and kill, where they pile the meat so high!" His arm shot out past my chin. "It is too much, and they do not know where is the head or the skin of that goat!"

He did not wait for a response.

"Madala!" Rre Segatlhe called out, signaling to Brian. "Madala!" he called again.

Brian toddled over to the old man's lap. Rre Segatlhe dipped his hand into soft, cooked meat, neatly piled up next to the skull. He dangled the revolting, gray mass in Brian's face. Brian ate it, and Rre Segatlhe delighted in his motions for more. They shared the meat.

"Madala," he said tenderly, "this is meat only for you and for me. Here you are the youngest, and I am the oldest. This is good for us. We have not all our teeth. The wisest, the oldest of the old men in Zululand is called *Madala*. And because you, and only you, are young and close to the Badimo—where I will soon travel—you, I will also call Madala."

After sundown, in the quiet of the lolwapa once again, I sat with Rre Segatlhe.

"Like this lolwapa and like this hut and like the shadow of this hut given by the moon, life is round. We travel in a circle from the Badimo back to the Badimo."

He turned to me.

"You are a mosadi mogolo. Certainly! You have a husband and you have two sons, growing to be men; you are a mosadi mogolo, so you are close to the Badimo. All the younger ones must hear you, and you must tell them things. Maria and Seipate, like you, they are mosadi mogolo, but they are closer to the Badimo than you because they are even older than you. You must hear them. But I am the *monna mogolo*—old . . . man," he emphasized slowly. "I am the madala," and pointing his finger at me with an air of authority, spoke out forcefully, "and I am the closest to the Badimo."

Hoyt blew out the candle that night. I covered the sleeping Madala, and we went to Keith's bedside. It was a very good feast, he reminisced. With all the boys—Moremi, Mosimanegape, Tiro, and Sejaro—he had raided the pot for leftovers behind Rre Sega-tlhe's back. They danced to the radio and played games in the sand.

"I know why Moremi doesn't name the goats. People are hungry here. A goat is meat," he said simply.

"Keith, you did a fine job helping today," Hoyt responded.

We bade him good-night and walked out under the clear, night-time sky to the fire.

It was early this morning that Keith, feeling quite left out, petitioned Rre Segatlhe for a Setswana name. The time had not yet come, the old man replied. He looked into a disappointed face.

"It is true, you were a man yesterday, but you are still a boy today. I will watch you . . . and I will find your name tomorrow."

Tomorrow came. It was on a relaxed Sunday afternoon. Neighbors visited while their children played around the lolwapa walls. The girls settled under a tree to play a game. One by one they tossed a stone high up in the air, and before catching it again, they grabbed for other stones which had been tossed on the sand. It looked to me very much like the game of jacks.

On the other side of the same tree near the lolwapa wall, the herdboys leaned forward in concentrated silence while watching two age-mates play *Morabaraba*. *Morabaraba*, like chess, requires both a long-range offensive and defensive strategy. The playing lines are drawn into a smooth hard sand surface. The two opponents each collect their pieces by finding twelve small color-matched stones. The object of the game is to capture all of the opponent's pieces through a series of moves along specific lines.

Tiro, with his black stones, and Sejaro, with his red ones, are recognized masters. When they compete, the other boys look on. Keith had tried unsuccessfully all week to defeat Tiro. He was not deterred when he noted that neither his father nor I could do any better. He had just suffered another loss when I pointed to the hut and asked him to bring me the scissors. Kicking up the dust, pouting, and shouting, "I don't want to," he walked off to retreat with a book.

"I didn't ask you if you *wanted to*—now, please get them!" I insisted. His continued open defiance and my attempts at persuasion visibly shocked both children and elders near us. The small group of women squatting on the floor around a fresh melon half stopped spitting seeds. One after the other, Maria, Seipate, and Ntatabo got up, kicking the floor and pouting, to imitate Keith's rebellious gestures. Polwane laughed, pointing to her children who mimicked and mocked Keith's glance and shrug, while repeatedly singing out their chorus version of his English "I don't want to!" The men, sitting on chairs, laughed in the sunlight of the lolwapa, and I, feeling very much ill at ease, sighed with relief when Keith threw the scissors into my lap.

Suddenly I became painfully aware that as long as we have lived here, I have never seen a child argue with or openly disobey an elder. A parent commands once, and the child runs to comply. Yet commands rarely need to be issued, since children clearly know their duties toward not only their parents, but any older siblings as well.

Children are a source of labor. It is important to have a large family to run the household. A family with few children must, at times, find other hands to help. How often have women sympathetically commented to me on my failure to have daughters to do the sweeping! Empathetic Seipate recommended that I see Rre Segatlhe for my fertility problem! Older daughters haul water and pound grain, while younger ones strap babies on their backs to sweep or collect firewood. While older sons go off to the cattle post, their brothers learn to trap wild animals or carve an axe handle while they tend the animals of the kraal at home.

As soon as they are weaned and walking, the primary goal of childrearing is to introduce the children to their rules and obligations in the hierarchy. Once this is accomplished, children can learn from older siblings the prerogatives they will have toward their juniors.

"What discipline techniques are used toward the disobedient child?" I wondered. Even if expectations and roles are clearly defined, defiance must be encountered now and then and reprimanded. Later on Hoyt told me that a child, if he makes excuses, refuses to obey, or sometimes even if he errs in the execution of a task, is lectured about his wrongdoing and punished. If it is a serious matter or a second offense, the child is usually beaten. Discipline of this sort is not only a parent's duty but also the accepted responsibility of another elder or older sibling in the absence of a parent.

Suddenly Rre Segatlhe called to Keith, *"Tla kwano, ngwana"* [Come here, child]. He motioned me to join them.

"There is a Tswana saying," he stated. *"Molemo wa ngwana ke go rongwa.* [The reward of a child is to be sent.] That is its honor." He turned to Keith. "Every older person in the village is your brother is your father is your mother. You know to greet properly, but still you do not know how to talk. Your manners are torn by town living."

"We see them come back," he said to me, "boys and men with manners rotted in town. They do not greet. They do not talk. They have sounds in their pockets but their have lost the Tswana law." And turning to Keith with a warm, yet chiding smile, he presented Keith his Tswana name:

"Wena o [You are] *Tsotsi!"*

"Tsotsi. Tsotsi," the children sang out.

"Tsotsi," the people of the lolwapa repeated with laughter.

"Keith, you have your Tswana name now," I explained to my bewildered son. He flashed a broad grin, repeating the name over to himself.

"Tsotsi—I like the sound of it!"

"A *tsotsi,* Keith, is a naughty town boy," Hoyt explained that night. Hoyt and I tried to translate Rre Segatlhe's message, which Keith, interpreting literally, had not understood.

"When you are no longer a tsotsi, you will get another Tswana name," we reassured him.

"But Tsotsi sounds good to me," he retorted. "I don't care what it means," and asserting his independence, he repeated, "I like Tsotsi!"

"Okay. Sleep well, Tsotsi," we replied, as we hugged him good-night.

Early the following morning, Rre Segatlhe told me to discontinue feeding MaMoremi and Moremi supper. They were to get their own food, he said. He took a blanket that I had given them

33

to use and put it in our hut, telling Hoyt that he did not want me giving them things. Then turning to MaMoremi, Rre Segatlhe told her that, except for Moremi, her family should leave. "Many hands I like at work, but I do not like them at meals," he said. They left as they had come, the old woman and three children, disappearing barefoot down the dirt road to town.

Often while washing clothes, I sit near Rre Segatlhe and we talk. Also, in the late afternoons, he likes to call me to his side for a chat. Priding himself on being my Setswana teacher, he patiently corrects my grammar and helps me with words. We both enjoy these moments together, but today as we worked side by side, there was tension between us.

According to Tswana custom, a comfortable preliminary chat must precede any specifically planned topic. It is bad manners to talk business before greeting and telling each other "the news." It was for this reason that we were now talking. I reminded myself to heed Tswana manners—to avoid disputing an elder. If my views contradicted his ideas, I would have to express them indirectly and inoffensively.

He was preparing what he calls his "medicals"—this time for a woman who complained of severe menstrual cramps and irregularities. He was peeling a root which looked much like a red onion but without its smell. He said that after cutting it up and pounding it into a fine powder, he would mix it with special herbs. He told me of his preferred specialty: fertility problems. With his "medicals" he had helped many women every year, and several of them had honored him by naming their children after him. At this point he put a piece of the root to his mouth to show me that it was not poisonous. Europeans, he said, did not believe in traditional cures. I assured him that I trusted his knowledge of plants, and that many villagers had told me of his curing powers. He was pleased. I had learned much of Tswana ways, he said, but every day there was more to teach me. Some lessons had been difficult for me, he continued.

"*Ee*, Rre Segatlhe," I agreed.

"You feed MaMoremi and Moremi too much! If Moremi is full, he only plays. A child must be hungry to work. Food is not something easy. Food is a great reward."

"Rre Segatlhe, you are right. Food is a great reward. Has Moremi forgotten his duties?"

"No. Certainly he must tend the goats! But you must weed a garden before it is overgrown. I see the shirt on his back. I see you

34

send him plates of food. You will spoil him if I do not stop you! I give him tea in the morning and mealies at night. That is his reward."

"You are a good man, Rre Segatlhe. You have taught me many things. You once told Keith that here every older person in the village is his brother is his father is his mother. You said I was the mosadi mogolo. Moremi is another son to me."

"Certainly he can be your son. But he is here to work for me, and you must give him nothing."

"You also must not spoil MaMoremi," he continued. "You give her blankets. You give her water. She is getting lazy."

"I will not give MaMoremi water. I will not feed her and Moremi if it makes you angry. But it makes me sad because I like to share what I have, just as you share your home with us."

"The nights are cold," he compromised. "She can keep the blanket. But you must know she, too, is here to work for me. Moremi is here to herd my goats. You must not get mixed up in this business."

"Ee, Rre Segatlhe," I agreed. But he knew, nonetheless, that I did not understand him.

It is difficult when learning the customs of a new culture to distinguish a person's individual stance from the culturally prescribed one. From my observations so far, however, I see that it is the custom to share resources in a homestead. I conclude, therefore, that much of Rre Segatlhe's reaction to my generosity toward MaMoremi and her son is based on his view of their role as servants. He is not willing to let them participate as family members. Relegating MaMoremi and Moremi to servant status makes me personally uncomfortable, even though Hoyt assures me there is a basis for stratification in traditional Tswana culture. Nevertheless, in this community, rather than stratification, we are experiencing only generosity and cooperation between households.

I can conclude, therefore, that Rre Segatlhe, for his own pleasure, wants nothing to interfere with his master role and Moremi's servant status. There is within me a strong desire to judge him harshly, yet further thought—as is often the case—must squelch this passion.

If, as Hoyt says, there is stratification within Tswana culture, tradition may tolerate a master–servant relationship for reasons that I, of a different age, sex, and culture, can never accept or understand.

When do ultimate humanitarian principles override cultural prescriptions? And then again, perhaps Rre Segatlhe's reaction is not culturally prescribed but a mere personal adjustment to his particular situation within his society. He lives alone in a society where a man's wife and children are his greatest assets. Clearly, in my ignorance of Rre Segatlhe's personal life and culture, I cannot judge him at all, yet a tremendous curiosity about this madala, Rre Segatlhe, has awakened in me.

It was not until just a few days ago that I first noticed why he always seems to be pointing with his right index finger. I had thought it was an authoritarian pose, but no, he is missing parts of his last three fingers!

"Rre Segatlhe," I uttered in surprise. "I did not know you were missing fingers—I'm sorry. What happened to you?" I asked.

"It is nothing. I am a madala anyhow" he declared.

"How did it happen?" I persisted.

"It is a long time ago—when I grew to be a man. Someday I may tell you, but not now, mosadi mogolo, not now."

The mealie meal pot.

4

No Harvest, but Flies

It is fly season. Rre Segatlhe hears our complaints and speaks to us of flies.

"Certainly there are many flies! Flies mean cattle. If there are many flies in the lolwapa, a man is said to be rich with cattle. It is not good to destroy flies, or harm will come to the herd. When the herd moves on, so too will the flies."

I used to wonder when I saw pictures of faces covered with flies why the victims were not brushing them off or twitching their skin. After these weeks, we have discovered there is no point in it. We confine such energies to mealtime. While dipping the spoon with the right hand, the left hand fans the dish; as the spoon approaches the mouth, the left hand quickly swats over the spoon before its entry. Both hands must then return to the starting position.

How long this will last is uncertain. Rre Segatlhe assures us that one day we will be free of the hectic buzz about our ears. Rre Segatlhe's calm assurance does not convince me, nor does his lofty rationale for these pests console me.

I complain about the flies just as I used to complain about the bats. Because everyone else slept through the invasion, no one except me seemed in the least concerned about them.

Nightly a driving fleet of bats entered our hut between the mud wall and straw roof overhang. Their hideous flutter just beneath the sticks of our ceiling woke me. I slept armed with a flashlight, and upon their intrusion, aimed my weapon, my beam of light. They flew off the perch directly above my head and left the hut while I waited for their inevitable return. I was convinced that if I could manage to consistently irritate them

39

when they entered, they would surely find another nightly lodging. They persisted, however, beyond my ability to stay awake, and consequently, my first chore every morning was to sweep up their droppings at my bedside. Planning flashlight strategies, I was too close to the conflict to think of a long-term solution.

It was Ellwyn Miller, the Vermont Peace Corps worker at the BAC, who thought of the final solution. We had found the Millers at home on a recent trip for water. Ellwyn Miller, bent over a bed of weeds, lifted his silver head of hair, squinted through the sun at us, and slowly straightened his back. "Ay-yuh," he pronounced in conclusion to his weeding efforts.

"How d'ya like livin' in one a' them huts?" he asked me.

"It's fine—nice and cool, really." The bats immediately leaped to mind. "But the nights are awful! I can't sleep at all. Bats fly in, and the pests leave their droppings all over the floor," I complained.

"Then spread it roun' on the flo'wah, why don't ya? Don't make no difference—not with all them other things I hear tell they use . . . Course you could jes tack up some nettin' where they fly in," he suggested.

There was my solution: block the entrance with netting. My gratitude to Ellwyn Miller!

We laughed through what was really a serious description of Ellwyn Miller's experience as manager of the BAC Farms. He went on to the lighter topic of their life as expatriates in government housing. Their garden was not tended by a "garden boy"; their living room was cluttered with unfinished projects; the kitchen was crowded with six Tswana youths baking bread. The British neighbors had complained of noise and riffraff. Clearly, the Millers were not living by expatriate "rules."

Beverley Miller left the Tswana youths in the kitchen to welcome us. Unlike her husband, she had been rejected by the Peace Corps for medical reasons. She intended, nevertheless, to contribute as much as possible during their two-year stay. She had taken leadership of a 4-B Club (Tswana equivalent of U.S.A. 4-H Club) and met with village children several times a week for group activities and projects.

We sat over tea and cornbread with the Millers. The Tswana youths politely greeted us in English: "Good evening, Madam. Good evening, Sir." With the Millers we spoke of Botswana, of Vermont, and argued over American politics. It was good to step out of our rural situation momentarily and liberating not to struggle for words. For Hoyt and me, it was our first long conversation in English since our arrival.

Hoyt filled the water drum while I searched in a neighbor's yard for our Madala. Running with a plastic duck in hand across a well-groomed flowerbed, he came to a full stop at the sound of a lady's voice. I caught his hand and greeted her with my apologies. She was pleasant and spoke English with a Dutch accent. She asked me where I lived and practically dropped her teeth when I told her.

"Well, I do miss some comforts," I admitted.

"The only thing I can complain about," she replied, "is that everyday is the same. It is boring here."

"Then it's a trade-off—your comforts for my adventures. If you like, come and visit us when you get bored." I told her the directions, fully expecting that she would never come.

With cameras slung over their shoulders, the Millers' neighbors arrived on Sunday—to break their afternoon routine, they said. Rre Segatlhe, throwing bones for Maria's grandchild, looked up briefly and continued his incantations. On the blue plastic chairs in another corner of the lolwapa, Hoyt and I sat with our visitors while they sipped hot tea and stumbled for words. They twitched and shook themselves, swatting the fierce flies. Cups half-full, they pushed away their chairs to make an exit. Hurriedly, they stood back to focus on our hut. To get a good angle, they ran around the wall—click! The perfect shot: an old, black man staring at bones on a mud floor, facing him a woman in pale blue rags scratching her feet, while to her left stands a fly-infested child wearing skins below its distended belly.

Bordering the field is the pit we dug upon arrival. We had expected to fill it with waste. By now, we had figured the necessity of digging another pit for disposables. Wrong. There is no waste. Any empty can disappears within the very hour we have tossed it into the pit. We might see Tiro clutching it in his arms as he runs home or Sejaro under some tree reshaping it to make a candleholder. Whatever papers Rre Segatlhe does not use to wrap his medicines or tobacco are burned in the kitchen fire.

The pit remains empty. Brian is careful to avoid playing near it. Until recently I had attributed his easygoing nature and accommodation to our new life not to his fear of the pit but to Rre Segatlhe's air of authority. Now I am not sure. Like a true madala, Brian prefers the fields and refuses to use the chemical toilet.

41

When finally I insisted that he try the toilet, he shouted his rebellious warning at my persistence.

"No, no! If you make me sit there, I am going to dig a deep, deep hole . . . and I am going to push you in . . . and I am going to give you some NOTHING!"

I, too, will occasionally rebel against my elders. Defying Rre Segatlhe, I sneak MaMoremi food left behind in my cooking pots. Keith scrapes our plates for Moremi, and any remaining garbage is gratefully gobbled by the pig. We toss the morning wash water into his trough. He slurps and snorts with great satisfaction.

The neighboring women come frequently for morning visits. Usually they are the same women, and Rre Segatlhe refers to them as my sisters—Maria, Seipate, Ntatabo, and Polwane. Maria and Seipate come everyday at least once or twice. Ntatabo, who lives farther than any of them, manages to join us almost every day. Although Polwane is the only one who lives within view of our lolwapa, she comes only two or three times per week. Rre Segatlhe says this is because Polwane has many daughters to pound her grain and fetch her water.

Sometimes if Polwane does not join us, we stop by her place to visit before going into the fields. She brews tea, and we take turns holding her new grandchild. Polwane is very pretty and petite. Unlike the others, Polwane never wears more than one dress at a time, but so far, I have only seen one dress on her, and it is so faded that the original color is indistinct. Whenever we visit, Maria looks around to see if her husband, Tabo, is near, and if he is, she shouts to him that the grandchild is destined to look like her grandmother—pretty Polwane! Every time he hears this, Tabo laughs with joy as if he has never heard it before.

Polwane is very quiet anywhere else, but at home in her lolwapa, she speaks freely. Her speech, soft and even, does not have the variety of expression that I am accustomed to hearing from the others, and she does not gesticulate much with her hands. It is difficult for me to understand her. I pretend and respond with any apt phrase that comes to mind, hoping it has some relevance. She is consistently gracious about my attempts, always smiling and accepting, never demanding.

I cannot say the same for Ntatabo. She demands to be understood by me, and if she senses that I have missed the point, she gesticulates madly, raises her voice, and engages Maria and Seipate for help. The three of them talk loudly past me. Invariably Ntatabo bursts out laughing, splitting open another seam of one of her two dresses. Ntatabo is rotund. Seipate chides her for not sewing her dresses properly. She replies that she does not bother sewing since both dresses together cover all the important spots. They dispute among themselves about precisely which spots are "important." Ntatabo suggests this may depend on the mood or man of the day. She flaunts her flare for fashion by pointing out that she alternates which dress is to be worn on top and which inside out.

We walk to the edge of a small grove of trees, the four of us, collecting wood for the hearth. There is a constant chatter of gossip and banter from which I feel left out. Sometimes Maria will tell a long story, and if she forgets a line, Seipate will interject to fill it in. We break branches and make bundles. They carry the bundles effortlessly on their heads while I, feeling the awkward load in my arms, struggle to look natural and comfortable.

"Oo, loo-loo!" Rre Segatlhe exclaims when I come back with the firewood. "Put it there," he points to the kitchen shelter.

The mealie meal pot is on after sunset, and we sit around the fire. The smoke helps clear some flies away. I scoop up mealie meal, add cooked, canned peas on top, and serve Rre Segatlhe first. Modise passes his plate; then I serve myself. The children come last. MaMoremi and Moremi join us by the fire, carrying their bowl of mealie. Moremi's eyes light up when he sees the can of peas. Rre Segatlhe asks for more, but there are still some leftover. We sit by the light of fire, and I am warm with satisfaction as together we consume my bundle of wood.

"You work well with your sisters," Rre Segatlhe observes.

"It is for you *tiro* on the lands, not like in town, where a woman's work is only *mmereko*."

"What is tiro and mmereko?" I asked Rre Segatlhe.

"Tiro is what you do here with your sisters. You work while you sing and talk. You are knowing each other when you are doing these things together. You are helping each other. And what you pick, you eat and you share with all in the lolwapa. It is tiro; it is good for you and good for all.

And if you and Maria and Seipate go to find a melon in the field, but there is no melon, you will come back with nothing. It is tiro; you tried to find the melon, and it is good. We will be sad that there is no melon in the field, but we are together, and we will share the head of a fly."

He paused and went on, "Mmereko is how they work in town. A woman will not go to find the melon with her sisters.

Maybe she must buy it, maybe she must cook it for somebody else, but she does not eat it. She works alone. If she is lucky there is a radio, and she sings with it. But, still, she does not like the work. She looks at the clock and thinks to finish it quickly. She does not know the people near her. Mmereko is only for the pocket . . . and if she has no mmereko, nothing for her pocket, she cannot buy food for her child. And in town, no one will share even the head of a fly."

Maria, Seipate, and Ntatabo came late one morning to teach me to pound grain. They had just returned from town with their purchase, a bag of mealie. They dropped it on the soft sand near our kitchen shelter and hauled the wooden tools into the sunlight. Like a huge mortar and pestle, the base, called a *kika*, was of heavy hand-hewn wood and stood higher than my knees; the pounding pestle, called the *motse*, was higher than my waist and must have weighed twenty pounds. We were to sing and dance to the pounding rhythm, while each taking our turn to stamp mealie. They laughed at my inefficient movements, and I entertained them when I, the youngest by far, held my throbbing arm muscle and gave up.

Maria poured kadi. They passed the gourd—a tense time for me. The taste was vile. Again I pretended to swallow with pleasure. Seipate strung together seed pods and wrapped them around our ankles. To their song, I followed their slow shuffle around a circle until I forgot myself. The chorus and rhythm grew strong; we sang, stamped our feet, and clapped. The tempo increased, and finally, Maria broke the chain, ululating a loud, long finale.

Grain pounded and distributed, we went our separate ways. With new rhythms and songs, I entered the lolwapa. The lyrics confused me; I would ask Hoyt for a translation when he returned from town. Rre Segatlhe, Tabo, and several other men were sitting near the wall. They turned toward me as I entered.

Tabo greeted me. Conspiratorial glances flanked Rre Segatlhe, who struggled to suppress his laughter and confront me with a serious demeanor.

"*Dumela, Rra, o tlhotse jang?*" and the Tswana handshake—I greeted them all. Rre Segatlhe and I eyed each other and played the waiting game. He won. I demanded to know what was going on.

He introduced Montsho, the man to his left, as an artist who worked wonders with hides. Was it hides that I smelled? Was it the dried blood on Montsho's caked fingers? He was bare-chested and wore only a loincloth. His face was handsome; his smile showed that he had all his teeth. But I backed up quickly after shaking his rough hand, for he had a putrid odor.

It was Montsho, Rre Segatlhe explained, who made the goat-skin mats and sewed together hats from bits of fur. Rre Segatlhe had summoned Montsho to collect our cat. The cat had committed an unpardonable crime—he had eaten a piece of *biltong* hanging from the roof of a hut. Since Montsho enjoyed eating cat meat and could use its fur creatively, Montsho was to take the cat.

Barring no emotion, mosadi mogolo that I am, an impulsive tirade burst forth. The cat, whose nightly vigil protects us from bats, spiders, and snakes, was to quench Montsho's strange appetite and ride his head! I stormed to our hut and returned with two cans of beans. "*Tsa!*" [Here!] I shoved a can at Rre Segatlhe and tossed the other in Montsho's lap.

"There's more nutrition in this can than in your dried meat, Rre Segatlhe. And Montsho will get more to chew and taste than he could ever get off our skinny cat." I grabbed the cat and retreated to the hut. The silence was broken by their chuckles, and it seemed to me, that with the crescendo of their laughter, I could hear Rre Segatlhe's above them all.

Colors of sunset faded away into darkness. After I fed him, Montsho spoke to me. Rre Segatlhe helped translate as we conversed, and before Montsho got up to leave us, he presented me with a traditional Tswana fur hat as a gift. I thanked him and spun it around to admire the various sections of fur. He, in turn, identified the donors: a skunk, a spotted wild cat (which he had shot two years before and had saved ever since), an impala (a piece left over from a sewing job he had done for a European), and for two sections—because he lacked furs—he had to kill a common house cat.

Nothing is in the fields. Food is scarce. We had better keep a guarded eye on our cat.

Hoyt returned from town with a curious specimen. He entered the lolwapa waving a white envelope. Several of us grabbed it at once before releasing it for Hoyt to display: an engraved envelope, smudged with our fingerprints, from the American

Embassy in Gaborone. It was a formal invitation to a party at the American Ambassador's residence in Gaborone to celebrate Independence Day.

Hoyt was reluctant to go until I pointed out that we were also invited to bring guests. We agreed that we should honor Rre Segatlhe by asking him to come with us. Certainly this would be the feast of his life! He thanked us and immediately accepted, but when it came time to leave, he excused himself, feigning a stomach upset. Hoyt had learned that refusal of an invitation is impolite. It was far better to make excuses and back out at the last minute than to refuse a person's hospitality. In a moment of candor, Rre Segatlhe explained to Hoyt that even though the feast would surely be delicious, its price was too high. He detested trips to town and could never enjoy an encounter with a group of fat stomachs.

Maria's son, Tladi, and Ntatabo's oldest son, Neo—both workers at BAC enjoying the leisure of a weekend—were standing nearby as we prepared to leave. Determined not to waste the invitation, I asked them if they would come along. They were delighted, and the four of us were off.

Laughing about our growling stomachs, we sniffed the barbeque sauce and approached the formal garden. We slipped through the gate, flashing our invitation, just as Guy Lombardo's strings dragged out "Oh, What a Beautiful Morning," violins from the left speaker, cellos from the right. Near the blue, sparkling pool, we found the Millers chatting with a small group of Peace Corps volunteers. Tladi and Neo lit up at the sight of Ellwyn Miller and shook his hand, Tswana-style. He was more than manager of the BAC. Unlike other office workers, he often went out into the fields with them. He did not just point and tell them what to do, they said; he bent down to the soil with them. His hands, like theirs, were hands of the soil. Hoyt offered to get us drinks, but Tladi and Neo, eyeing the opulent bar, returned the favor and went off to get us drinks.

They never returned. Milling through the crowd, I looked for them: green grass and blossoms; garden chairs and tables; plaid slacks, pastel dresses, laughter, ice cubes clinking glasses; now the Mormon Tabernacle Choir singing Stephen Foster's songs in stereo; hamburgers, hot dogs, and chicken coming off the grill to passing paper plates. Hoyt grabbed my arm. "I found them. We're going."

It was an Embassy official, a Mr. Duncan, who, in a state of inebriation, grabbed Tladi and Neo and showed them the gate. They did not belong, he said. They could not produce an invitation. "Find Modise, find Mr. and Mrs. Miller," they urged, but he could not or would not understand their appeal. It was not the blunder alone that irritated Hoyt; it was the fact that Mr. Duncan, after hearing Hoyt out and seeing our invitation, refused to apologize to our guests.

"Duncan? Duncan? Oh, you mean "dill pickle"—that's what we call him," the Millers tried to humor Tladi.

We left, but not without sustenance. Halfway home, we stopped the truck in a field, settled on a few rocks, opened my bulging purse and sweater parcel, and toasted warm beer cans. Even cold hot dogs and mustard make a splendid feast in the bush!

From feast to famine we returned home. One afternoon as I poured the last of the dishwater onto the remains stuck to the bottom of the breakfast mealie pot to feed the pig, Brian ran through the lolwapa shouting, "Traffic! Traffic!"

I dropped the pot and ran out of the kitchen shelter to see cattle moving swiftly across the field. Rre Segatlhe looked across his bones and up to me.

"The fields are bare. There is nothing here for cattle. They drive on behind Mosimanegape's whip—far off to better land. The flies go with them, and you, my mosadi mogolo, will have nothing to squawk about."

Rre Segatlhe was right, of course. Cattle dung, dried hard in the sun, no longer attracts flies. Relief at last! And it is true that I sit longer with Rre Segatlhe for Tswana conversation. He speaks slowly and teaches me words. Although he often laughs at my response, he is careful to correct my every mistake and then insists that I repeat the phrase to his satisfaction.

MaMoremi asked me to help her collect dried cow dung to use as coals for our morning fire. As we walked through the fields, an idea struck me. I left her side and returned to the hut. I mixed a dough with ingredients Hoyt brought from town, rolled it with a glass bottle, and cut out biscuit shapes. Arranging the biscuits inside the large lid of a black pot, I covered them tightly with another lid of the same size. I prepared a bed of hot coals with the dung, and then placed my makeshift oven, the two lids pressed against each other, on top of the coals. To completely seal the apparatus with heat, I shovelled coals on top of the lids until they were out of sight. Certain that a high heat had been achieved, I

47

waited for what felt to be about ten minutes. After scraping off the coals, I threaded the handle of the top lid with a stick, lifted it up, and *voila*! Perfect biscuits! Never had I felt such culinary pride.

Who would want my recipe? Women here do not have flour and butter, and those elsewhere with the ingredients have easier methods. My thrill upon lifting the lid was, no doubt, a sense of victory over the plethora of specialized kitchen gadgetry I had deemed "essential" at home in America.

No more flies: to me that is reason to celebrate. We feast, and feeling somewhat like a heroic housewife who has created and conquered, I pass the plate.

Montsho, who generally manages propitious arrivals, walks in just as we divided the last of the biscuits. I want to hold my breath as his odors waft about.

"Modise," Montsho complains. "How my arm hurts!"

"Why does your arm hurt?"

"Because all night long, I was sleeping like a baboon."

"How does a baboon sleep?"

"A baboon sleeps on his arm."

"Why does a baboon sleep on his arm?"

"A baboon sleeps on his arm so as not to forget where he left his food supply. You see, he sleeps on his arm which is pointing to his food, so that when he wakes up, he need only follow the direction to which his arm points."

Montsho's face brightens. He reaches for another biscuit and continues, "Of course, when I woke up this morning, my arm pointed straight to Modise's place!"

A good, strong sip of kadi.

5

Crossroads

The pig is causing us some consternation. Rre Segatlhe and Hoyt tried to dig the sticks of the enclosure deep enough to thwart the pig's escape attempts—all to no avail. The sand is easy for him to dig up.

The pig is attracted to the shade and privacy of the green canvas covering of our chemical toilet. He spreads himself out at the entrance so that we have to step over him to get in. This could be considered quaint bathroom decor. We have given up on the concept of privacy here anyway. If the pig could just peacefully coexist, all would be well. It is when he blissfully chooses to roll himself about that problems occur. The toilet tips over while the canvas collapses. If he could meet us halfway, if he could facilitate matters by at least effecting a clean getaway, that would be one thing. But it is quite the *other* thing. Tangled in the ropes, he drags the canvas and poles so that his escape could be confused with a peacefully moving caravan were it not for the plaintive squeals which, of course, summon Hoyt's curses and rescue efforts. The ensuing duet often draws a crowd of onlookers.

It was at the conclusion of one of these events that little Leta, Polwane's four-year-old, discovered a game far better than running after chickens. She encouraged our Madala to overcome his fears and join her; now the two of them have spent many happy afternoons, sticks in hand, chasing down pig Nixon (so named by Hoyt because the soaked caravan reminds him of Nixon's Watergate).

Privacy is a rare occurrence here. This is much more difficult for us to get used to than any lack of modern conveniences. Except for bedding down, our daily activities are out-of-doors.

Recognized as a good witch doctor with a stock of herbal cures and tobacco for sale, Rre Segatlhe has a steady stream of customers throughout the day. Whenever a child is born, parents come to Rre Segatlhe for him to throw his special bones and read the infant's future. Now that MaMoremi is steadily brewing kadi, people come to buy jars of refreshment. They sit here to drink. Tswana custom demands a greeting upon each encounter. If I am washing clothes in the lolwapa. I must stop when someone enters to get up and offer a greeting in Setswana. Even if I withdraw to the hut to write in solitude, any woman or man my senior who calls my name from outside must be properly acknowledged with a greeting and a show of hospitality. Face-to-face relationships have priority over the immediacy of any task. A job cannot be more important than the people you must know to support your life-world.

One morning after chores, Keith and I withdrew into the hut for a math lesson. Just as we were getting our heads together, old Maria shouted outside the door. Resentful of interruption, I nonetheless obediently stepped out into the lolwapa to greet her. Maria and Seipate returned my greeting and sat down to await my hospitality. Tsotsi happily skipped away out of the hut and out of sight.

As soon as I asked Maria and Seipate if they would like some tea, I knew it was a mistake. Maria pouted at my ignorance. The question itself indicated choice, and that convinced her that I was withholding kadi. She snapped out her order for kadi. Seipate nodded her approval. They sat awaiting my attentions.

There are still patterns of past social interaction which I engage in without thinking. It is only when they are inappropriate that I even become aware of them. Here a host does not question visitors as to their preference. After all, there is no choice. If kadi has been brewed, the beer must be offered. If there is no kadi, tea is cooked and served. When serving, a host does not ask visitors whether they wish a refill, for to a Tswana, such questioning reveals a lack of generosity and true friendship.

Maria's demanding voice rang out again: "Mpha kadi!" She reduced me to servility. Seething with anger, I visibly complied by entering the hut.

Just to get away from them, I put the kettle on the paraffin burner inside the hut rather than on the logs outside. Waiting for the water to boil, I tried to control my rage. I could not risk showing my irritation at the timing of their visit, their misunderstanding of my intentions, and their command for service. Hoyt's work and our presence in the community required good neighborly relations, and yet, if I could not openly express my differences and feelings, I remained an actor on stage.

For several months I had watched, listened, and conformed. Performing my role and routine, I had greeted and spoken Setswana with increasing comfort. I knew names, families, and a few homesteads. I had worked side by side with my age-mates. We shared efforts and smiles as I learned songs and dances, but what did I know about their personal lives and dreams? And what did they know of mine?

In trying to be accepted as a Tswana woman, I did not dare reveal any feelings which conflicted with what was expected of me. I did not feel free to express any negative emotions toward the people or circumstances around me. My relationships could only be superficial, and I was isolated. In my loneliness, I prepared to socialize once more.

They came into the hut to find me. Maria sat on the bed; Seipate pulled up a chair. I poured tea and passed the cups. They looked for kadi.

"*Kadi, e kae?*" Maria asked as she looked around the hut to find it.

"*Ga e yo!*" I insisted as I spread my arms to prove I had none.

"Maria, Seipate—*ga ke na kadi!*" I insisted again. Maybe they believed me. They looked around once more. I grabbed the sugar bowl and spooned extra sugar into their cups. "*Gape?*" [More?] I asked.

"*Ee,*" they both demanded.

"*Gape?*"

"*Ee,* don't ask!" they commanded. They finally stopped the sugar after five or six teaspoons, and then Maria broke the silence. She asked if the hen had laid eggs. Yes, every morning I went looking, I said, but so did the pig, and it was a matter of who found the eggs first. They laughed. Maria finished her tea. I automatically asked her if she wanted more.

"Don't ask. Just pour," she retorted impatiently.

"I did it again!" I spoke out in disgust, and spontaneously burst out to defend myself. Life was very different here for me, I explained. They nodded. At times we did not understand each other, and I felt angry but could not show it. They asked "why" and "when." They were interested. We spoke of our two worlds. I admitted how I had felt when they arrived, when they ordered beer. Maria, shocked at my interpretation, assured me that she was making sure that I had not forgotten about kadi. After all, she added, it was clear to everyone that even though I sipped kadi, I was only pretending to like it. A monkey does not see its own hollow eyes. It was time, she said, that I felt comfortable to be myself. She spoke Setswana slowly so that I might understand.

"You are a mosadi mogolo here. You get angry. You get sad. You cannot hide yourself here. With us you are a Tswana woman, but you are white. You are our friend, but you must remain who you are. You must share who you are with us."

Maria continued, "We see you with Tsotsi reading books. We have children, but we cannot teach them. The village school wants uniforms and shoes and money. Only some of us can send one or two of our many children to school."

Seipate elaborated, "I can send *none* of my children to school. Maria and Molefi have sent their only boy, Tladi, to school. Because Tabo works at BAC, Polwane could choose two children for school—the oldest boy, Lekoto, and the oldest girl, Lerato. You know Polwane's son, Tiro—he wishes to go too much . . . but he cannot go . . . there is no more money for shoes! Ntatabo, whose husband, Keokilwe, earns some money, sent only one child—her oldest son, Neo—to school; but the little one, Sejaro, who is much too clever, cannot go to school because Neo, now working at BAC, does not give the money. . . .

"And because Sejaro must keep the goats," Maria interrupted.

"We see you read," Maria continued. "We see you write words and teach your child. You speak our language. You must teach us. You must teach our children."

The old woman lifted her cup. I poured. Underestimating their ability to perceive me and tolerate our differences, I had not thought of an exchange.

"*Maria le Seipate—ditsala tsame!*" [Maria and Seipate—my friends!] I hugged them, immediately agreeing to start a school.

Hoyt, as *Modise*, had a mission; his anthropological rounds kept him moving every day from one lolwapa to the next. I saw him less every day and was left to sit with Rre Segatlhe or do chores with my "sisters." Now these very sisters, Maria and Seipate, were giving me a purpose beyond my daily routine, one in which I as an individual could contribute to the homesteads beyond my own lolwapa.

54

"You will see—I will teach better than I can carry wood!" I added enthusiastically.

"Still, you must carry wood and learn from us," Maria cautioned with a warm smile.

I was euphoric and at the same time bemused at my change of mood.

We walked out of the hut together and bid Rre Segatlhe good-bye.

"I have never been to your places, Maria and Seipate. Show me the path so I can visit you soon." We walked a few kilometers together and parted at the crossroad to go our own ways home.

I arrived back at our place just as Hoyt returned from town. He stepped out of the truck holding high an item claimed at the side of the road: a worn tennis ball. The boys, Tiro, Moremi, and Tsotsi, ran toward him, shouting, "mpha! mpha!" Hoyt threw it in the air, and the boys leaped after it.

After putting the animals to pasture, many of the herd boys meet regularly for a soccer match. The tennis ball, so small and by now the color of the dust, is barely visible. Barefoot, the boys speed through the flying dust in pursuit of goals which they never care to tally. Meanwhile, the goats and sheep wander through parched brown grasses, nibbling at crackling leaves. There has not been a drop of rain or even a cloud in the sky in three months.

On the morning that I decided to visit Seipate, Brian and I met the herd boys at the crossroad. Their goats grazed on thorn bushes while Tiro, Sejaro, Moremi, and Tsotsi played soccer. Running and yelling, they madly scrambled into each other and kicked up the dust. Brian and I left them behind as we made our way to Seipate's place. "If he were not such a big and heavy three-year-old Madala," I thought, "I could carry him on my back and make some progress." The going was slow as he stopped to investigate grass sounds, peer down sand holes, or haltingly touch the sharp, long thorns of bushes.

"Maokeef! Madala!"

Seipate greeted us and entered the hut to seek chairs. Madala left my side to join three small children by the lolwapa wall. He watched a young girl who had one foot in a pan tipped forward. She looked up, greeted us, and scrubbed her leg with a bit of water. An older girl swinging her arms and motse up and down into the wooden kika briefly stopped pounding to greet me. The wooden thuds went on as Seipate pulled out two chairs. We carried them to a shaded kitchen shelter made of branches. Inside a girl sat by the fire breast-feeding her infant. She looked as if she had just reached puberty. Seipate introduced her daughter, "She will marry Moses when he comes back from the cattle post." We greeted each other, and I admired the child. Seipate looked on proudly and told me of her family.

"It is here that I live with my dying mother, my son, four daughters, and my two grandsons. Molefi visits me on and off, but he stays with Maria, his first wife.

"Molefi and Maria were married for several years without producing children. This caused them great suffering. Finally, after receiving medicals from Rre Segatlhe, Maria succeeded in giving birth to her son, Tladi. To this day, he is their greatest joy, for the medicals lost their power, and they were never able to have more children.

"It was for this reason that Molefi took me as his second wife," Seipate explained. "Even though three returned to the Badimo, I produced five children who are still living. The oldest daughters are not yet married, but they have given me grandsons. My son has hot blood. He thinks he is a man, but he has lost his manners. He went to the gold mines in South Africa and came home with shoes and new clothes. But for me, he brought only very little money to buy mealie and sorghum.

"He has changed his ways; he has changed his name. Every day he tells me, he will go away again—back to the South African mines. He thinks only of himself. What good is such a son for me?"

From her description, I could recognize him when he joined us by the fire. He introduced himself as "Number 19" and asked me about America. Was it true that there was no apartheid in America? Was it true that all people in America had cars?

He spoke of the mines, where the white man ruled and shouted numbers. "I was beaten and treated like an animal. Deep in the earth where air was fire and falling rocks deafened my ears, I lay on my back blasting for the White Man's gold. But I did not cry in pain, for it was man's work. There in the mines—unlike here on the lands—I was a man equal to the elders. I ate the same food and drank as much beer as the older men.

"With my age-mates, I got a pass to leave the compound. We walked in city lights. I fought. I gambled and lost, but next time I will win and buy a radio.

Work in the mines is heavy; the Boers and Boss-boys are cruel, and no matter how hard I work, it makes no difference. But now I walk with shoes on my feet. I will go to the mines and the big city again, and the herd boys who touch my clothes and see that I am a man will follow me!"

Seipate shook her head with these words. "He thinks he is a hero and walks like a peacock!"

We stepped out of the kitchen shelter. "Before you leave," Seipate instructed, "you must greet my mother." Behind the hut, in the shade of its roof, her mother's coiled body lay motionless. Flies circled the protruding bones and wrinkled skin. When Seipate roused her, the mosadi mogolo slowly propped herself up and made efforts to focus on us. She did not return my greeting but meticulously picked her nose before lowering herself back onto the burlap mat.

"She can get food in her mouth to keep herself alive, but that is all. She does not get off the mat anymore—even to defecate. We wash her blanket again and again."

"She is the closest to the Badimo," Seipate told me as we left the old woman's side. "Like my grandchild, when she speaks, we cannot understand her. She speaks now only to the Badimo." Rre Segatlhe's words when he named Madala came to mind: "life is round."

I told Seipate as we walked out of her lolwapa that I would soon take a trip to town to buy school supplies. I would teach reading and writing to those who wanted to learn. There would be a regular time and place for lessons.

She scampered off into a nearby bush and emerged clutching a hen. Thanking me, she thrust it into my arms. Madala, anxious to see it run, moved steadily along the path, for he knew I would not let go of its feet until we were home again.

It was not long before Seipate's son, Number 19, left for the mines. He came to bid us farewell. His recruits, two older herd boys, walked at his sides, and Seipate tagged along behind. Hoyt, just leaving with the truck, offered to take them down the road. They slammed the truck door shut and waved back to us. At the crossroad Seipate and I stood looking on at the flying dust—perhaps thinking the same thing. "He has gone not to earn his cattle but to win a radio."

We turned to speak to each other, and at the same time, asked the same question of each other, "Do you think Number 19 will ever return?"

I thought about Number 19's road ahead. The Induction Center for the Mine Labor Organization is just south of Gaborone in Khale. It is a white building on a watered lawn with dormitories at the back. Young boys coming from southern parts of Botswana wait there for transportation to the gold mines of South Africa.

Hoyt went there once to get data for his research and described the scene to me. One group of boys waited for medical inspections. Another group lined up, one behind the other, for formal induction. The recruiting officer officiously held up a pencil at arm's length. One by one they filed forward to touch the pencil. One tap of the pencil, and they were committed to nine months of labor for the gold mines of South Africa.

"*Ow!*" Seipate exclaimed as we watched the truck disappear behind its tracks. "*Ruri*, Maria's one son, Tladi, does more for her than my many children, will ever do for me! . . . Come, Maokeef, I'll take you to Molefi and Maria's place."

Unlike any other homestead, Maria and Molefi's place is considered to be particularly opulent. They have dug both a dam and a well. Their fields have been plowed for early planting. A bright, red bougainvillea drapes across a trellis placed near the entrance of their lolwapa. The walls are not only neatly built but decorated with a two-tone color pattern.

The first thing Maria showed us was her new cement floor inside one of the rondavels. Like any other visitor, I was amazed, and immediately appreciated the fact that it would not need the maintenance of a dung floor. "Someday," Maria said, "all our floors will be cement!" Molefi explained their success by forethought and hard work.

"As a young couple, Maria and I left our family and crowded homeland near Mochudi for the unsettled lands area of Kgaphamadi. At that time it was just a cattle post, but because the land was good, we decided to make it our home. We went to the Bakwena chief, and he gave us this land. Alone, we cleared it and built our home. We worked from sunup to sundown. Segatlhe was our first neighbor. He came in 1946. Not long thereafter, others came to settle nearby. Close neighbors made the harvest easier.

"A sharing community was growing, but for us there were no children to fill the lolwapa. No children to work! We could not rest. Even after our son Tladi was grown to boyhood, we had to toil, for no other children followed. After his grammar school, we sent our only son Tladi to the mines to earn cattle for himself.

Alone again, we decided that I, Molefi, should take on another wife to produce children. For Seipate, I built a homestead not far away. Maria stayed home and dug a well. I went to Seipate. When I returned to Maria, we worked together to build the dam which everyone now enjoys. We visit and drink kadi, like everybody else, but work always comes first."

Maria added that Tladi, her only child, was worth many children. Seipate poked me knowingly, and Maria continued. "Like Molefi, Tladi is a good worker. He went to the mines as a young man. He did not spend his earnings but brought them home to buy cattle."

"*Ee*," Seipate agreed.

Maria told me that Tladi looked for opportunities open to young men of his day, just as his father had done. After the mines, he found a job in Gaborone. He worked hard, and his firm sponsored him for extra training at the Botswana Training Center. Thereafter, he found his present job at the BAC. He gave many cattle to marry a good woman. They built their homestead nearby.

"Tladi cycles to work every day," Maria continued, "and often he returns home with new ideas to improve our homestead. It is Tladi who brought the clay for my wall. It is Tladi who poured the concrete. See here the flower Tladi has given me to grow! This year we will try a new way of planting and use different seeds. Tladi has many ideas. We will try them all."

Rre Segatlhe's place is off a major crossroad. A few feet from his kraal two dirt roads and many sandpaths come together. When news travels, it comes to us quickly and moves on in many directions. News from across Mopane Hill, news from Mochudi, Mogoditshane, or Gaborone. There is news to sit and ponder over, news to discuss and dispute about, and most importantly, news demanding the interruption of one's day.

Neo cycled in at daybreak. "*Ke* Neo!" Rre Segatlhe called out. We greeted Neo and listened to his words—his sister's baby had died in the night.

"She married just last year. She is young, and that child was her firstborn," Rre Segatlhe explained to us. "We must go this noon to her lolwapa."

Down the long, winding path to her hut, we greeted others and walked together without words. For a winter's morning, the air was strangely still, the sun hot. But we covered our limbs to

59

honor the dead and show our grief. Field birds called; dry grasses rustled with life; and our pace played a continuous rhythm on the sand beneath our feet.

Filing into the lolwapa, the men went to chairs beneath the shade of a tree while I followed the women toward the hut. One by one we greeted the relatives and then sat with them on the floor near the entrance. Each in our own silence, we sat as one facing the shaded doorway of her hut.

Straining to look through the sunlight, I saw my own memories in her darkness. She cradled her head in the agony of her hands. She sat in the empty netherworld of loss. In this single moment—as I confronted sorrow and death—my world and hers united at last.

The sun moved far across the sky before Maria spoke. ''The gift of birth is a gift of Badimo. It is to Badimo that every living person will one day return.

''This child was given to this mother one year ago. When it smiled, cooed, and later when it babbled, this child was conversing with Badimo. We could not understand these words, for they were not the words of men. But they were words of Badimo, and that made us joyful.

''Only the Badimo know why this child could not grow into the world and language of men. Only the Badimo know why this child returned before it was ripe. We cannot know why this happened because we, as living people, are far from the knowledge of the Badimo.

''We know only the great stomach sickness that gathers many of our children. What woman here has not lost her most precious gift to the ways of disease? What woman here does not know the pain of loss?

''Today we sit together to grieve with the mother. We share her pain. From this moon to the next, we will tend this mother. She is tied to her child, and she will stay in her hut. She will sleep over the grave in her hut, and she will keep the child warm and safe on its journey back to Badimo.''

The men built a coffin using a bench and a few planks. They nailed a black cloth to it and buried the child under the floor of the hut. We sang.

Women pounded sorghum. Men slaughtered a goat and cooked the meat. We passed the drinking gourd. Death was not a shock; it was a part of the living. They spoke of the child and its mother. They spoke of the dead and of the Badimo. MaMoremi gave birth seven times; she told of the two that returned. Seipate had eight children; three died and were buried in her homestead.

An infant or child who died while still suckling its mother's breast was buried in the hut. A child who had been weaned was buried in the lolwapa, its place of play, and a child who had died after puberty, having entered the adult world, was buried in the fields. The ties between mother and child are recognized even after death. The intimate link between parent and child is evident from the child's burial ground.

Next to Maria, Ntatabo heaved a sigh, "My only grandchild has left." Near us was the household water supply in a bucket hanging from a tree. I noted its brown color and thought of its source: a stagnant dam where I once saw goats drinking. The water was not boiled. The child probably died of dysentery or gastroenteritis. No doctor was called. The child was sick, and death followed.

Or maybe not. As Maria said, we cannot know. I sat in the sun of this lolwapa listening to Maria's words, "we cannot know," and heard the echo of my past. My own daughter, Kirsten, died. The label "crib death" or "S. I. D." could not explain her death to me. In a society that does not consider the frailty of life, her death was a shock, and I its victim. Physically and psychologically bound to her being, I mourned alone. Where the living protect themselves from thoughts of death, there is little room for grieving. There is an awkward silence. To comfort, in our society, friends attempt to divert the victim from grief.

And yet, when a loved one dies, there is no victim, no diversion, and no consolation. This the Tswana accept; they stare straight into the difficult conditions of being human.

"We have been to a funeral, Rre Segatlhe. When will we go to the crossroads and down the sandpath for a marriage?"

"The oldest and youngest die on the lands. It is the best place for it. But many young ones move to town and do not come back—even to marry! Seipate's daughter will marry here . . . when Moses has earned his cattle. We will see."

"You want something good to happen?" he continued with a mysterious grin. "I have something for *you*," he said, stroking his bulging pocket.

"*Ke eng? Ke eng?*" I begged to know.

Rre Segatlhe knew well my curiosity and impatience. He

stroked his pocket, took his time to enjoy my plea, and reluctantly came forward.

"The sandpath is not the only way for news. It can come in my pocket as well . . . I have some things from my mailbox at Mogoditshane Primary School!"

Slowly he reached in his pocket, pulling out a bundle of soiled, folded envelopes. "Your mail, mosadi mogolo," he exclaimed with some sense of drama.

"They were lost because it did not say 'Segatlhe.' You must tell your Americans to write 'Segatlhe—Gustav Ernst Segatlhe."

Finally, the replies to what I thought were unanswered letters! Eagerly I read through our mail, but it soon became apparent that our friends were getting a distorted view of our life from the snatches I chose to write them.

Dear Marianne,

Thank God my husband isn't in anthropology! That you had to actually smear sh—is incomprehensible. Couldn't you assert yourself and refuse? (If you want to come home early, Suzanne said Ted has finished their new addition to the house and they would consider renting out the extra . . .)

Another,

. . . the latest thing is Support Groups. I've joined the Wednesday night group for Single Parents, and Helen goes to one for mothers of preschoolers. Do they have them in Africa yet? I suppose not. Your experience over there certainly sounds exotic. Could you please send some African recipes in your next letter so that I may try one for the Gourmet Club? . . .

Rre Segatlhe watched intently as I read the letters.

"Do you miss your sisters in America?"

"A little, but I will be too busy here to think of them."

"I have heard," his voice was distant, "Maria and Seipate are taking the news of your school down the sandpath to all the crossroads."

"The children are now so eager that they wish to extend their school day."
(A group practices English conversation with Tsotsi.)

6

To School

Sunday afternoon, Hoyt and I went to our neighbors, Polwane and Tabo, to inquire about the village school. About half of the homesteads in this area send a child to the government school near the BAC. They are homesteads where some sort of income is realized. For some, like Tabo, who work tilling the soil of the BAC, there is a small monthly salary. For others, there may be support from a relative working in town. A few with particular skills such as thatching, making pottery, or carving wooden household items have their own source of income.

Tabo told us that, although fees for elementary school levels are low, it is the required purchase of a uniform which places school attendance out of most children's reach. Yet attendance is highly valued, and families will often sacrifice basic wants to send one of their children to school. It is hoped that a properly raised and educated child will become employed and will continue to feel responsibilities toward home. Older siblings who successfully enter the job market in town are expected to share their resources by sending a younger sibling to school or by financially contributing on a regular basis to their parents' homestead. This is not considered a burden but a natural exchange for the nourishment provided during childhood.

Tabo and Polwane are sending their oldest son, Lekoto, and their oldest daughter, Lerato, to school. Mosimanegape, the second son, keeps the cattle. Tiro, the third son, tends the goats and sheep. The second oldest daughter, herself a mother, tends the household and younger siblings with Polwane. Lekoto, in his final, seventh, year at school, will take exams in the spring to qualify for secondary school. Whereas most children, regardless of exam scores, cannot hope to enter secondary school, Lekoto's father will sell cattle and his family will eat only a minimum to meet the high costs of secondary school.

Keith had been curious about the village school. Early one morning he woke me to look out of the hut window. Children were running into the moshu trees toward the low, red sun. One behind the other, they headed down the path to the BAC fields. They returned in the late afternoon, parading in uniform past the herdboys corralling goats, past the girls hauling firewood and water.

On the next trip to town, Tabo advised, we should buy Tsotsi a uniform, and on the following day, he too would go off to school. Lekoto offered to take Tsotsi on his first day. Tsotsi, still reluctant about leaving the freedom of the fields, expressed polite enthusiasm. As we returned home, Hoyt remarked that a Tswana child chosen to go to school receives the news with a sense of privilege and pride. To Keith, however, schooling was clearly an obligation taken completely for granted.

It was time for a trip to Gaborone, not only to purchase Keith's uniform, but also to buy the supplies for the "bush school" which I had promised Maria and Seipate.

Gaborone, the capital of Botswana, is only about eighteen kilometers from our lolwapa, and yet it is an entirely different life experience. Paved roads, electric lights, and telephone lines pass government buildings several stories high. A three-block shopping mall with parking lots on either side has grocery shops, pharmacies, furniture and clothing shops, variety stores, travel agencies, banks, a post office, a hotel, and a movie theater. The grass is green even before it rains, and flowers blossom in the tidy beds of traffic circles and office entry ways.

Gaborone is theoretically a town of about 20,000 residents. The official population, however, cannot keep up with the actual population. Rural people abandon fields that cannot feed them in hope of employment in town. Alongside political refugees from neighboring countries, they find housing in the southern section of town—away from the central district. Crowded together in mud houses, cardboard shelters, and structures made of junkyard finds, they seek jobs to improve their circumstances. The vast majority fail; they become trapped. Many want to return to their rural homes, but they cannot raise the funds which they promised to bring back. A few others who achieve a modicum of financial security remain in town and move to small, concrete, iron-roofed houses in another neighborhood. Those who have an education, and receive good salaries settle in two- to three-bedroom concrete houses with plumbing and electricity in a middle-income area closer to the center of town.

Set apart from these local Tswana areas are the northern residential areas of the white expatriates, the diplomats, and the upper-echelon Tswana bureaucrats. Among these inhabitants, there is recognized status in owning a Class 1 type house as opposed to a Class 2 type house, although to the casual tourist, the distinction is difficult to discern. They are all large three- to four-bedroom homes with patios and courtyards. Some have swimming pools; only a few diplomatic residences have tennis courts, but all have green lawns and lush flowers behind fences and gates decorated with brilliant bougainvillea and the "Tsaba Ntsha" sign. Discreetly blending with the background are the quarters for the maids and gardener.

Everyone was wedged so tightly into the metal back of the blue Mazda pickup that even the biggest ruts of the dirt road could not dislodge them. I checked the rearview mirror to catch sight of Tsotsi and Madala between MaMoremi's knees, Polwane's baskets, and Ntatabo's elbows. Maria and Seipate sat quietly at my side until we bumped onto the pavement, felt the wheels rolling smoothly, and exclaimed delight in unison. We cruised past a few embassies and residences. Seipate poked Maria to tell her that the makgoa servants must carry huge vessels of water back from the river just to feed the grass. They laughed. We pulled into the parking lot, but before unraveling the back and dispersing, I pointed up to a position in the sky where the sun would be when we should meet at the car again for the trip home.

In the open square of the shopping mall, Keith and Brian dangled their legs off the bench while sipping ice-cold "Appletizers" through a straw. Ecstasy! Gaborone is but a small African town, yet seeing it with eyes accustomed to the bush caused me to sit mesmerized by the pace and fashions of the day. Knee socks and safari suits strode briskly to the bank. Under broad-brimmed hats and British caps, moustaches brushed envelopes for their final seal and swift deposit down the letter slot of the post office wall. High heels—pedestals for bronze legs and stylish hemlines—glistened in the sun and tapped the concrete. A pink, fleshy child held its mother's free hand as they proceeded to the parking lot with a basket of groceries. Two women paused by my bench.

"I couldn't find crabmeat anywhere!"

"Try Food Town. I saw some there last week."

Here were the makgoa, and here too were the Africans of town. The young man in a safari suit dropped his briefcase to shake his hand of rings with the gentleman whose wristwatch sparkled like the fluorescent shirt tucked into his bell-bottom trousers. They exchanged words and, parting, crossed paths. Polished shoes and bureaucratic white shirts with ties passed the *monna mogolo* slumped over his cane, squeezing his toes back through the hole of his shoe. African prints, swirls of green and red, prints of brown and blue, wrapped heads and hips. From one shop a woman with baby bundled to her back stepped out into the sunlight, placed a box on her head, and continued on her way. Office girls, with coordinated sweaters and skirts, clicked to the take-out lunch line and, chatting, ignored the ragged street urchins on the corner. Young boys shared a Coke, tossed it, and scattered to pursue more pennies. Some carried parcels for makgoa or invaded the parking lots with aggressive sales pressure to buy oranges. Some found other means. Women clutched purses or stuffed change in their bodices.

Beware of sticky fingers! I checked the bags by my side with Keith's new uniform, school supplies, and groceries. At our first stop, the Indian shopkeeper returned my Tswana greeting with a baffled stare and British reserve. The Tswana clerk at the bookshop, delighted at our transaction in Setswana, asked me where I was from as if I did not fit the image of her usual white customer.

From the bench I scanned through the crowd for familiar figures and faces. Rounding the corner by the President Hotel, MaMoremi and Polwane headed for the parking lot. The sun was high; it was time to meet at the truck.

Bodies over and under bags, we drove out of the parking lot and came to an abrupt halt at the policeman's signal. He motioned me to pull over. I fumbled across Maria's lap to get my driver's license out of the glove compartment and looked up into his face at the window. Gruffly he commanded me to get out of the car to see another police officer. The second officer apprised me of my offense: illegally exiting out of the parking lot entrance. This was no gentle reminder.

". . . Here in Botswana, we British could not do just what we wished . . . Botswana has laws . . . but British think that . . ."

Irrelevant as it might have been to assert my American citizenship, I was willing to give it a good try. But before I could open my mouth, he slapped on the fine—20 rand ($30)—to be paid immediately at the Police chief's desk. In staccato motion, he pointed to the police station, conveniently located directly across the street. It was clear from his frozen stance that he did not want to hear a response from me. He watched me leave my carload of passengers to head across the street.

Officers in various uniforms—short pants, long pants, hats, and stripes—begrudgingly directed me around the next corner or hallway until I finally reached the man in charge. He sat alone in a concrete-block room painted patriotic blue with a picture of President Khama staring down from behind him. Although he heard me enter, he didn't look up from the stacked papers on his desk. I waited. I had learned from Rre Segatlhe. I put my violation slip on his desk and watched him take it. He lifted his eyes and stared at me. He waited.

"*Rra, Ntshwarele Rra, ga ke na madi.*" Without thinking, I pleaded submissively in Setswana. His eyes blinked; his shoulders moved; he melted. Where did I live? Yes, he had heard of us living with Segatlhe. Addressing me as a "Mokwena"[one of the Bakwena tribe], he gave me a gentle reminder on traffic rules and said he was pleased to meet me. He would let me go this time, he said in English, and then in Setswana he reminded me to please be careful.

"*Ke itumetse thata, rra.*" I thanked him as I turned to leave.

"*Go siame, mma. Tsamaya sentle,*" he returned with a smile.

"*Ee. rra. sala sentle!*" I called back.

Maria and Seipate were relieved to see me slam the car door shut and drive off.

"Hoyt, we are famous!" I exclaimed upon arrival in the lolwapa.

MaMoremi was so impressed with my floor smearing that she suggested I teach American women this skill upon my return home. The humor of it went past me because I was still thinking about Keith. That morning, for his sixth day at Boitumelo School, he had been spared the five-kilometer walk. A fellow classmate, Joseph Pulanka, came to our place with his bicycle. Still shivering in the early morning air, they set off down the path—Joseph pumping furiously through the sand; Keith riding on the back fender.

Keith had complained of being touched by everyone in the school. Wherever he went, he was followed by a retinue. This was particularly awkward when, because the school lacked toilets, he, like others, sought to hide himself in the bush. No privacy was possible. We assured him that after a few weeks the children would forget about his differences and treat him like anybody else. He must have been disposed toward attending school, for he gave us no argument and left the next morning with alacrity.

While proud of his self-confidence, I did harbor some anxiety. This was only aggravated when Hoyt came home from the BAC and jokingly remarked that Keith's attendance at the Boitumelo School has hit the gossip circuit of the expatriates. Beverley Miller, who lauded our participation in Tswana culture, was genuinely pleased to hear of Keith's attendance at the local school. The expatriates around her, however, had noticed a white child in the schoolyard. His presence there appalled them. Why didn't his parents join their carpool to attend the elite school in Gaborone? How could they send their son to a Tswana village school? Even though intellectually I could dismiss their vehement reaction, emotionally I felt vague apprehension.

I probably would have walked off toward his school to peek in on him if it had not been for expectations of me here at home. My own "bush school" was to start off under the tree by Rre Segatlhe's goat kraal. Down the paths of our crossroad the news had traveled: a chance to learn writing, reading, and perhaps some English from MaoKeef at Segatlhe's place.

"When the sun is so high," an outstretched arm measured one hand's length west of the noontime position.

"*Go siame*, fine, the chores will be done," a voice replied.

MaMoremi and I finished our section of the lolwapa floor. We left it to dry in the hot afternoon sun, and I gathered clipboards, papers, pencils, and rulers and headed for the tree.

A dozen children between five and fifteen years old were already waiting for me. Their mothers, aunts, and grandmothers grouped themselves to one side, I assumed to watch the spectacle. One by one the children were called on to stand up and introduce themselves. I entered their names in my rollbook and began by taking roll. This, I explained, we would do before every lesson. I proceeded to pass out the writing materials, and it was then that the older women came forward. They had no intention of being left out. One grabbed a clipboard, while the rest clamored for pencils. I pulled back the clipboard, sat on the papers, and held tightly to the rulers and pencils.

"No, I cannot teach the old women," I tried to say respectfully.

"*Ka Goreng? Ka Goreng?*" They demanded to know why. They pushed their way toward me and positioned themselves between myself and the seated children.

"I am only one teacher. There are many children, and there is much to learn," I tried to explain. The women stared at me. At last they were quiet. They waited for me to give in, but I delivered my final rebuff, "Either I teach only the children, or I don't teach at all."

Grumbling to each other, they retreated, but rather than leave the scene, they sat together in the background looking on. I returned my attention to the children. No one knew how to hold a pencil. I wondered if limiting the class to children was overly ambitious.

Not until long, late afternoon shadows appeared did we disperse. I had not noticed Keith's return from school. Perhaps he was relieved that I did not pounce on him with questions. At supper the family commented on my far-off gaze. Never had I taught children with such intense desire to learn. Their motivation overwhelmed me. What I had anticipated as being a mere afternoon's diversion was already, after just one session, proving to be an extraordinary challenge.

Rre Segatlhe broke my pensive mood when, upon receiving his plate of spaghetti, he exclaimed, "This is my very favorite thing. I like these worms too much!"

Before retiring for the night, he now routinely comes by our hut to say good-night and get his vinegar. He likes me to pour him one tablespoon of vinegar while he braces himself for the taste and opens his mouth for me to feed it to him. He gulps it down, slaps his chest, and bellows his satisfaction. It is his conviction that a person of his age is susceptible to blood clots and that daily doses of vinegar are an effective preventive measure. To use his expression, "Vinegar thins the blood."

To my dismay, the number of children to arrive under the tree for lessons more than doubled the next day. I tried desperately to pick out the children who had come on the first day, added a few more, and told the remainder to go home. In order to achieve worthwhile goals during my limited stay, I had no alternative but to limit the class size. Watching the downcast faces turn to leave depressed me. As it was, accepting twenty-five students was already more than the maximum I had set.

I recorded the new names and called the roll. So that I could

71

learn their names, I explained again that we would start school this way everyday. We worked on small motor movements with the pencil, and they enthusiastically took pencil and paper home to practice.

At full moon, bright beams stream into our windows. I waken to close the wooden shutters and lie restlessly listening to the confused rooster crowing intermittently throughout the night. Finally at dawn, he struts and scratches around the yard with his last calls and then retreats exhausted to his perch in the tree.

Rre Segatlhe shuffles through the lolwapa to set the fire. He washes himself in the twilight. The air is cold. Keith and I rise reluctantly and dress quickly to join Rre Segatlhe and MaMoremi by the fire for the morning greeting. I cook porridge, and Keith eats his share, setting the bowl on his lap to warm his shivering knees.

On the path outside, the workers of the BAC cycle past us. Those we know—Tabo, Neo, and Tladi—stop by the fire to greet us and then move on. The school brigade rushes past, running to keep warm—boys in khaki shorts and shirts, girls in short, mustard-yellow dresses. For several miles they run barefoot through the sand, the smallest five-year-old keeping pace with the bigger boys. What continues to amaze me is the sight of the young barefoot girls swiftly moving along the path: glinting in the morning sunlight is a glass ink bottle expertly balanced on each wooly, black head.

Joseph Pulanka arrives with his bicycle. Keith hops on the fender, and they, too, are off.

This morning I did not stay by the fire to wait for Hoyt to rise. MaMoremi would do my sweeping. I dressed sleepy Madala, straddled him over the front bar of our bike, and rode off behind Joseph and Keith to the Boitumelo School. We caught up to the running brigade but did not leave them behind. They sped up at the sight of us, and to my amazement, maintained their speed, ink bottles and all! They even had breath left to laugh at my praise!

Here was natural potential for the Olympic Games. Tiny legs running long distances through sand, not panting but laughing. But who here has heard of competitive sports? Who here would accept the status and glory of such pursuits?

We arrived at the schoolyard and one long concrete building with a facade of about eight classroom doors. Just as Keith described, he was immediately surrounded by a coterie of classmates. I greeted the ladies cooking mealies in big black pots for the midday meal. The bell sounded; a flurry to the classrooms, and all was still. The teachers marched through the open doorways. Chairs scraped the concrete floor, the students rose, and a chorus of "good morning, teacher," rang out. Another scraping of chairs—they seated themselves. They sat in rows at small wooden desks; some, like Keith, sharing books and desk because there were not enough for each to have his own.

The headmaster walked into a classroom—scraping chairs, "good morning, sir," scraping chairs, and silence. His voice boomed out. I looked in from the door outside and listened.

"Many of you still do not wear shoes to school. Brown or black leather shoes are the uniform. Those who do not wear shoes today will leave their desks now and go with me. You will do the washing today."

He led my Olympic runners to a small concrete house, his own. His wife passed out clothes, and the children bent down to scrub them over large tin pans.

I waited with Madala by the headmaster's office, the second door of eight in a row. He greeted me cordially and told me of his school. Keith was placed in standard 4—even though he was younger than the others—because at this level classes are first taught in English. It did not matter that he could not write well in script. He would catch on quickly, but I must provide my son with fountain pen and ink.

Soon they would start preparing a plot to raise vegetables. The children may be kept later than usual when work duties take time. They are fed hot mealies in the afternoon to satisfy them for the day. Did I have any questions? he asked me.

I told him that Keith had come home from school very tense the other day. He would not tell me what was wrong. He read his chapter in the history book and studied very hard. I finally asked Keith's friend, Joseph, if anything had happened that day. Joseph laughed. No, nothing unusual had happened, except that it was the first time that Keith was beaten. Our conversation continued.

"Is it true," I asked, "that Keith's teacher beat him?"

"No, his teacher did not touch him. I, the headmaster, beat him," he said, proudly taking the credit. "I beat him only three times across his fingers, one time for each question that he could not answer on his history test. There were others who needed many more beatings. Keith is not a bad student."

"Keith has never been beaten in the school in America," I started, just beginning to get wound up for an educational debate on the merits of positive as opposed to negative sanctions. But he interrupted me, and looking down at me from the high seat of his chair behind his square wooden desk, he proceeded to put me in my place.

What?! Did they not beat in America?! He did not know or care about my "American" ways. Here in Botswana, adults have responsibilities toward the growing child, and as headmaster of this school, he would see to it that children who did not learn properly were beaten. Children were to copy from the blackboard the lesson which the teacher wrote out. They were to memorize it well. If this was not done, then they should expect a beating . . .

Hoyt and I agreed that because our Tsotsi had not directly complained to us, he should continue at the village school. Along with his classmates, he would find ways to cope with the system. It would only single him out and harm his adjustment to our rural life if we sent him off to another school in town. The strict, authoritarian educational structure would not harm him; maybe it would do him some good, we rationalized. It would certainly help him to conform to the expectations placed upon him as a Tswana child in the rural society. As to our fears on what long-term effects his present experience might have on his attitude toward schooling, we rationalized again that, after all, this experience would only amount to a matter of months, not years.

Although we could appreciate that the discipline of the school, like the rearing patterns of traditional society, was based on a system of deference to elders and proscribed societal decorum, we were convinced that, in the long run, inculcated patterns of docility and submissiveness would not be conducive to the development of independent, critical thought. Later, in a conversation with the Millers, they told us that their fellow Peace Corps workers who arrived in Botswana to teach were continually frustrated by pupils who had only learned by rote, rarely expressed themselves creatively, and certainly had never contradicted a teacher. While the latter had its positive effects, the exchange of experiences which some teachers had hoped for was not possible in the classroom.

As for my purposes under the tree, the deferential attitude of my students is most beneficial. There are no interruptions. Their cooperation, however, clearly is not based solely on their upbringing but also on their own desire to learn. They listen intensely, repeat after me, and try again and again until they receive my approval. We are progressing faster than I ever dreamed possible. They are printing letters and repeating their sound values. There is a group of about ten children—Moremi, Sejaro, and Tiro among them—who are catching on so fast that I am sure they will be reading before I leave. It is certainly helpful that written Setswana, transcribed by the missionaries of long ago, is phonetic.

Relieved, I bid Rre Segatlhe good-bye and watched him pedal off to Mogoditshane. It was a perfect conclusion to the tension between us that morning, and pedaling through the deep sand, I thought, might restore his sobriety. I tried to put the morning's events out of my mind, but the nagging fear that it could happen again kept me thinking about it.

MaMoremi had taken Madala with her to Polwane's place. Hoyt, as usual, had gone out on interviews. Tsotsi was off at school, and I sat alone in the shade inside our hut planning my school lesson. Meanwhile, Rre Segatlhe, whose kadi consumption had put him in high spirits, entered the hut to join me. He closed the door behind him and moved to my side, sitting very close to me on the bedframe.

"You do this school business too much!" he declared.

Having successfully arrested my attention, he proceeded to praise me in Setswana. He spoke of "my beauty," leaped forward with poetic proclamations of love, and then solemnly stated his physical demands. Gasping, stunned, I backed away, dropping a crayon to the floor, and when I moved over on the bedframe, I crushed it under my foot. It was beginning to feel like a comedy skit, but I nevertheless clicked into the gear that any emergency situation demands: swift strategy. To recuperate pause for thought, I feigned ignorance of his Setswana. He repeated himself, and I could only think that our entire presence or all of Hoyt's anthropological research now depended on my response. Above all, I could not offend our host.

"I love you too much," he repeated.

"*Ee*, Rre Segatlhe," I stressed, "I like you and respect you as well."

He did not tolerate my misunderstanding and bluntly demanded my affections. Grabbing for threads from heaven, I found none. Striking my most pious pose, I told him of my strict religious code which forbade me adulterous deeds, even in these most tempting times. He stopped to ponder this, and sensing that I had gained some advantage, I rose, quickly opened the door, and walked out into the deserted lolwapa. He followed me into the sunlight; we were still alone. He was not impressed with my God, he said, and begged for a kiss. He grabbed me and kissed my lips. Jovially, I returned his kiss with a peck on his cheek, hoping thereby to minimize any significance he might draw from our interchange. We sat in the chairs outside. I waited for anyone to come along. While I tried to make light of the morning's episode, he assured me that my God could make exceptions for me. No, I insisted, I could not jeopardize my place in heaven for earthly desires.

Perhaps, he suggested, it would be good to pay a visit to his girlfriend in Mogoditshane. I rushed to fetch his bicycle and polished his boots while he pumped the tires. He changed into a clean white shirt, fastened the cuffs of his trousers, and put on his old Boer War helmet. I untwisted his suspenders and admired him, gently reminding him to take special care until the effects of kadi had worn off. He smiled in my direction, and the proud macho announced that possibly he would not return that same evening; in all likelihood, he would not return until tomorrow morning.

He was gone not one night but two. I started to worry about him and worked myself up to feeling guilty that I had happily supervised his departure. Weaving down some sandpath was a very elegant and very drunk seventy-three-year-old madala on the rusted frames of a vintage, balloon-tired bicycle. Madness. Most likely he had landed in a ditch somewhere.

But Rre Segatlhe finally cycled in at noon and strode into our lolwapa.

"Certainly I rode all the way to Mogoditshane!" he protested my doubts. ". . . and I slept with my lovely mosadi for two nights," he swaggered. He continued to elaborate such fascinating details that, much to his pleasure, I was his captivated listener and late, as a consequence, for the children waiting beneath the tree.

The children are now so eager that they wish to extend their school day. When we finish with Setswana reading and writing, they urge me to teach them more. I finally relented, so that what originally amounted to a couple of hours a day now takes up all of the afternoon.

For Setswana it was necessary to split the class into three groups. While one group repeats oral exercises, the other two groups do written work. Two of these groups are still reviewing letter-sound values; the third is blending sounds with ease. It was only a few days ago that Sejaro discovered he was reading words. His toes curled in the sand underneath him, he shifted his body forward onto his raised heels, and holding his page up high, he slowly read out words that he himself had constructed with the sounds he had learned, "SALA, LALA, BALA." The moment was magic. Moremi and Maria Maloma understood. "KALA, KWALA," they shouted out one after the other. The contagion spread. When I passed out their first Setswana readers, they bent open the covers with reverence and lost themselves to the wonder of the printed words. Along with them, I rode a crest of joy, capturing moments of recognition, discovery, and meaning.

As a large group, we worked with rudimentary mathematical concepts, and sometimes we would explore answers to anyone's questions. One day a child asked if it was true—as she had heard—that the sun did not travel around the earth. A lively discussion followed, and it ended, much to everyone's entertainment, with our tree representing the sun and various class members rotating around it in elliptical fashion, while, in turn, other classmates circled them as moons. We attracted various onlookers with muffled laughter among Boitumelo School children in uniform returning home. They had often lingered around us, but now they ventured forward out of curiousity. It was here that I took my stand: drawing a line far beyond our tree, I forcefully told the uniformed school children that they were to pass by that line without coming near us or looking on. We were very busy learning and did not wish any disturbance. The class in rags cheered and gleefully watched their privileged peers move on.

There is a strong feeling of solidarity and seriousness of purpose under our tree. At the conclusion of every day we gather for their favorite subject—English. Along with Setswana, English is an official language of Botswana. All government workers must know English; for a Tswana in town, mastery of English is a sign of success. The children have learned English words here and there on brief trips to town, from community members with work experience, or from our family conversing in the lolwapa.

Using an oral drill method, I called out common Setswana words to which they, in unison, were to call back the English equivalent. *Ntsha*—dog; *dipudi*—goats; *dinku*—sheep; *dikgomo*—cattle; and upon hearing the Setswana word for pig, *kolobe*, they proudly called back "Nixon"! They expected delighted praise, not an uncontrolled fit of laughter.

He pulled a chair forward for me. "Sit," Rre Segatlhe commanded.

"You are too much with children. You teach them too much. One small lesson is good, but not many for the whole of the day!"

Avoiding my eyes, he fixed his sight beyond me. His voice shook with anger.

"You spoil children. Moremi, Tiro, and Sejaro do not look at goats but at numbers in the sand. You are blind! Do you think little Maria Maloma fetches wood in the afternoon? No, she sends her sister and hides with a book! The children forget work; they get lazy. Your school is no good."

"Have parents told you this, Rre Segatlhe?"

"No. But I say so. I don't like your school."

"Rre Segatlhe. *Ke a utlwa.* [I hear you.] Since it bothers you, I will not teach on your land anymore. It was not my idea to start this school. I will ask the parents what they think, and if they feel as you do, I will stop teaching. If they do not share your ideas, I can only promise you that we will not meet in your sight. I am truly sorry that I caused you this anger."

"School or no school, Moremi must go. You have spoiled him. You still give him food. Do you think I am blind? Moremi is no good to me just eating and writing numbers. He must go tomorrow. I have already found another boy."

He stared straight into the horizon. I waited politely for moments to pass and, relieved that he said nothing more, left his presence.

In our field there is a sandy hollow behind a termite hill. His words, "Moremi must go," echoed in my mind. Alone, I sat questioning. Was I wrongly interfering with traditional life? Did some parents now feel as Rre Segatlhe that school matters would adversely affect children's commitments to rural labor? Or was Rre Segatlhe's anger a result of his own personal discontent? Did he demand strict servile behavior from Moremi to the exclusion of all other joys? Was he jealous of the daily attention I paid the children?

Suppose all these questions could be answered in the affirmative. Then what? Stop teaching? Moremi would still have to go; that decision was obviously final. But what about the other twenty-four eager minds? What hopes had I built up in them—and, yes, in my own mind too? Stop teaching. Admit it—how could I? Was my teaching a sentimental, self-indulgent pursuit disturbing routines of village life?

Crying. What for? Blotting cheeks and messing my shirt—a maudlin heap by the termite hill. Every doubt was dredged up and tossed about for surrender.

I crept back through the darkness into our hut. The boys slept soundly, Tsotsi buried under his blanket and Madala with his ragged stuffed cow "Hedgy" slipping from his arm. Hoyt looked up from the candlelight.

"Where the hell have you been?"

Moremi packed his things into one compact bundle. He tucked it under his arm and waited by the morning fire. MaMoremi finished her tea. I looked for the car keys. While starting the motor, I looked into the rearview mirror to see MaMoremi rise to join me. Moremi bid Rre Segatlhe good-bye with a formal Tswana handshake: a handshake, a firm grasp of thumbs, and a final handshake.

The old madala did not rise from his stool but looked on solemnly as Moremi turned toward the car.

"MaoKeef, I told Moremi what you told me last night—that you will get him into a school in Gaborone! He is boiling over with happiness."

"I said I would *try* to get him into a school," I corrected her.

"*Ee,*" she agreed with a confident smile.

Although determined to do everything possible to get Moremi into a school, I had no idea what was involved nor what likelihood there was of success. I tried, however, to conceal my doubts. After all, MaMoremi—believing that all had already been accomplished—continually broke the silence with her thanks to me. Her firstborn son, she explained, would have the chance she had always hoped for—a chance to determine his future, not by the dictates of others, but by his own initiative and labor.

"*Ke itumetse, mma,*" she thanked me again.

"It is not just for Moremi—this stroke of luck," she went on.
"It is for the whole of my family. Think of it! Moremi in school!
And when he finishes and gets a good job in town, he will pay to
get Leraka and Elina to school . . ."

She had all her children educated and employed. They were
paying her old-age support by the time we finally pulled into the
government school in the Bontleng area of Gaborone. Although
built in the same style as Keith's village school, this school had
not one, but several, long rows of concrete-block classrooms. The
door of each classroom opened onto the common courtyard
where we stood wondering where to go. We approached the first
passing adult who promptly directed us to the door of the headmaster's office.

"Good morning," he greeted us. His English was as superbly
precise as the rules in his book.

"I repeat, Mrs. Alverson, we would be perfectly delighted to
enroll this boy in our first grade—standard 1. It is truly unfortu-
nate that he is too old. He has turned thirteen years. There is a
government rule of the Ministry of Education: after twelve years
of age NO child is accepted as a new student."

He ushered us to the door.

"We are very pleased that you are delighted to enroll Moremi," I managed to say with enthusiasm. "We will now go to the
Ministry of Education and try to get special permission for him,
and hopefully, Mr. Molefi, we will be back this afternoon!"

"It has not happened before. Do not get your hopes up," he
warned us judiciously.

"*Ee, rra,*" I replied in agreement. "*Sala sentle, rra.*" We took our
leave.

"*Tsamayang sentle, bomma,*" he broke into Setswana, and,
"Good luck to you," he rang out as we turned to go.

MaMoremi's undaunted faith in her "great stroke of luck" had
had its effect on me. We went directly to the Ministry of Education. We negotiated a series of stairs, hallways, doors, and refer-
rals until we were finally face-to-face with a Tswana government
official who was sympathetic to our cause. Although he had no
power to make any decision in our favor, he helped work out a
strategy. The age barrier, he insisted, would be impossible to
circumvent. We would have to consider Moremi as a transfer
student and try to place him in standard 2. It, however, remained
to be decided whether the Ministry of Education would accept his
previous bush schooling as transfer credit. This decision could

only be made by the Minister herself. Unfortunately, he added, the Minister was not in her office but at home recuperating from an operation. MaMoremi and I, ignoring the official's polite signals to leave, remained seated and waited for something to happen. He finally offered to call the Minister at home. I could speak to her and plead our case over the telephone, he suggested.

Starting with a Setswana greeting, I tried to create a good impression speaking Setswana but soon found it necessary to rely on English. I described Moremi's abilities and progress in my class. I assured her that he would be supported financially by us. This would be our gift to Botswana, for Moremi had much promise. She was kind. She heard me out and agreed to transfer credit if he could pass a test for the standard 1 level. He was to proceed to the school at once, and she would arrange for his testing.

There was little I could do to prepare him in the half hour that we waited for his test. Nevertheless we tried. He listened anxiously; he concentrated; he was very determined. When he left us for the classroom, I tried to prepare MaMoremi for the letdown, but she would not listen.

"He passed math but could not read well. He does not know much English. But he is good enough," Headmaster Molefi declared.

Showing no surprise, we calmly registered him to begin the next day. Once in the car again, we screamed out with joy. "Good enough Moremi" got his uniform and shoes.

At the agreed-upon tree they waited: twenty-four children, their mothers, carrying infants, younger sisters and brothers, and some fathers and grandparents. As soon as I arrived, a few children with no representatives apologized for their parents who could not come. There was absolutely no understanding as to why school should be discontinued; to the contrary, couldn't more children be included? My questions were shrugged off. For a while there was chaos as some older women pushed forward to insist again that they too wanted schooling. In a moment of silence, I persisted with my query. They did not seem to understand what worried me. School was a good thing, they called out. If they could afford it, they would send many more of their children to school. Little Tebogo, the youngest member of the class, stood by her father. He commanded order, stepped forward and spoke out, directly addressing the concerns which I had raised.

"You have asked a question we have asked ourselves. We do not know the answer. There are those of us who dislike town living. We have seen children of town who have lost manners toward their elders and have chosen to beg rather than to work. But our children live on the lands. They know their duties. This school does not—as you fear—make them forget. This it cannot do. Things are changing whether we like it or not. Can the elders teach our children all that they will need to know tomorrow? They can teach them many, many things, but not all. With our taxes the road to Gaborone is being paved, and a clinic will be built in Sebele. Who decides what is to be done? The government. I cannot understand the government officials who come here with English. I cannot write a letter in Setswana to tell them of our needs. Our children will inherit our animals and our fields, and, in their time, to protect our way of life, they will need to know how to write and read."

This justified my efforts and buoyed my spirits. They were not curious about my reason for a new meeting place. Maybe some of them could guess, for it seemed to me that for several weeks there were lively conversations between Rre Segatlhe and his visitors.

Rre Segatlhe noticed my reserve. He tried to humor me. As I passed him his dish of rice, he exclaimed, "Ah, a plateful of little white ants. I like them too much!" He is never so happy as when I serve him. The cat sidled up to his leg, and he refrained from giving him the usual kick.

"Tsotsi, come get this worthless cat," he chided affectionately.

It was time to make peace. No matter how selfish, jealous or domineering he acted, he would always, I had to admit, command our love and respect. Having lived alone for most of his life, he was comfortably pursuing his own self-interest, even if it conflicted with others. He had gained a respected position as herbalist and witch doctor by dint of his own hard work and planning. Botswana was his home, but it was the home he had chosen.

I knew that he had traveled far and learned the ways of many people. In this rural community, he was the only elder who spoke English, and he received patients and visitors from distant places. It was nothing to see a strange car in front of Rre Segatlhe's lolwapa. Rre Segatlhe was worldly. Rre Segatlhe was knowing and proud. If anyone could, it was he that understood the adjustment we were daily making while we lived as his children under his rules; and, despite our differences, he tried to be understanding and supportive. As best I could, this is what I told him.

Affectionately he patted my knee and called me mosadi mogolo. Many times I had asked him to tell me about his life; now he asked me to fetch the kadi. We should settle in comfortably, for it was a long story.

". . . I went to Kopong, Botswana, to learn to be a doctor in the hands of a Mokhalagadi." (Rre Segatlhe, wearing a fur hat made by Montsho, sits with his Mokhalagadi visitor.)

7

A Tswana Life-World

It is I, Gustav Ernst Segatlhe. Yes, you know, mosadi mogolo—because you also have a German name that I have two German names. Ow! You are surprised. You did not expect to find any German names in Botswana! I was born in 1899 as Segatlhe on the Tswana lands of South Africa near the border of what the British, the whites, then called Bechuanaland. In those days, like today, there were many Tswana people living in what the whites called South Africa and Bechuanaland. The border was nothing. It was easy to go back and forth. I did not receive my German names, Gustav Ernst, until I ran away from home to a German Lutheran Mission.

But I am jumping too far! As I have said to you, at the time that I was born the British called this place Bechuanaland. The British were not truly interested in our land or our people. Like many white nations in Africa, they stayed here to make themselves rich and powerful and to keep out the other nations wanting to take land for the same reason. As you know, Maokeef, it is good to keep a cat in the lolwapa to eat the things we do not like to see crawling in our mealies. For us, the British were like the lolwapa cat. And there were many pests crawling the sandpaths to the lolwapas! First, there were the Boers, coming from South Africa, taking our land, stealing our cattle, and worst of all, trying to take our boitlopo (self-esteem). Second, the Germans who took the lands in East and Southwest Africa were also looking to our lands. The Germans and Boers were ready to hold hands and cross over to Bechuanaland. But our cat, the British, kept them out. That is why they called this place the British Protectorate of Bechuanaland.

But as I have told you, I was not born here, but on the Tswana lands just south of here in what was named by the whites in 1910 the Union of South Africa—what is today called the Republic of South Africa. My mother died just after the birth, so my father took me to another woman who was nursing her infant. She cared for me well until I was about twelve years old. Then I returned to my father's place. My sisters kept the lolwapa, and with my older brothers I herded the animals. This was as it should be. A boy must know the fields and the animals.

But after some time, I ran away. My father, he gathered beans into a bag with holes. My brothers were two bulls who could not share the cattle fold. I have told you of pests. As you know, some worms are good to eat. From other herd boys, I had heard of free schooling at the German Lutheran Mission near our lands. I left the herds and ran to the Lutheran Mission. There I was baptized and confirmed and given my names. I am no heathen. I am Gustav Ernst Segatlhe. I learned many things—to read, to write, and to speak English and Afrikaans. Of course, this did not mean that I would forget my own culture. This the Mission did not understand. So when the time came, I went with another boy from the mission, to be circumcised. We were initiated together. It is a good thing to be a man among others.

Now hunger cannot make a person wise. While in the Mission School, I had to keep myself alive by stealing from the fields. It was time for me to look for work. My first two jobs as a boy of twenty years were tending cattle for Boer farmers. They fed me well, and after a year, I was lucky to receive a cow. But there was no pay in it, so I moved on to find other work.

In those days, not only young Tswana boys went to look for work in South African towns, but also Tswana men with families and land in Bechuanaland. Why is this? It is because of the South African gold mines! I can say to you that when the gold mines first came to collect workers from the Tswana lands in South Africa and Bechuanaland, no Tswana man wanted to leave his family and land. Why did he need metals jingling in the pocket if he had mealies and goats? Why should he ride a bus to a strange place? But our British cat and our Tswana chiefs smelled gold for the stomach. They made a tax called the Head and Hut Tax. To pay the tax to the British and the Tswana chiefs, men and boys were sent to work in the mines. And when boys discovered that the coins they earned could buy a cow, some went to the mines to earn bogadi. These Tswana men and boys thought that they could work a month or two to pay the tax or buy a cow and then go straight home to the lolwapa. Ow! But the mines were too clever for them!

The mines made them sign a paper, a contract, for a long time of work, such a long time that many were swallowed up by the city and its strange ways. Women were left alone in the lolwapa too long. Boys came back from the mines wearing shoes and thinking they were men when they still could not even skin a goat! I say to you, Maokeef, the South African mines changed our Tswana ways!

As a young man I had no lands and no family to care about. I could read and speak English and Afrikaans. Why should I go to the mines with the others? I was ready to find my gold my own way. The winding road does not let you sleep. I can say that I went a long, long way and did many, many things in my lifetime.

In Potchefstrom, I was cook at a military base. This was my first paying job. From there I went to taste the life of the big city. I went to Johannesburg. I moved through the townships like a fox. Indeed, I lived the life of a fox. Always on the move, living with different relatives. Leaving the farms, leaving my home, and going to Johannesburg removed me from the bondage of poverty for sure. I fared well in town. In 1921 I went to Natal, where first I signed a contract to work in a coal mine. Open-pit. None of this underground work for me. What can you learn of life if you're buried alive half the day? I worked at the mine six months, living in the mine compound.

No one gets anywhere working in the mines. So I went to Vryheid in search of better work. Really, I was looking for lots of things at once. At that age the thorn of young love makes one's blood run hot. I was constantly chasing after girls.

I landed a job as plumber's apprentice. I worked with a certain Mr. Long. I learned much from him. As you know, the white men don't go out of their way to teach or to help you to understand what it is you're supposed to be doing. They just point at tools, or work, grunt, and bark orders, and yell and kick you if you do something wrong. But I was a clever fox. I used to watch Mr. Long every minute; I followed him and watched what he did and how he did his work. I learned a lot that way. If I had just been able to get more schooling, I'd be in America right now!

I liked to watch and learn to do things on my own. Now this plumbing work was heavy for a young boy like me, and no matter how much I could learn and do, I knew that only a white one could get good pay. Besides I had other interests and wanted to move on, so I quit in 1923 and went to the cane fields near Durban. That was rough work. Ow! Those Indian foremen were a mean lot. They would beat you. And if you tried to beat them back, you'd wind up in a hell of trouble. This was useless work. So I ran away to Durban. To hell with the contract!

In Durban I found a job at an SAS [Suid Afrikaanse Spoorweg] refreshment hotel. There I had a job as second chef. That was relaxation and good food for me. I would wash pots, peel potatoes, watch the cooking food, clean fish. Pay was pretty good. I got £ 2 4s., with 4d. increment per month each three months. I worked there for two years.

Now as you know, I was still a young man at the time. And I enjoyed going places, visiting people on my bike when work was slow. Why should I bust my ass for £ 2? When my boss asked where I was going, I told him he wasn't the only white in the world. I just left the place and sought work elsewhere! I knocked around in Pietermaritzburg for a long time doing odd jobs. In fact, I did everything imaginable except commit murder.

Of course, I could move from place to place! Sure they had the pass laws, but as long as I found a job, I could always get another pass. I had to renew passes at different times, but this was easy if I had a job. It was not like today. Back then, passes were just to help a place hold on to its worker. After all, if they spit on his skin and did not pay him, why should a worker stay too long? If a man ran away from the contract and tried to get a job somewhere else, they could see it from his pass, but as long as they had a worker to hire, what did they care where he had been? To become a rich nation, South Africa needed workers everywhere; they needed the black workers who, no matter how hard they worked, how much they learned, could never get rich themselves! This is what I finally learned!

I can tell you that four years after I left South Africa—in 1948—when Malan came to power, things started to change with the pass laws for the Tswana workers. Malan was the first President of the Boer Party, and just like a Boer and all the Boers after him, he kept black people down, down, down. Imagine! The Boers want a Tswana elder to say "Yes, Sir, Boss," to get on his knees to scrub the floor or cut grasses with scissors! The Boers use pass laws to keep apartheid planted, and it is growing so big it will choke them all!

But I am jumping too far! In 1929 I got a job at Grace Hospital as an apprentice to an electrician, a Scottish fellow named Mr. Helsey. I even used to go to his house and eat rice and drink tea and savor all kinds of delicacies of the white people. At this time I was living at a location called "Settlers." This guy, Helsey, used to have me do everything. He'd send me on errands to buy groceries, go do things for his wife. And as payment, he'd let me buy things for myself. I particularly like a variety of food. Eating like Europeans is nice indeed. Pork is my favorite. I ate well working with this electrician. But suddenly my luck changed. I suspect to this day I was bewitched by a certain policeman named Cele. He used to earn £ 2 per month, and he was jealous of me in my position, being in charge of the electricity in the hospital. Anyway I was burned on the hand and fingers by an electrical wire. That's why I can't use my hand to this day. I was hospitalized for some months and received pay of £ 4 and 10s. And £ 36 workman's compensation. But I lost three of my fingers. I had to quit late in 1929, and for one year I was out of a job. I had to live off my wits, planning all the time how to get through the day, the week, the month.

Finally I got a job helping a fellow in his shoe repair business, Mr. Ntombela. He paid me 6d. per shoe for stitching the heel or sole. I learned the art of shoe repair from him, something I would use later on.

In 1931 I decided to leave Natal and go back to Johannesburg, where I could live with one of my sisters. I had no fixed job at that time, but I managed to save close to £ 300, not in the savings bank, but in the house where I was living, buried in the ground.

Now if you die, that kind of money buried in your place becomes "ghost money." When I got back to Johannesburg, some friends and I once tried to dig up some ghost money we'd heard about. But do you think we got anywhere? This was in Mayfair, a suburb of Johannesburg. We hadn't even gotten into the place when the cops spied us. They were mounted on horseback and pointing revolvers at us. There we stood with our picks and shovels. Lucky for us, they just told us to beat it.

I did a lot of things in Johannesburg. I was working as a peddler of soft goods with a certain Indian shop owner. He would provide me with the wares and sales price. I would go off, sell, and we divided the profits. But that job got me into difficulties. The cops caught me because I didn't have a hawker's license. Lucky for me, they just fined me 5s., which I could pay, and I was released. Another time I was passing near a shop when a Boer cop yelled at me, *"Kom hier jy kaffir"* [Come here, you nigger!] I had no pass, so I had to escape. I jumped on my bike and took off. Now the roads were slippery, wet from recent rain. I was pedaling like mad, with the Boer behind me on his horse. Off we went down the road, cop on my tail. Bad luck got me. I crashed the bike, but I was far enough ahead of the policeman that I made it to a barbed wire fence, slipped through, and got away. Sometimes, if it's a matter of survival, you can do amazing things.

By the end of 1932 I was established in the private business, hawking from my bicycle to sell intestines, heads, and hoofs of beasts. This was not the best line of work, but I got enough money from it to open my own shoe repair place in Brixton, where I took advantage of the Boer trade. What a pain having to deal with Boers! One day a Dutch lady came into the shop and said to me (mind you, no greeting or anything), "Hey, Jim!" Now my blood boiled. "How much do you charge to attach this heel to a lady's shoe?"

I said, "I'm not Jim. Jim's in the backyard. So if you don't know me, which you don't, then you'd better call me by the trade I'm in: Meneer Skoenmaaker."

So I took the shoe and threw it out the window. Hours later her husband pitches up, and he had with him the same bloody shoe. He was very polite. He called me Meneer Skoenmaaker. So I took the shoe and fixed it.

Shortly after this, I moved my shop to Sophiatown [an African township] where I had business opportunities.

Now in 1933 I had decided I'd better get to Botswana, Kgaphamadi, to learn about witchcraft. Now I'll tell you why. Just before I left Natal, when I was staying in Pietermaritzburg, I had sought out a witch doctor who could help me to become a witch doctor myself. The "accident" at Grace Hospital made me aware that if I was to succeed in this life, I would have to learn to defend myself from the jealousy and envy of those with medical power. So I had begun my studies as a doctor. Now while I was running my shoe business in Sophiatown, I was practising with new medicals to help people on occasion. It was then I realised that I could make much more money as a witch doctor than I could as a shoe repairman. Also, I was hit by too many misfortunes—and I was convinced they could have been avoided completely if I had known how to take proper medical precautions. I was arrested for a pass offense. I had neglected to renew my day laborer's permit for two months. I was taken to Newlands police station, booked, and kept there one week. Again, I was once arrested for playing cards (gambling in the street) at night. This time I was fined and discharged. Now all this would have been unnecessary if I had known how to protect myself. So in 1933 I went to Kopong, Botswana, to learn to be a doctor in the hands of a Mokhalagadi [a Tswana from the Kalahari Desert] who lived there. There I became a powerful doctor.

I went back to Johannesburg, but I dreamed of going back to Botswana one day. During this time I tried a lot of things. Some friends and I had heard about the diamonds down in Losotho. So we walked down to Maseru to see if we could turn up some. We spent months looking for diamonds but had no luck. We were running short of food and money, so we had to do something in a hurry. We got into the business of delivering *dagga* [marijuana]. It was a good line of work but risky. I never got caught—it was good luck. A week after I left to come back to Johannesburg, all my friends who had stayed to deliver dagga were arrested by the police.

For the next ten years I did odd jobs in Johannesburg. I got into the taxi business with my brother's car. I was driving all over Johannesburg. All went well 'till 1939, when I was arrested for not having a driver's license. Actually, at that time I had hired a driver who had no license, and I had no business license, so we were both arrested and fined. This license business is hard to figure out.

In 1936 I decided to try work in the gold mines, so I signed on a nine-month contract. I worked one day underground. It was horrible. You could lose your mind doing work like that. So I ran away. I was found by the police and arrested for running away from the mines. I was fined £ 1 10s. and discharged.

The next few years I did odd jobs, but nothing big came along. My blood was beginning to cool. I grew tired of the fast life. I had been doing quite well with starting a medical career in Johannesburg, but I longed to try my hand in the lands of Botswana. You see, my reputation as a witch doctor was spreading quickly.

To this day, people still come from Johannesburg to see me. They pay cash and plenty of it! Here on the lands, people simply tell me of a cow or a sheep some place or another. Most likely, I'll never see it. And if I begin to press for payment, the patient might seek out another doctor to have me killed. So I wait and sell tobacco and kadi. The people from town and from cities, they pay plenty of cash!

I've had good fortune in my medical practice. No one has ever died at my hands. Many barren women whom I have made fertile again have named children after me; they're testimony to my success. I have helped many keep their work by preparing medicines against their employer's wrath.

Well, mosadi mogolo, you know I am a powerful doctor. I was telling you that in 1944, I finally decided to leave Johannesburg for good. I gathered together all my belongings and packed them in my wagon and rolled my way to Botswana . . . no, no, Bechuanaland. When I came to this land, it was still—as before—the British Protectorate of Bechuanaland.

Certainly things had changed! There were some new roads, and some places had water. Schools and medicals could be found here and there. The British still were not interested in these lands and left many things to the chiefs. When first I came here, I bought a scrap van to haul and sell wood in Lobatse. But my heart lay in farming, so I got these fields, you see there, from the Chief in Mogoditshane. There were thirty hectares of cultivated field here. With my savings I bought cattle to start my herd. I was alone on the land. My closest and only neighbors were Molefi and his wife, Maria. I became a successful farmer.

But as I was farming, I can say to you, things were changing here in Bechuanaland. No more pests to fight, the British cat wanted to wear the Tswana hat. I say to you, they wanted to decide more and more things for the Tswana chiefs! Tswana chiefs were going back and forth with each other and then with the British. I believe the British are not Boers; they knew in their hearts the Tswana hat belongs on the Tswana chief. But one does not always like what is known by the heart, and it took the British some time to give Bechuanaland to its people.

Before this time, Khama III, Chief of the Bamangwato Tribe, sent his son, Seretse Khama, to be educated in England. Yes, Oxford University, it is! And the young Seretse Khama learned many good things for Bechuanaland, but also, he fell in love with a British woman, a white woman. Now it is not the Tswana custom for the son of a chief to just fall in love and marry. This is not the son's decision. But the young Seretse Khama learned many things overseas, and he married the woman he loved without his father's blessing. Ow! There was much talk about this marriage all over the world! Such a noise because the black son of an African chief married a white British woman! Ow! Ow! I say to you there was too much noise! The British cat had no more pests to keep out, so it kept out Seretse Khama and his bride. The British refused to let Seretse Khama come home with his wife! For eight years, Seretse Khama could not come home, but finally in 1956 the cat gave up and let him come home with his wife *if* he promised never to be chief.

You know, mosadi mogolo, that the people of these lands cannot be told by the British cat that suddenly a man is not the son of a chief when he *is* the son of a chief! And why all the noises about a white wife? People are people. To separate people by color is a strange idea invented by the whites. In 1966 the British cat passed the Tswana hat to its chief. Bechuanaland was erased from the maps forever, for these lands are Botswana. I can say to you our first President, President Seretse Khama and Lady Ruth Khama are good for us, good for South Africa, and good for the world!

You know, mosadi mogolo, there are many who have come to live here on the lands—your sisters Maria, Seipate, Polwane, Ntatabo, and all their families. I live alone. Certainly this is not a good thing! I had a wife—and two sons. She disgraced me and left many years ago. She took the children with her. I do not talk of it. I know that my downfall in life has been women. I tell you, mosadi mogolo, had I not gotten bitten by women, I would be a rich man today.

"And the greatest work of woman is to fill the world."

8

To Fill the World

Even the melon supply has dwindled, and Hoyt travels to interviews with bags of mealie. Last week he wanted to interview some of the men whom he had not seen for several weeks. Kgosana was among them.

Kgosana and his wife, Keledi, came to this rural community to escape crowded living conditions in the village. They are recent arrivals, and having just finished building their hut, they are now preparing for spring plowing. While his wife, pregnant with their first child, clears fields, Kgosana goes off into the hills with his axe to look for wood. He hauls it back and carves household items—motse and kika for stamping grain. With his earnings, he will buy seed for their first planting.

At noon Hoyt arrived at Kgosana's place. It looked deserted. He stepped into the lolwapa and called out. A faint voice replied from within the hut. Keledi, sitting on a goatskin mat with a newborn infant lying at her side, weakly called out to him, "Modise!" Reaching for Hoyt, she begged him for food.

Kgosana, she explained, had left to search for the special wood he needed to carve. He had been gone two days and still had not returned. The day after he left, the baby came. Keledi was alone. After the birth she was weak and sick. Walking was painful. She could not fetch water. Only a little was left, not enough to cook mealie, and she feared that she would not have enough milk to feed the baby. She waited for Kgosana, and in the meantime, she also waited for someone to cross the field to help her.

Hoyt returned to our place to seek my help. He planned to take me to help Keledi so that he could continue his work, but I was not within calling distance. He threw down his interview schedule, loaded the truck with food supplies, and left for Kgosana's place. He collected wood and set a fire. Keledi cooked a meal. He filled her water buckets as she swept the loose dust from her lolwapa and sat with her and the newborn until day's end.

Kgosana, Keledi, and their infant arrived one morning for tea. The child, they said would be named Modise. Hoyt bounced off his bike, beaming with pride, and abandoned his interviews. Everyone listened while Rre Segatlhe threw bones for the infant, Modise. The group of men sitting in the lolwapa clamored to see the infant, and Rre Segatlhe passed the baby bundle, like a rare treasure, from one to the next. The infant, Modise, was passed around and coddled until he uttered his first fretful cry. Thereupon Molefi passed him to Keledi, who nursed him to quell his discontent.

Babies are not left to cry. Until they are finally weaned at about two years, they are generously cradled, cuddled, and carried. Parents and elder siblings lavish them with attention and affection; to each baby, the entire community is family.

"We have cattle. We have goats and sheep. But the greatest gift of God is the infant child," exclaimed Tabo.

"And the greatest work of woman is to fill the world," added Kgosana.

Tabo had held and looked at the infant with such wonder and delight that it would seem he had never seen an infant before. Yet Polwane had delivered infants to him ten times, seven of which had lived. And just last month, his fifteen-year-old daughter, Gomolemo, delivered her firstborn, his first granddaughter.

Gomolemo has no husband and still lives with her parents, yet the birth of her daughter was greeted by the same enthusiasm as Keledi's. More than half (some say ninety percent) of all first children are born out of wedlock, and there is no stigma attached to such births. Like Gomolemo, a young mother often stays with her family until marriage. The infant is cared for by everyone in the lolwapa, and when grown to childhood, it is expected to contribute to the household along with its age-mates. In rural society, where the smallest unit for survival in a homestead is six to eight people, women and children are sources of life-sustaining labor. With the high infant death rate, each birth, each "greatest gift of God," is a potential contributor to the group's survival. If an unwed mother cannot remain at home with her family, there will be other homesteads to welcome her. To bear children gives any woman status.

"It is good to have children, husband or no, but to be a wife with no children is a woman's greatest sadness," Maria told me.

Since birth was not tied to the concept of marriage, I asked Maria, "when or how do young women decide to marry?"

"What do you mean *decide* to marry? This is not something for a woman, alone, to decide. This is a matter for families; it is what keeps us all together."

"When a daughter leaves her family for marriage," Maria continued, finding a comfortable position to settle on our lolwapa floor, "she can no longer help her own family everyday. She goes to fetch water and to work for her husband's family. It is only proper, then, for the husband's family to honor her family with a gift of cattle. This is what we call bogadi. The parents of both daughter and son must give something to marriage, and in their old age the marriage will give things to them. If there are problems in the marriage it is not just a problem for the couple, it is a problem for the families. The families must help to keep things together."

"Some people say that bogadi is bad because a woman is traded for cattle; it looks like she is bought with cattle," I told her.

"Nonsense! Those people do not know what it means to give a cow, and they do not know what it means to be a woman. Those people are makgoa, I know it!"

She looked at me for confirmation, but my silence showed my ignorance.

"People who say bogadi is bad," she continued, "confuse us with the Bamangwato who live near us. A long time ago, the Chief of the Bamangwato became a Christian, and they were forced to change. No more bogadi; only one wife—even if you do not have enough children! But I ask you, MaoKeef, what do these makgoa know about bogadi that is bad? What do they know about our family ways? And how can they say it is bad if they do not know anything about us?"

"Fetch me the kadi, MaoKeef, I will tell you the Tswana way." She held snuff to her nose, pulled in a deep breath, and began to reminisce on the occasion of her only son, Tladi's marriage.

"Things worked out very well from the start. Tladi fell in love with the very girl that we, his parents, had always preferred—Mariga. Mariga was a good worker, respectful of elders, and beautiful as well. When Tladi asked us for permission to marry Mariga, we were delighted. And so, according to tradition, Tladi's father, Molefi, went to Mariga's parents with the formal request.

"'We want something to draw water,'' Molefi said.

"'We do not know what it is you want,' Mariga's parents replied.

"'*Re batla se ga metse,*' Molefi repeated the same request.

"'*Ga re itse sentle gore o batla eng,*' they replied a second time.

"Molefi repeated his request again; and throwing up their hands to display their ignorance, Mariga's parents declared again, 'We know not what you want.'

"After a moment of wonderful silence, Molefi finally said to Mariga's parents, 'We have a son, Tladi, who said you have a daughter whom he loves and with whom he hopes to make a family. Her name is Mariga!'

"Mariga's parents then, of course, had to say that they needed time to think things over. After all, one must never be hasty or anxious.

"After they agreed to the marriage, I went with Seipate and Ntatabo to bring engagement gifts to Mariga's mother—blankets and dress material. And, of course, the elders from both families met to decide the number of cattle for a proper bogadi. They agreed that all cattle would be delivered on the wedding day. Because Tladi loved Mariga, he worked day and night to earn his cattle for bogadi. As you know, he went to the mines.

"Many days before the marriage, the walls at Mariga's home were smeared new with color and beautiful designs. They also prepared much food for the wedding guests.

"Finally, on the day of the wedding, all of Mariga's relatives gathered together to eat *Seswaa*. It is pounded meat. In this first light of the day, they could barely see us coming down their sandpath. We carried with us the wedding dress and ring for Mariga and, of course, we brought the cattle. We were quite a procession, and as we got closer to them, their women sang out with the highest, most lovely and long ululation!

"Tladi's father's brother led the procession of cattle to Mariga's parents. That was a sight: the uncle in front with three men of the family, then the cattle—and they were beautiful ones—and five more men behind them! Upon entering Mariga's parent's place, the very last man at the back of the procession announced their arrival, '*Re a tsena*' [We are entering], and calling attention to one of the cows, he shouted out its colors. Tladi's uncle and all the men approached the kraal and knelt down to pay respects and to greet the men of Mariga's family. Together the men all gathered at the fire to kneel down again. It was Tladi's uncle who spoke first.

"'*Re batla se ga metse*' [We wish something to draw water].

"'What do you want?'

"He repeated his request twice more until he received the answer, '*Go siame*' [It is all right.]

"Using Tladi's surname, the uncle then mentioned the cows. The men of Mariga's family stood up to show their sign of approval and went to see the animals.

"Meanwhile, women gathered. They spoke of drawing water and prepared the wedding feast. At the same time as the hide was removed from the slaughtered animals, the young pair, Tladi and Mariga, were to dress for the wedding. It was a grand feast! One hoof, of course, did not get cooked. It was presented to the oldest man of Tladi's family. The hoof—the same shape as what makes a woman—was the symbol of Mariga's innocence. If Mariga had come to her marriage with children, the hoof would have been cooked to show that she was used.

"That day was some years ago, and Tladi and Mariga already have given me two grandchildren," Maria said proudly.

She fumbled in her skirt pocket for more snuff, unwrapped the last bits, and pushed them up her nose.

"You know, MaoKeef, that Molefi and I have but one son, yet we will have many grandchildren . . . Tladi is a good son. He was raised to follow tradition. He earned many cattle for his bogadi. He, his wife, and their children live on our homestead. We all work together in the traditional way. Tladi brings new ideas to us because he works in the fields of the BAC, and we try them if they make things better. This is good for everyone. We can bring in new ideas to make things better, but we do not change the traditional ways."

News came this morning with the old woman, MaMoremi's mother. Rolling up the sleeve of her sweater, she displayed her badly bruised arm. MaMoremi and Rre Segatlhe sat listening intently. Out of curiosity I left the dishes to soak and joined them to hear the old woman's report.

The old woman had slept at Morwadi's place for the last few nights. Sixteen-year-old Morwadi, her granddaughter, was hav-

99

ing marital problems. For several weeks, Morwadi's husband had not provided her and their one-year-old son any support. One day last week Morwadi arrived home from town and found another woman's clothes in their hut. She gathered them up and took them to the elders of the village to be kept as evidence in case the need for a court proceeding should arise. This action infuriated her husband. He beat her, but she did not recoil in fear; she fought back with anger. This aggravated him further. He wrestled with her, successfully pinned her down, and beat her brutally. Slamming the door on her sobs, he left her. She feared his return, and it was for this reason that Morwadi went to find her grandmother's protection. Thus, the old woman stayed with Morwadi and her infant son waiting for the husband to return so that she might speak with him.

Late one night the three of them were sleeping soundly on their mats when they were suddenly awakened by an abrupt intrusion. Morwadi's husband returned with his parents. They did not pause to talk things over, but attacked, screaming angrily and striking out at Morwadi and her grandmother. The parents tried to hold the old woman down so that their son could get at Morwadi. Morwadi ran behind a mealie sack. The moonlight streamed in through the open door, and the old woman could see him go after her granddaughter. Lunging towards Morwadi, he pulled out a knife. The blade flashed in the darkness. The old woman struggled to free herself. Morwadi screamed. As quickly as they had come, the intruders fled. She lifted her sore limbs and went to her trembling granddaughter. She swabbed the wound on the young girl's breast. The cut was long but not deep. They stopped the bleeding, barred the door, and waited for the end of night.

She wanted Morwadi to leave the hut, but the young girl refused, fearing further reprisals if she deserted her home. At her granddaughter's request, she went straight to the Council of Elders to ask their advice. Perhaps a *kgotla*, a village court proceeding, could be convened to settle the dispute.

The old woman walked all day to reach our place. She now pleaded with MaMoremi to convince her daughter to leave the hut. She was certain that Morwadi's life was in danger. Rre Segatlhe shook his head. He knew Morwadi's husband's parents. Their son's actions did not surprise him. "Kittens of the wild cat are known by their mewing," he said. Rre Segatlhe and the old woman talked while MaMoremi sat stone-faced. Aware that I had heard only one side of this marital dispute, I nevertheless could not remain a casual bystander. To MaMoremi I felt loyalty, and Rre Segatlhe's words encouraged me to take sides. I offered to drive MaMoremi to Morwadi's place as soon as Hoyt got back with the truck. MaMoremi expressed her gratitude and returned to her thoughts.

That evening, MaMoremi and I left for Morwadi's place. We drove up to Morwadi's hut. When the motor stopped, all the main characters presented themselves by the lolwapa wall—Morwadi and her baby, her husband, and both of his parents. MaMoremi stepped toward her daughter and said, "We hear you are sick. We have come to take you home." Morwadi replied that she could not come. MaMoremi repeated her words, and this time Morwadi did not respond. There was a strained silence.

Morwadi finally spoke up. "You must go," she said. "I will walk you to the car." In a hushed voice she said she feared for her life. The situation was bad, but she could not leave. Her husband had threatened witchcraft on her if she dared leave him. MaMoremi told her daughter that her grandmother had arranged for a *kgotla*. Morwadi seemed relieved, but the parting, nevertheless, was tense.

The next morning MaMoremi and I sat on a goatskin in the shade of a morula tree. She was unusually quiet all morning, and I realized how little I really knew about her. My continuous questions broke her pensive mood. At first she answered simply and to the point, but as I asked for more details and showed increasing interest, she warmed up to our conversation. With a bit of paper, she rolled tobacco, lit her cigarette, and took a long, satisfied puff. In the end, I was her captivated listener as she told me of her life.

"Dreams. I still dream of childhood, of the dark warmth of my grandmother's arms, of working in the fields and getting food without knowing its source, without thinking of when there will be none. This is the dream from which I awaken on cold winter mornings. When I was a child, I dreamed other things—I would be a nurse or a teacher. A man would pay my parents bogadi—not just a few cattle, but many. We would be rich with many children, and I would work as a nurse and teach my children.

My parents lived in Mogoditshane. My brother, born in 1937, and I, born four years later, are their only children. It was difficult for my parents with only two children. I worked with my mother in the lolwapa and the fields. My brother watched the animals, but often, because there were only two of us, he too had to help out in the lolwapa. He dominated me in every way—even took my few possessions. This I had to accept, for he was my brother and he was older, and our parents were good to us. My two age-mates, Nsepinyana and Leta, often played games with me when I went to fetch wood. We saw others go to school, so secretly we played our game, "go to school." We ran in a line singing songs, sitting together in a row—one, two, three—we scribbled lines in the sand. Ha! I begged my parents to send me to school, and finally they agreed. Three years of joy. How I loved school! But when I was barely fifteen, my parents forced me to leave school; it was time, they said, for me to marry. I cried just thinking that I would have to leave school.

"I disliked the boy intensely, but my parents could not accept my refusal because they were close to the boy's parents in every way. Their son had helped my father plow fields and herd animals. The marriage was arranged long ago when I was four and the boy was fourteen. To refuse my parents' wish would be to insult their dignity. I had no choice; we accepted blankets as engagement gifts, and I prepared for marriage. There was a feast at our home. A cow was slaughtered for our engagement, and the boy moved into my hut. We did not move to his place because he had not yet paid bogadi. For this he left for the Johannesburg mines: to earn the bogadi of just two cows. But—in truth—I never saw him again.

"At first he wrote letters and sometimes sent clothes. I was pregnant. But soon he was quiet. And then his parents told me he had impregnated a girl in Johannesburg. I figured he was working on two wives. His family changed toward me; they favored the other girl. And I gave birth to my son—a strong one! One month later the baby died. He was not sick. Of course, I know what killed him—witchcraft. My fiancé's father's brother was a witch doctor and preferred the girl in Johannesburg. Actually, he wanted to kill me. He sprinkled poisons around the lolwapa where I worked. He failed—I lived, but my baby was dead. No, I did not see the poison, but I am sure this is what happened. Everyone knows witchcraft is too powerful. My grandmother had eight children, and four were killed by witchcraft.

"There is only one man I ever truly loved. He was father of Morwadi, Mpho, Moremi, and Leraka, but we could not marry because he was of a different tribe and also he was not my senior. We were the same age, and he was a Kalanga.

"Do you know where the Kalanga live? It is far from here—in the north of Botswana. Most of the Kalanga live north of the Botswana border. I met him after my baby died. I ran from the witchcraft to visit a friend in Francistown. There I met him. He was working at a poultry farm. We were both young. He had a friend in Maun. We went there together, and together we saw a place of dreams—the place of the Okavango River.

"The Okavango River is a great waterway in the north of Botswana which flows around palm-covered islands, through more green grass than you have ever seen! Leaves grow so big there that they can shade you, and when a bird sits on the tree, you cannot know if that bright color is a bird or a blossom! MaoKeef, this great river flows straight into the sand of Botswana, the sand that drinks it dry! . . . so, too, did my own happiness sink into the sand.

"We lived there with his friends—even ate fish for dinner! But we could not stay, and his family, farther north, told him it was time to marry, to settle down. They would not have me—our marriage would be against tradition. With no marriage, there is no bogadi; with no bogadi, a man's children are not his own. We separated, both to marry others.

"I had great hopes because the man who offered to marry me was a skilled builder. He gave the engagement gifts, and we moved to Molepolole where he had a good government job. We lived with his parents along with my four children. I gave birth to his child, but it died the same afternoon. My fifth living child, Elina, was born in the next year. We lived there for two years. His job took him sometimes to other towns, and then one day, he came home with another wife. She was pregnant. Now, a man has a right to marry a second wife, but if he forgets the first wife, the first wife owes him nothing. He neglected me. I gathered my five children and headed for my home. Yes, *my* five children. He never paid bogadi!

"My brother lives far away. My grandmother and father died in the same year. Now my mother, the grandmother to my children, is with us. She is the old woman, but I too am getting old. Like her, I followed traditional ways with Morwadi. She refused to marry that boy. Why did I force her? Because he had a good job and could pay bogadi. I thought things were better for her than for me. He paid bogadi but does not care about the child. It is not right for men to beat their wives, but they do it. No, I was never beaten, but I know this happens these days. Times are changed. Traditionally it was right for parents to arrange the marriage. Nowadays such a marriage is no good. Men are slippery things! They are like water, trickling away through the fingers. See what has happened to Morwadi! The family says nothing! The kgotla will teach that boy!"

Whereas Botswana as a modern African nation models the higher levels of their judicial system after previous British colonial rule, its traditional system of justice, centered in the kgotla, has remained paramount at the local level for settling minor, internal village disputes. The Council of Elders represented by senior men of various lineages in the community convenes the kgotla at the request of a senior household member who presents a grievance. Recently Rre Segatlhe, a member of the Council of Elders in Kopong, officiated at a kgotla convened for a household which accused a man of stealing two piglets. The accused was found guilty. He was ordered to return the piglets and fined one goat to be paid to the household from which he stole.

The kgotla system not only expedites legal matters efficiently, it serves to reinforce traditional laws and customs. It takes place in an open courtyard designated as the official kgotla, and invariably members of the community join the proceedings as spectators. The headman presides, and the respected elders—the old men of the community—are the jurors. After both sides of a case have been heard, the jurors deliberate until a consensus is reached. The headman presents the decision of the jury of elders to the community, often grounding it within the framework of the history and custom of the tribe. As participant observers, the community-at-large offers social sanction to the rulings of the court.

Lacking a senior male member in their family, it was Morwadi's grandmother, the family's senior member, who requested a kgotla to settle Morwardi's marital problem. The meeting was scheduled six days later on the following Tuesday. MaMoremi left our place a day early. We arranged to meet her at the kgotla on the following day. Hoyt drove the truck down the dirt road, and Madala bounced back and forth between Rre Segatlhe and me, alternating laps.

The kgotla is not scheduled for a particular clock time. There must be an understood time, however, for the courtyard seemed to fill up all at once. In midmorning, when the sun was high and chores were done, people gathered. When all participants arrive, the kgotla is called to order. The precise time may vary from one kgotla to another, yet if I compare my one experience in an American courtroom (where, after waiting nine months for a hearing, I was scheduled for 9:00 a.m., along with fifty other small claims, and waited all day for my name to be called at random), this system is more efficient many times over.

We spotted MaMoremi immediately. She had not yet seated herself but was leaning against a post on the periphery of the courtyard, dragging deep puffs off her rolled cigarette. The elders had taken their seats on the row of chairs next to the desk. Calmly nursing her son, Morwadi also sat in a chair, facing the crowd of villagers seated on the ground before her. Her husband sat on the opposite side of the area with his parents and a few age-mates. When we greeted MaMoremi, she motioned me to sit on the ground with the old woman near Morwadi's chair. Hoyt, hoping to remain outside of the proceedings, sat down on a rock in the very back of the arena. Upon seeing him, an elder rushed over to him with a chair. No man was to sit on the ground during kgotla, and a rock was no seat. Rre Segatlhe, who often sat with this Council of Elders, could not join them for this case. Being party to the case, he sat as an observer on a chair near Morwadi. As tradition dictates, the headman and the counselor arrived and took their seats behind the desk, and for current, government records, a court transcriber joined them. The kgotla was called to order.

Chronologically Morwadi slowly and clearly stated her testimony. When the counselor spilled the contents of a cardboard box onto the table to show the clothing to which she referred, there was not a flicker of recognition from the audience. When Morwadi unbuttoned her blouse to show her wound, no one edged forward to see better, and there were no murmurs. A respectful, unemotional calm reigned as people carefully listened. The transcriber wrote furiously to keep up with her words. When she concluded, the counselor questioned her at length, demanding that she repeat aspects of her testimony and asking for additional details. Did she want to remain with her husband, he asked, to which she gave a firm "no." When he was satisfied with a complete account, he dismissed her and called her husband to the chair.

His report was brief. He denied the accusations. He did not know where she got those clothes. He knew nothing of her wound. He described his workday and insisted that he provided adequately for his wife and son. The counselor questioned him.

He asked him to account for his actions at particular times on particular days. He was quick to pick up on minor discrepancies between the accused's opening statement and his response to questions. He repeated verbatim segments of his earlier testimony which conflicted with his present statements. This confused the witness. He wiped his brow and squirmed—a sign of guilt. He admitted difficulties with his marriage. He regretted past actions. He wanted to remain with his wife.

The jury of elders met briefly and found him guilty of lying to the court and of failure to support his wife and child. The headman lectured him on familial duties and fined him 20 pula ($30), to be paid to the kgotla within one week or spend three months in jail. He was told never to beat or injure his wife. Any grave disputes were to be brought to the kgotla. The couple was told to live together again in peace. If the husband was again found guilty of any transgression before this kgotla, he would be expelled from the community.

MaMoremi was pleased with the outcome, but Morwadi was disappointed. She did not want to go back to her husband. Downcast, she strapped her baby to her back and walked off with him. His parents went their separate way, as did we.

Driving home, Hoyt and I were still stunned at the counselor's abilities for precise recall. He had quoted large sections of earlier testimony during his cross-examination without reference to the transcriber's notes. Rre Segatlhe explained that he was raised to do this job. His father had been a well-known counselor, and as a young child, he apprenticed with him, going to every kgotla to listen and learn.

"He never attended school," Rre Segathle explained. "To this day he cannot read or write. This is a good thing. Clever ways of speaking and exact memory for what is spoken take up the whole of his brain."

There was much talk of Morwadi's kgotla at the crossroads and in the lolwapa. I sat with the women at Maria's place. They agreed with MaMoremi that for Morwadi and her son the kgotla's decision had been wise.

"Her boy of a husband must learn to walk straight."

"*Ee*, his hot blood will have to cool."

"But what about Morwadi?" I asked. "She did not want to stay with her husband. Her feelings were not considered. She lost the case!" I concluded.

"Ow! Ow!" they shouted in return. "She is a young girl with a baby. She has a hut of her own with him. Her husband has a government job. If she runs off with the baby, MaoKeef, she will return to MaMoremi or her grandmother."

"*Ee*", MaMoremi added," and her boy husband will grow fat while the baby starves. I have nothing to feed her. She would have to go to work with her grandmother or brew kadi somewhere else."

"She is young," I argued, "She could try to train for a job somewhere so that she could live on her own."

"Ow! In town? Where would the family be, MaoKeef?"

"Look in town, MaoKeef," Maria spoke out. "Children grow up in the streets and sleep on the curbs when there is no family to keep them. That is not good for Morwadi's little son, Deêpe. These children of the streets do not greet their own father's brother! They do not even know the touch of the cattle whip!"

"Where I live," I ventured forth, "there is an idea which many women now think about. They wish to make their own decisions and have the same chances to work and earn money as men. They say there should be no jobs a woman cannot do and no jobs a man cannot do. Some women go to the office while their husbands sweep the house."

The image of husbands sweeping produced an hilarious uproar. MaMoremi remained pensive.

"In your America, the husbands and wives are very confused," Maria declared. "They must fight over everything to decide on who does what on what day . . . and how will their children grow up if they don't know what it is to be a man or a woman?"

"How can they marry? How can they live together as a family?"

"Each person, whether man or woman, is to be free to choose a way of life that brings personal happiness," I began to explain. "A man and woman choose to live together if they agree on how to live together. It is not a family decision. It is their own decision," I continued.

MaMoremi listened, but Maria was quick to interrupt me.

"There is no happiness without the law of the tribe and the law of the family. A woman is a woman. A man is a man. There is no family if people do not know the difference. A man and woman together with children are family of the tribe. They must live by the rules of the tribe. They cannot live any way they want! If they live without the tribe, they will be alone as a family. And if they live without knowing what it is to be a family among others, they will be alone as man and woman, thinking each of themselves. Then why have a family? Why marry? Why have man? Why have woman? Why aren't we all sticks, looking the same but each on our own?"

"Baboons live better than that!" she asserted as the other women laughed at Maria's conclusions.

"Do you think that women have it as good as men in Tswana society?" I tried another tack.

"Ee!" Maria declared emphatically.

"Nya!" MaMoremi disagreed. "A man can sleep with all the women he likes. If he pays no bogadi, he is a free man. The woman, alone, is left to feed all the babies."

"The babies grow up to do many chores," Maria countered.

"Still they must eat plenty and that makes more chores," MaMoremi returned.

"MaMoremi," Maria dropped her voice, "it is not whether you are a man or a woman that keeps you in the shadows. It is whether you are rich or poor. It is whether your people have honor or not. Basarwa [the Bushmen] have a bad life because their own husbands are treated like servants by the Tswanas. Tswana women have a bad life if they must scrub floors for makgoa.

"We must keep to the traditional ways," old Maria instructed.

I did not argue with Maria. Yet the question remains in my mind—are Maria's happy experiences and favorable personal circumstances responsible for her strong defense of tradition?

MaMoremi did not have it so good. With her daughter, Morwadi, she hoped to find defense for the Tswana customs and values of her upbringing. She forced her daughter to marry. Yet finally, as her own dreams and those for her daughter were frustrated, she reluctantly questioned traditional ways.

Morwadi, reared by her grandmother and mother, grew up in a matriarchy, apart from the tradition which MaMoremi sought to recover. She was forced into marriage that now proved to alienate her from her mother's dreams. She relived and shared the same disillusionment, long harbored by her mother. What lasting support could a kgotla give her? At fifteen years of age, she was a woman, alone with her child.

Rre Segatlhe listened to my questions that night and replied with his usual transcendence.

"Mosadi mogolo," he said, "life is uncertain everywhere—

whether you are a man or woman, rich or poor, here or in America. You don't ask where a person is going. You ask where a person is coming from. Even that, you cannot see clearly. You must look to the bones."

"Then tell me how the bones work."

"That is only for me; it is not for you to learn."

"Stout one of arms, Preparer of Liquid Food." (Rre Segatlhe with his cattle.)

9

Intruders In The Desert

Hoyt, looking for future research sites near the Kalahari Desert, decided on a trip to the settlement of Letlakeng. Upon hearing about this, Rre Segatlhe exclaimed, "Ah! Letlakeng, I know it well. It is by the Great Thirstland, near the lands of the Bakgalagadi and the Basarwa [Bushmen]. These people know the sand floor better than you know the heels of your own feet!"

"My heels?" I immediately felt for a heel which, admittedly, had never received any scrutiny. "Why should I know my heels?"

"This is just what I am saying to you. You do not need to know everything that is closest to you. You pick and choose what to look at, what to know. But the Basarwa of the Great Thirstland must come to learn the whole of themselves, their people, and their lands."

He drew a circle in the sand by his feet.

"What do you see here?"

"A circle of sand."

"Ha! Sand? Is it all you see? Tell me all that you see in this circle of sand."

"I see sand . . . here a twig and some footprints . . . a little weed growing here by the edge of the circle."

"Certainly. But you have told me nothing!"

"The Basarwa will see here that it is your heel in the sand, that it is the heel of a woman who is not bearing a child, but she is still young. The woman walked slowly when the sun was there," he pointed at the sky and continued. "The woman walked on a day with very little wind, a day with no rain clouds nearby. She walked from southwest to southeast and stopped right here for

111

something. She walked past the twig, broken by the foot of one in man's shoes who was moving quickly east to west when the sun was higher in the sky. Here, a beetle was moving to that morula tree. This is the beetle which eats the leaves of the morula tree, and it is the beetle to collect and make poisons for the hunting arrow. The woman who walked here was not a woman of the Thirstland because she had her own food and water. Why would she leave behind a good eating root with water?"

"A good eating root? Where?"

"This here!"

"This?" I pointed to the skimpy vine at the edge of the circle.

"Certainly! It is not enough to see what is on top of the sand. You must know what is underneath!"

"Modise," Rre Segatlhe called out to Hoyt, "I must go with you to Letlakeng. It is the best place for skins! There the Tswana people walk completely covered with fur!"

"In the desert?" I questioned.

"Certainly!"

To spare him another lecture, I merely nodded my head with approval.

Listening to their plans and sensing a mood of excitement, I insisted on joining them. MaMoremi, perplexed as to why anyone would want to go to the Great Thirstland, agreed to stay home with the boys. Her reaction could not discourage me, keen as I was for new adventure. I declared a holiday for the bush school and was ready to go anywhere. We loaded the truck with blanket rolls, a box of food, and five gallons of water. The children bid us a cheerful good-bye, and as we waved back, I felt the sheer joy of emancipation from all school, household, and motherly duties.

Leaving behind the limits of our daily experiences—our lolwapa, the kraal, and the fields—we headed west on the road to Molepolole. Had I traveled the same road months ago, I would have seen it with different eyes, but the footpaths between thorn bushes toward huts and kraals were a familiar sight. In the morning sun, women walked single-file with empty buckets. One ducked into the bush while the others waited. This immediately reminded me of an awkward moment of initiation to bush life. Once while walking side by side with Maria, she suddenly squatted down on the edge of the path. I rushed to her for fear she had suffered some kind of stroke. If anyone was capable of communicating ridicule with one significant stare, it was Maria. Blubbering apologies, it took me some time to recover from my rescue mission. . . . Only in retrospect could I now divulge it to my travel companions.

There were individual rural settlements—much like ours—all along the road to Molepolole. We passed huts decorated with two shades of color, extracted from different clays; a lolwapa wall displayed contrasting colors in a spectacular geometric pattern.

"I would like to make a wall like that," I looked out with envy.

"The soils with such colors are not near our lands," Rre Segatlhe noted. "But look, there, at the stacks of bojang [long grasses]. These you will have. Soon it will be time for us, as well, to prepare for the rainy season. Before pula comes, two of our huts will need new thatching."

We stopped for cattle, sauntering across the road behind a herdsman's whip. Three barechested boys with whips of their own stopped momentarily to look curiously at our car.

"We have a saying," Rre Segatlhe said, "To corral the cattle is done only by a man with sons."

Cattle are the pride of Botswana. For the nation they are a major export item; for the homestead they are a sign of success and wealth. Asking a Tswana how many head of cattle he owns is equivalent to asking an American how much he has in his bank account. It is a private matter. As Maria described it, a young man accumulates cattle wealth to start his homestead, and at marriage he expresses his solvency by presenting bogadi cattle to his bride's parents. Throughout his adulthood, he tries to increase his herd for his own economic stability and prestige and for the inheritance of his children.

"Truly, this is a beautiful herd of cows!" Rre Segatlhe exclaimed as, again, we waited for cattle to cross the road.

"Makgoa of the BAC Farms would say to kill them," he mumbled under his breath.

Quizzically, Hoyt and I both turned to look at him. Intently watching the cattle pass, his voice rose. "Men of cattle from America—from a place in America with many cattle—from—" he paused.

"Texas," Hoyt suggested. He knew of a current project led by cattle experts from Texas to advise Botswana on livestock.

"Yes, you know, Modise. These people are coming here to teach us of cattle. But they think only of meat. They say to kill the cow when it is still young! When it is still good for bogadi, for plowing fields . . . ha! for boloko! I say to you they do not think what cattle are good for in Botswana. What can they teach us coming from a place in America when they know nothing of Botswana?"

Rre Segatlhe lamented the time of the great *Rinderpest* [hoof and mouth disease] which swept over the countryside some years ago.

"If they want to do something for Botswana, they can stop the Rinderpest. Many, many Tswana people lost all their cattle. I am saying to you *only*." There was a pause as he prepared to confide in us. "I, myself, lost so many that only four are left."

Quantities of cattle are not discussed, yet particular animals are often the subject of detailed conversation and spontaneous poetry. They are heralded in praise songs. Rre Segathle described his cattle. Hoyt followed his words and spirit. I felt obliged to look at each cow on the roadside with new vision. Hoyt translated lines of some praise poems he could remember. Rre Segatlhe, evermindful of his role as my teacher, repeated every line in Setswana as Hoyt went along.

"Stout-one of arms
Preparer of liquid food . . ."

"Arms?" I queried.

"Stout-one of *weapons* . . . No," he interrupted. "*Arms* is better," he corrected himself. "It refers to the horns, of course."

"Preparer of liquid food,
God with the long, straight nose,
It lows, saying 'moo'
Ah! Animal of my father—red female.
God with the moist nose.
A short sip of something hot.
Animal with the moist nose."

"There is another," he continued. "It starts like this:

Beast with such palatable gravy
Animal with the moist nose
Sniffer with both nose and tongue
I lacked one, I lacked sleep . . ."

"I *had* one, I lacked sleep," Rre Segatlhe continued.

Approaching Molepolole, Rre Segatlhe pointed out several

small concrete houses on a hillside. These were government houses, he explained.

"Molepolole is the tribal capital of my Tswana tribe, the Bakwena. The Chief of all Bakwena lives here. His lolwapa is for all; it is the kgotla meeting place for all of the Bakwena. We are one family, and he is the head of the family. We can all go to him for important things or problems. It is here that, long ago, I went to the chief to get my lands, for it was the chief that knew all the lands and gave it to farm.

"I told him I would not live in the village but stay on the lands. The chief had a good laugh seeing me staying on the lands all the year.

"He laughed?"

"Certainly! He was pleased. He knew I was a doctor, and it is a good thing for me to be near the fields to make my medicals. In those days, a family did not live all year where it farmed the land," he continued. "Families lived in a village or town and only went to the lands at the time of planting for the rainy season. Women went to the lands, and their sons stayed at the cattle post, bringing the cattle to plow when it was time."

"What about the men?" I asked.

"Men went back and forth from the lands to the cattle post, working on the lands and on the cattle post. When there were no more crops, the family lived together again in the village."

"But I never lived in the village . . . even when I had a wife to go to the lands. From the very beginning, I wanted to stay only on my lands. It is the beauty of Botswana! When Maria and Molefi came to the lands, they still had a place in the village, but after a few years, they, too, decided to stay only on the lands."

"Why?"

"It is as many are doing today. They are staying only on the lands. Why? I can say to you it is because the village and towns are changing. Many young people do not want to stay on the lands so they run to live in town. Towns in the east, like Gaborone and Francistown, near the railroad line, are getting full of people, people coming from everywhere . . . people who do not know the Tswana way. . . . It is too much people! And it is not a good thing to leave your place behind.

"Molepolole is to the west, not too close to the railroad," he continued. "Molepolole is still like a big Tswana village—not too crowded. Here many people can live in the old way, going from

115

their lands and cattle post to the village lolwapa. You can see they are living here with the goats and sheep, but soon many will go to live on their lands."

We passed a one-room general store. Two sleepy mules did not even twitch as the driver loaded their burden of sacks onto the cart. Worn wheels still intact, the cart was simply the rusty shell of the back half of an automobile. Separated by decorated walls and thick bushes, family compounds were pressed hedge to hedge. In one open space, a queue of women and young girls with infants strapped on backs and toddlers at their sides waited their turn at a water pump. Goats and sheep wandered about, probably wending their way to the nearby fields. Behind them a group of herd boys ran playfully pushing each other. Two of their companions rushed to catch up but stopped abruptly by the side of the road as they saw us approach. "Sweets! Sweets!" they sang out in unison, and as we passed, they leaped across the road to join the others.

In Molepolole, we turned westward onto a narrow, sandy road. This was to be our track for over forty kilometers to Letlakeng. Our Mazda was merely a miniature model truck with three-speed gear shift and no more clearance than an ordinary city sedan. To allay any misgivings, we stopped an oncoming four-wheel-drive Bedford truck to inquire about the condition of the road ahead. The driver assured us that without four-wheel-drive the going would be difficult, but, he added, if we proceeded with care, we could probably manage it. We drove on.

After fifteen kilometers we were accustomed to the rough ride. Hoyt commented that the track was worn down so much that the center aisle was quite high. The differential seemed to be dragging slightly in the sand as we drove steadily downhill. Rre Segatlhe and I nodded and continued our conversation.

"Mosadi mogolo, I am telling you Letlakeng is a beautiful place for skins!" he exclaimed, affectionately patting my knee. "I will buy two pair of pants," he declared expansively.

"Rre Segatlhe," I interrupted his ravings about skins, "when we get to Letlakeng, I want to see the Bakgalagadi and the Bushmen of the desert.

"Certainly! You will see them . . . but you will see them like they live today . . . tending the cattle post, waiting for the mine bus, or serving the Tswanas who live there."

"What of reading footprints in the sand? What of the beetle for the poison arrow? What of the good root to eat? Rre Segatlhe, what are you saying to me! How does serving Tswanas and cattle post duties fit in with reading a sand circle?"

"Oo-loo, loo! Mosadi mogolo, you are shooting too many bullets at once."

"What do you mean, 'waiting for the mine bus?'"

"Before the Tswana people came to Letlakeng, only the Basarwa [Bushmen] were living here. They hunted and gathered food and, yes, read the sand. Then the Kgalagadi, who were running from the Tswana people, came with their cattle to farm. They had weapons and made the Basarwa their servants. Because the Basarwa knew these Thirstlands, they hunted and herded animals for the Kgalagadi. Then, of course, the Tswana people caught up with the Kgalagadi, and so today, the Tswana people use Kgalagadi and Basarwa as their servants—mostly to tend the cattle post because there is no longer any rain here for planting."

After thirty kilometers we left behind the last huts and kraals. We crossed a broad field of bojang. But for the white sandy soil, the high golden grasses catching the breeze and playing out its rhythm passed for a fertile wheat field.

"This hardly looks like a desert to me. If those grasses can grow, why can't crops?"

To Rre Segatlhe this idea was absurd and warranted a lecture. Here there was very little rainfall. Only a few trees could grow big enough for shade. Many varieties of thorn bushes, grasses, and vines covered the sand, but only a few could provide any sustenance. Here on the perimeters of the Kalahari Desert, the Tswana, like the Bushmen who lived farther west, could not grow crops. They knew which roots were edible but depended on the hunt to stay alive.

"And if there is no rain, there is nothing near to hunt," he continued. "Everybody is hungry . . . the Basarwa, the Kgalagadi, and the Tswana people. To drink warm milk, hungry boys leave home for the cattle posts, and if they are lucky, they can earn a calf after a year or so. Other young men do not think of the cattle post. Unlike the elders, they cannot bear the pain of hunger. They lie in the sand holding their stomach and wait for the mine bus."

"What about hunting? What about digging roots?"

"Only the Basarwa who stay far west of Letlakeng, deep inside the Thirstland, who do not mix with the Tswana ways, they can live very well. They have no lolwapa. They move with the wild herds, leave a place when the water dries up and move again to another place. But this life for them will soon be gone—gone like it is today in Letlakeng. You know that it is not the Tswana way to be moving all the time from place to place!"

"Wouldn't it be better for the Basarwa to just stay in the desert and live their own way?"

"Certainly! For *them* it is better. But they are not anymore alone living there. People come everyday—the Kgalagadi and the Tswana people looking for new cattle posts, making new boreholes. You know that some wealthy Tswanas of town have large cattle posts, not only with water wells, but with diesel pumps! And the Tswana government will move these Basarwa away from their hunting lands to live and stay somewhere else. I can say to you that I know this is true. I have heard this from an elder who has spoken with the chief and the government people."

"This is sad, Rre Segatlhe," I offered. "Why not treasure the Bushmen for their knowledge of the sand and protect their life the way it is in the desert?"

"Ha! Do you think these changes are just from the Tswana ways?"

"Makgoa in big trucks and jeeps climb over all the sand hills, shooting animals with cameras and bullets, giving sweets and tobaccos to Basarwa for skins and ostrich egg beads."

He looked directly, accusingly, at me. "Ha! Ostrich egg beads, like the ones you bought in Gaborone, are not anymore for the Basarwa to wear, they are for makgoa to buy! And do you think the Basarwa get the moneys?"

Our conversation was ended abruptly as we sighted a long stretch of deep white sand directly ahead of us. Hoyt picked up speed. Our Mazda plowed through a few feet, sputtered, and stopped.

"Far over that sandhill, Basarwa run with light feet. The Great Thirstland is not fooled by four wheels trying to fly," Rre Segathle observed.

"Next time we'll come in a Landrover," Hoyt countered.

We pushed the door open into a sandbank to step out. Two wheels and the differential were completely buried in sand. It was at this point that we realized our failure to bring tools. We had no shovel, no boards. Our Madala, Rre Segatlhe, did not look on, but joined us on his knees to scoop sand.

Scooping sand. Scooping sand gave me time to think of the meaning Rre Segatlhe attributed to my ostrich egg beads. 'I wear them in honor of the Bushmen,' my inner voice repeated as I scooped more sand. 'I wear them in recognition of and admiration for . . . yes, . . . in recognition of and admiration for their way of life,' I repeated to myself while scooping more sand. We scooped sand in silence until clear, at last, we pushed our way out—only to get stuck again after driving a few feet further. Just ten kilometers from our destination, we looked down the sandy stretch ahead.

Resigned, Hoyt concluded," We'll have to turn around and go back."

Each feeling the measure of our own disappointment, it was a disappointment overshadowed by the question we dared not ask out loud. "Turn around and go back . . . HOW?" I comforted myself—five gallons of water, if used sparingly, would surely do until help came by; Rre Segatlhe knew the edible roots; forget what lions there may be lurking about, goodness knows how long we could survive in this very spot!

Looking helplessly ahead of us while waiting for someone to come up with an idea, we spotted a heavy-duty truck barreling down the track toward us. In no time at all, a dozen hefty men piled out, lifted our car up and around, and bade us good-bye with the reassurance that they would be back down this very same road five days hence—just in case we got stuck again.

We actually laughed at the thought, confident that our return could be managed with ease. What we had not considered was that upon returning we would be on an uphill grade. Going downhill our differential had merely dragged along the median strip; now, with no downhill momentum, it buried itself again and again. After digging ourselves out several times, we tried riding the right wheels up on the bank and the left wheels on the track. The only difference was that we stopped now to dig out wheels rather than the differential. At one point when the right wheels rode onto a particularly high section of sandbank, the car teetered as if about to roll over when, just in time, the wheels slipped off the sandbank. Sand piled down with them, and we were buried again.

This time an impressively healthy thorn bush tangled into our rear wheel complicated matters. And it was here that we realized our failure to bring an axe or a knife. Rre Segatlhe and Hoyt wrapped their hands in an oil cloth and pulled at the thorn bush while I twisted myself under the car to scoop sand. The wheel was almost free when the sandbank collapsed in on it. I started all over again. There was plenty of time. After all, the men grappling the thorn bush with a shredded cloth were still planning strategy concerning their maneuvers.

"I prefer digging out the differential to the wheels," I volunteered.

"From now on, let's stay on the track and dig out the differential," I shouted at them.

The men wrestling the thorn bush said nothing. When the car finally pulled out of that spot, we figured that no dig-out operation was beyond us. With new confidence, we continued along the middle of the road and, when the differential was stuck, automatically went to our dig-out stations. Too tired to talk, we returned to the car. Waiting for the car to lurch again for our attentions, we drove ahead in silence.

As the road leveled out, our stops became less frequent, and when we had gone a considerable distance free and clear, we allowed ourselves sighs of relief. The sun settled down. One black bird with a tail twice the size of its body swooped heavily across the darkening sky. A bush in the shadows straightened up—an ostrich, startled by the sound of our car, ran to its partner in the distant field.

Night rolled in. We, intruders of the desert, were relieved to see the dim lights of Molepolole scattered in the hills. Battle-weary, we turned onto the main road and sped toward Gaborone.

"Kabo's ladder is up against our roof."

10

Pula

The strong spring wind blew clouds to us. They billowed over our lolwapa for some time and then moved on. "Rain, rain, pula, pula!" Tsotsi shouted, as he gleefully raced around the courtyard. Perplexed, Madala looked up, held out his hands tentatively, and repeated his brother's words while discovering what he had long forgotten. There had not been one cloud nor one drop of rain since our arrival.

Sand swirled up against the lolwapa walls. Spinning with the whirls, leaping through the gusts, the children danced to pula, and Rre Segatlhe and I took refuge for our stinging eyes in the kitchen shelter. There the cat lay coiled up by the fire, twitching his ears at the intrusions. The rooster and hens scattered. Some slipped into MaMoremi's hut before the door banged shut; others fussed and scratched up settling places behind some logs in the shelter.

Their tree and roosting place swayed heavily nearby. Among its green leaves the old brown, crackled ones had hung tenaciously all winter, providing us with shade. With each blast of wind, twigs clicked together, and a few old leaves finally let go, scudding across the sand, drifting into piles along the lolwapa wall.

Seasons are different here. There is no sudden exodus of old leaves in the fall, no bare-branch monuments to the dead in winter, no jubilant veneration of youth in spring. Our tree regenerates imperceptibly, new growth pushing forward behind the old. Synchronous rhythms of growing and aging prevail throughout the winter, and the tree is never left bare. As in rural Tswana life, it seems that even in nature, age is revered.

The experience of a life-world is the wisdom of every elder. Rre Segatlhe shows Tiro how to distinguish the succulent, edible roots from the poisonous ones. Seipate takes her daughter where seed pods grow to show her how to prepare them to make shampoo. From one generation to the next, there is scrupulous care to use every potential in nature. MaMoremi's grandmother has taught her the power of witchcraft. Old Maria, fetching water with her daughter-in-law, Mariga, chides her youthful optimism by quoting a traditional proverb: "Jackal brags, 'I am a fast runner.' Sand replies, 'Ah, but I have already spread.'"

"No matter what you think you have learned, no matter how much you can do, there is always more ahead of you," old Maria explains to Mariga. Mariga helps the old woman lift the bucket on her head, and the two return to their household. Seipate's dying mother, still in the shade of her hut, is beyond the wisdoms of life. Because she is in transition—on her way to the Badimo—it is to her that the newborn granddaughter is brought for a blessing. Generations living together depend on each other.

Now sheltered from wind and dust, I sat with Rre Segatlhe, and he told me his view of my society.

"Urban life changes things. When the young move to the city, they can no longer value the life of an old man. The family and the community are not what support them. It is the market that holds the plow for them. The shops are the center of the White Man's life. They sell many things, and when people see these things, they say they need them and buy them. Soon the fat stomachs fill up whole garbage cans with things, and trucks come to empty them to make room for more. Yes, they throw out the old and get the new. *New* and *young*: that is the spirit of the White Man's world; it is called 'progress.'

"People even want to stay young! When the young of town visit the lands, they have no manners because they cannot see the elders. They only see themselves and tomorrow. But life catches them. Tomorrow arrives; they are ashamed to grow old! They try—many ways—to hide it because just like old things, old people are useless. They look behind them at times when they were young, or they look ahead with envy at those who are young. Elders are not content to be what they are. They waste their years and do not live a whole life.

"This word 'progress', it is a waste, a waste of things and a waste of people."

The problem of waste in our society was a concern of many

people, I said. The problem, as he recognized it, was the result of industrialization and urban growth. Throughout history, many others shared Rre Segatlhe's wisdom and had written of the waste of human potential. It was true that as people benefited from industrial development, they were also its victims.

I now eagerly recited poetry from Wordsworth and Goldsmith, lines committed to memory with minimal understanding a decade ago,

The world is too much with us; late and soon
Getting and spending, we lay waste our powers.

Ill fares the land, to hastening ills a prey,
Where wealth accumulates, and men decay.

"These are wise words," Rre Segatlhe said. "The madalas of your poetry see that man can become weak from the waste of having too much. As you know, mosadi mogolo, our wisdom here in the fields comes from the opposite. The world is not too much with us—no, not at all! There is a Tswana saying: 'People of a stomach divide the head of one fly.' That means that we, living here together, are all of one stomach. We are weak from the same hunger pains, and even when there is only one head of a fly left to eat, we must share it."

The cloud passed on. The cat lifted himself, stretched, licked the ashes from his fur, and ambled into the courtyard in search of insects. As Rre Segatlhe and I emerged from the kitchen shelter, we met Molefi, who had come with news.

Mariga's older sister had been ailing with great pains for about a week. This morning she died. Had she seen a doctor or been to the hospital? No. She was tended by the family. He knew not of what she died, nor did it seem relevant.

Solemnly and calmly, as though this were just another task of life, the old men discussed the funeral arrangements, and I stood in shock. To me, this was an abrupt interruption. A young woman—dead! No medical care! I did not know her. Do I have to go? Do I have to think of this and be reminded once more?

Again the confrontation of the inevitable; again the need to support a grieving household. We found MaMoremi and the boys and gathered sweaters to cover our arms. Hoyt, out on an interview, would hear the news; he too would come to mourn.

A procession, shuffling through the sand. In my society, funeral rites include close relatives and kin of the deceased;

casual acquaintances usually do not become involved. Sickness, aging, dying, and death are in the care of professionals, removed from our everyday presence. Professionals make plans. Professionals bear the responsibilities, and we send flowers, bake casseroles, make donations, continue our routines, and protect our consciousness from unpleasant thoughts. If this were not the case, would our individual and societal emphasis on youth and focus on progress and growth be possible? Could we rush to the phone and fill up the calendar? Could we successfully shove our mortality to the recess of our minds to punch the time clock?

From far away, from all directions, lightning flashed. Even with the distant mountain and far-stretching fields, we felt closed in. Goats and sheep stood stiffly pressed against each other under nearby trees. Clouds gathered closer, darker, and school children raced home clutching skirts and jackets in the wind. Late afternoon storms often played themselves out on a horizon, but now several storms converged directly above us. A breathless Tsotsi burst through the doorway, relieved to find refuge in the hut. "Father's home!" Rare occasion: the wind blew him in from interviews. By lantern light Hoyt and Madala lay curled up on the bed for storytime. Tsotsi grabbed a blanket to huddle up and listen. Winds brought pula. Muffled by thatchwork, the torrential rain persisted. Its sonorous drone lulled me into half-sleep.

Drips on the metal table roused me from my stupor. Here and there straw gave way to the force of driving rain. Pushing the beds together to a dry spot in the center of the hut, we tried to reassemble ourselves back into comfort, despite a curtain of rain now falling all around us. Then Madala urgently expressed interest in going to the fields. He climbed on my back, Hoyt threw a plastic cloth over us, and we rushed out through the downpour. Barefoot, I splashed across the lolwapa floor and ran the fifty meters, dodging thorns, to our green canvas enclosure. Nixon grunted mildly at our intrusion. Madala, never once taking his eyes off Nixon, climbed cautiously onto the seat as rain pelted in through the canvas flap. The plastic cloth slid off somewhere during the return trip; we arrived drenched. Strange feeling: suddenly a surfeit of water!

Maneuvering the suitcase out from under the bed to find a change of clothes proved difficult because the stream of water coming down near the bed allowed no dry clearance. The paraffin stove was accessible; we held our plates of steaming beans, daubed with chutney, and felt some sense of victory, but the night was long and restless.

By morning we emerged into bright sun again. Rre Segatlhe and MaMoremi rejoiced over pula. Looking at the damage—the lolwapa and hut floors were broken, walls were crumbled—I could only think of the tedious repair work. As long as water was only a truck-ride away and I had a chest full of food tins, this would be my perspective.

At midday Hoyt came for the first-aid kit and returned to Nkabo's place near Mopane Hill. Nkabo's wife had spilled boiling water on her foot. Her foot had not been bandaged well and was badly infected.

Burns are common injuries. On winter nights, when the blanket, goatskin, or flattened cardboard box cannot seal out the cold to bring sleep, some abandon caution to settle by the fire. They still speak of Kgetse who rolled into the fire and did not survive.

Summer storms bring lightning. It crackles and streaks the sky from one horizon to the other. The flash blinds our eyes, and we seek shelter in the hut. The next morning we hear Radio Botswana news:

Three huts belonging to the family of Lekoma Nkwane were destroyed by fire yesterday evening. It is said that lightning struck the thatch of one roof. Mrs. Nkwane and three of her children escaped injury, but two, Sebego and Maseng, were killed. The victims were two and four years old. One child has suffered burns and is in critical condition.

Rre Segatlhe spoke of the preparations we must make for the rainy season. We would hire a thatcher to repair our roof. Tabo and Polwane's son, Mosimanegape, would bring the cattle for us to plow the fields. Tiro, Sejaro, and Rre Segatlhe's new goatherd would be put to work preparing a plot for his herb garden. I, too, would prepare a garden, I added. He looked at me skeptically, which only encouraged me to verbalize my fantasy: I would get seeds from town and grow carrots, cabbage, beans, tomatoes, onions, Swiss chard, corn. Every bit of leftover wash water would go not to Nixon, but to my garden. We would feast with fresh vegetables!

"O tlatsa molomo wa me ka maswana a senang sepe" [you fill my mouth with empty spoons], Rre Segatlhe replied.

Manaka, Rre Segatlhe's new goatherd arrived. He is a boy with large quiet almond eyes above wide, hollow cheeks. Beside other Tswana, his mustard-colored skin is rather fair. The gaping shirt stretched across his narrow chest displays his skeletal detail. Patched, ragged shorts button tightly across his distended stomach. His legs, thin and delicate, contrast with his wide, bony knees. Thick knees, crusty with grime, like sturdy pads—pads like his wide feet that have never known shoes. He is perhaps twelve years old. Rre Segatlhe does not know his age; Manaka's mother does not remember just when he was born. Since she dropped him off at our gate last month, neither she nor his family has come to visit him.

Rre Segatlhe loaded a bag of mealies on a car headed toward Kopong, payment to his parents for Manaka's services. Manaka himself receives nothing but enough food to stay alive in exchange for his labor. Dependent on Rre Segatlhe for food, and slave to his every whim, Manaka, still a young boy, is emotionally alone. At the start he was so very shy and withdrawn that Tsotsi's attempts to engage him met with repeated failure. Yet when the monna mogolo, Segatlhe, yelled out "Manaka!" he picked himself up and ran to the old man's side. Rre Segatlhe stretched himself out on the goatskin mat for a midday snooze, and the boy, on his knees, bent himself over the old man's feet, scraping callouses off the soles.

Again in the early afternoon clouds gathered, there was a light drizzle. I retreated into the hut, only to hear tapping on the wooden shutter minutes later. I peered out to see two of my school children imploring me to come to our meeting place. The whole class was waiting. In the rain? Yes. In English we did warm-up exercises and thereafter reviewed some English dialogue. I cut the class time short and told them it was not necessary to hold classes on days like this. Disappointed, they did not move but sat shivering in the rain. Uncomfortable and unable to ignore the weather, I should have stuck to my decision and left. But their faces were glum, and Sejaro stood up to tell me through his chattering teeth that pula was good for the fields. I have been here long enough to know that children do not directly dispute an elder. They would not protest my decision, but they certainly made an effective appeal. Perhaps catching sight of the broad white smiles across their wet cheeks was worth my change of heart. New school policy: classes are to meet daily, regardless of cloudy, cold, or wet weather; they will be canceled only in case of thunderstorms.

Tonight the sky is clear again. The boys are asleep under blankets and goatskins. Hoyt, Rre Segatlhe, and Manaka are out by the fire to keep warm. When the sun disappears, it can still get cold at night.

I just went to the storage hut to find something and forgot what I was after. It was the sight of Manaka's sleeping place that diverted my attention. He had left burning a small, paraffin lamp which he had made of a discarded ink bottle and a wick. Its dim, flickering glow cast light on the bed he had carefully laid out on the floor: a burlap bag covered by a thin piece of torn sheeting and a flattened cardboard box. Under the lamp, lined up neatly beside his bed, was a piece of notebook paper and a pencil. The entire sheet was filled, line by line, with meticulously formed loops and crosses, spaces, and tidy zigzags. Alone he found the resources to make his lamp; was the silent Manaka now trying with pencil and paper to discern written language? Could this display of Manaka's worldly possessions give me a hint of his concealed spirit?

Whereas I can learn from my ill-fated, direct method of attempting to improve Moremi's living conditions, Rre Segatlhe's attitude toward his herd boys is something I cannot accept and to which I refuse to adjust. There are, after all, certain basic physical needs—food, warmth, and sleep—which go beyond cultural differences, but Rre Segatlhe and I disagree on what they are.

Woman that I am in a male-dominated society, I must find indirect ways to influence Rre Segatlhe. I must employ a Tswana woman's art of persuasion. To begin with, tomorrow I shall pour him plenty of kadi. I will praise him and refer to the training he is offering Manaka. Then, at just the right time, I will make him a gift of our extra blanket, suggesting that if he does not need it himself, he could offer it as a reward to Manaka for his excellent service.

Rre Segatlhe accepted the blanket with no comment, but proved stubborn about giving it to Manaka.

"Seipate," I asked in exasperation one day, "the madala of my lolwapa can be too stubborn—how can I exercise my authority as mosadi mogolo over Rre Segatlhe when I feel he is wrong?"

"Brew more kadi," was her immediate response.

"MaMoremi brews it . . . but I already tried giving him kadi."

"What about your chickens," she suggested.

"My chickens?" I queried.

"*Ee*, your chickens! Rre Segatlhe is always scolding that you do not tend to your chickens . . . that you just let the meat scratch around the lolwapa without cooking them!"

"Rre Segatlhe," I said one morning, "I see you are not using the blanket and that you have neatly folded it and put it on your chair to give to Manaka. Shall I carry it to his sleeping place for you while I go there to fetch the axe? I was thinking that perhaps we should kill a chicken for meat tonight." He watched me pick up the blanket. "Rre Segatlhe, you know how difficult it is for me to think of my chickens as meat; would you please kill this one for me?" I said, as I continued toward the storage hut.

Cradling it in his arms, Manaka thanked Rre Segatlhe for the blanket. He leaned in the doorway of his hut stroking the fleece. His face aglow with wonder, his calm, rough hands turned the edges over and over again.

We sat by the fire that night, trying to recover from a gluttonous meal. Rre Segatlhe came for his vinegar, praised the meal, and retired early. Because the laying hen had changed her hiding place and Nixon had not yet found it, I succeeded in collecting eggs. Thus, in addition to the chicken, I baked a cake for dinner.

My recipe: Place a rack over a paraffin burner, turned down low, and put a pot on it, covered tightly with another pot which fits upside-down onto its rim; the effect is that of a preheating oven.

Mix whatever "cakelike" ingredients you have on hand (flour, ground mealie, eggs, a can of fruit, some sugar) in whatever amounts you happen to have or feel right about and pour into pot. The cake with—granted—an unusual texture and flavor was savored by all, but it is hardly a recipe I can send home.

We sleep outside in the lolwapa all week because Kabo, the man who thatches roofs, arrived to start the job. He leaned his hand-hewn ladder up against the walls of our hut and climbed to the roof with a few wooden hand tools he made especially for thatching. His teenage son worked on the ground, evenly stacking bojang [grasses] into piles. Kabo's father taught him the skill, and he, in turn, was passing it on to the next generation.

Rre Segatlhe explained that traditionally, it is men who build and repair roofs. Although many families do their own thatchwork because they cannot pay a specialist, the advantage of hiring Kabo is that his superb craftsmanship builds thatch of greater durability. His fee is about one dollar a day, plus a midday bowl of mealie for him and his son.

Other aspects of building a hut also require specialized skills. It is common, however, that many homesteads do the work themselves. Men work with wood, constructing wooden doors and window shutters and building the door frames into walls. Women work with earth and stone, setting up the foundations, building the walls, and smearing floors.

Rre Segatlhe said it had become the fashion in some areas close to town to buy corrugated iron sheets to use for roofs and doors. To accommodate the iron sheeting, people had built square, rather than round huts. Square huts with iron roofs resembled town houses. Perhaps bojang was difficult to acquire in town, but he thought that some people were not satisfied with traditional ways and vainly strove to look like, to think like others. He laughed, "But a beautiful shoe can pinch your foot! If you wait out a rainstorm in a hut covered with corrugated iron, you will hold your ears tightly. And if you escape from the hot sun to the shade of one of those huts, you will find it worse inside. With no space between the wall and the roof to let the breeze through, it will feel like a slow oven!"

Kabo's ladder is up against our roof. The floor of our hut is strewn with straw. Tonight we bed down in the lolwapa, but it is difficult to fall asleep under the nighttime sky. Stripped of all so-called necessities, life may be simple here. Yet this very simplicity, entailing none of the diversions of "civilized" society, often forces us to confront ourselves. This simplicity becomes complex. Looking up at the immense sky, I feel miniscule, like a spark that fades too quickly.

We woke to daybreak and the rooster's call. At morning tea the lolwapa was full of workers. Manaka, Tiro, and Sejaro worked bare chested in the sun, while their shirts, hanging off the kitchen shelter posts, flapped in the morning breeze. They dug Rre Segatlhe's herb garden. Kabo and son, both on the roof, worked side by side brushing thatch with short, firm strokes. After sweeping, I continued digging my vegetable plot behind our hut. Usually bending over to sweep the lolwapa hurts my back to the point that I must raise myself again very slowly. Now after the two jobs, racked with pain, I groaned so loudly as I straightened up that I momentarily attracted everyone's attention. Rre Segatlhe, dressed in his finest clothes, tucked his cuffs into his boots, and pushing his bicycle, walked over to me. "One hair from your head may draw more than a team of oxen, but if you pull too hard, you will break it!" That said, he straddled his bicycle and rode off on the path to his "lovely mosadi" in Mogoditshane.

Propping a pillow against my back, I sat in the sun watching the boys who, now aware of the old man's absence, interrupted their digging to tussle in the sand. The sun was still low. Laundry was piled up; our bedding, full of dust, was bunched up by the crumbled wall. Madala, stick in hand, poked the long, fat *chunga-looloos* inching their way across the cracked floor. There was really no point in sweeping the loose dust back and forth. The wall needed rebuilding, the floor resmearing. MaMoremi was fetching water for the midday mealie pot. For just the two of us, there was too much work to be done.

Perhaps Seipate, Ntatabo, or Maria might come by to lend a helping hand. Together we could sing and tell stories while the work got done. But they were probably at their own homesteads repairing the damage of the rain. Were I a true Tswana woman I would have daughters to help. Seipate was right: to live here I needed daughters.

Tsotsi, the privileged school child, was not here to help. Rre Segatlhe was off to his girlfriend in Mogoditshane. Hoyt, appearing quite anxious to leave the chaos of the lolwapa, cycled off down the sandpath. Modise, I mused resentfully, would not alter his interview schedule to help me. Had he conveniently identified himself as a Tswana male and shunned this "woman's work?" At least Madala, contentedly in pursuit of the centipedes of the season, did not clamor for my attentions. Listless and alone, I sat waiting for companionship. No one came.

I rose, holding the pain in my back, and headed for the mirror in Rre Segatlhe's hut to see if I actually looked as old and tired as I felt. The stringy hair hanging limply to my shoulders was supposed to be blonde. The long, thin face was tan, or was it dirt? Eyebrows, bleached by the sun, were hardly visible. Squinting through small, flat eyes, I inspected the circles under them. Coming closer, I scrutinized the lines about the eyes and the wrinkles framing the straight, thin lips. Backing away, I recognized my part: mosadi mogolo. This time, though, there was more pain than pride. This was a hard life. The image of myself—before Botswana—came back to me. It was not what I saw. Turning away from my reflection, I was ready to fall onto Rre Segatlhe's bed and give in to depression.

How could I, just last night, distance and diminish myself to a fading spark and then this morning be totally absorbed with and overwhelmed by my self that it becomes as great as the universe?

Madala pushed the door and let the sunshine in. He wriggled with delight when I answered his plea for a bike ride with a resigned yes. We pushed on through the sand and the moshu trees toward the BAC farmland. I took a turn off to the right where I had never been. We cycled away from the trees to a freshly plowed field. I stopped. Madala climbed down, ran off, lifted clumps of soil, and threw them in the air. He watched the sand break apart and scatter, clouding the clear air. We left the bicycle to walk along the empty rows far out into the open.

We bent down to look at the stand of newly sprouted sunflowers. "They will grow this high!" I exclaimed as I raised my hand above our heads. Madala looked up, shielding his eyes from the sun. We walked more carefully between the rows. Even little Madala could understand not to trample new life.

Madala lay down between the rows. I too stretched out to feel the soft soil. We drifted off: Madala to sleep and I to the consolation of the warm sun. A tuft of cloud passed on above us. How this landscape could change my mood!

"Why are they sunflowers?" Madala asked, as we pedaled home.

"That is just the name of the flower," I replied. "They will grow large and bright and yellow, like the sun. And like every flower, they need sunlight to grow. Everything alive needs the sunlight."

"I'm glad I don't need the sun to grow. I'm glad I'm not alive," he said.

"Brian! Of course you are alive! We are both alive!"

"No," he insisted. "If you're alive, you will die. If I am alive, I will die," Brian repeated.

"Wake it!" I remembered him demanding when he saw the goat corpse hanging. What had his three-year-old mind understood when he played in the periphery of funerals?

Like a Tswana, today the growing Madala observed that death was inextricably bound to his life. He waited for me to assure him that he was of a different category—something other than alive—and realizing that I could not, he was content to accept my assertion that it felt good to be alive and then change the topic.

We returned home in good spirits, composing a simple song to the rhythm of the pedals. It was about the sunflowers and had

"Rre Segatlhe has tolerantly left Suzy to Tsotsi's affections."

11

Witch Doctor or White Coats?

The thatchwork of our hut is completed, and with a great sense of relief, we move our bedding back under its roof. Even though the hut does not offer complete privacy, at least when everyone else is asleep, we can close the door and feel alone.

One night when bedding down in the courtyard, we were awakened by a young man who came charging between our beds and tapped urgently on Rre Segatlhe's door. Rre Segatlhe lit a wick, opened the door for the young man, and closed it again. They conversed in hushed tones for quite some time.

Hoyt and I found it difficult to get back to sleep and started discussing something which led to disagreement. We strained to keep our voices down as our argument grew more intense.

"You said that I said . . ."

"No, I did not . . . You're the one that said that . . ."

There was a slow, steady crescendo as we argued and refused to abandon our positions, whatever they were. Infuriated with Hoyt and frustrated at not being able to yell, I swung myself out of bed and stomped off in anger. Striding barefoot across the lolwapa. I rushed into the dark open field. There, dancing with pain, I came to an abrupt halt. With every move, my feet felt sharp prickles. I had escaped into a patch of thorns.

Trembling in my nightgown, I stood in one spot ready to scream or laugh or cry when Rre Segatlhe's door opened and the young man emerged. I think I expressed all three emotions in rapid succession. Hoyt, who could see the horror on the young man's face as he spotted a figure in the field, would have explained the situation, but the young man flew off in desperation.

I whimpered my way out of the thorns into Hoyt's perfunctory arms. Rre Segatlhe shut his door and blew out the wick.

The next morning Rre Segatlhe explained that the young man had been haunted and pursued by witches and had come to him to get rid of them. After a lengthy discussion, Rre Segatlhe determined that the witches had been sent by his brother-in-law because the young man had insulted him. To rid himself of the witches, the young man needed to perform good deeds for the wronged brother-in-law and thereby regain his favor. Rre Segatlhe promised to help him by holding on to the witches in his field so that the young man could return safely to his brother-in-law's home to make his amends and solve his problems.

I commented that it was a fortunate coincidence for Rre Segatlhe's credibility that I stood screaming in the field. He shook his head at my ignorance.

"Certainly I kept the witches. What do you think caught you?"

"Thorns."

"No! No! Why do you think such simple things? You must look under the surface to find meaning. You cannot just look at what is there to see. Just as you cannot hear all sounds with your ears or smell all things with your nose, you cannot see all that is with us. And just because you cannot see something, that does not mean it is not there. Thorns! Ha! Modise struggled with evil spirits in you. You ran to the witches because of evil spirits in you. But you escaped, leaving them behind. Then Modise could welcome you back to his arms."

Rre Segatlhe told me that I must try to understand the hidden powers in myself and in the world. If I had trouble, I could come to him; he would throw the bones and show me what I could not see. What we have here is a resident psychiatrist.

"Rre Segatlhe may not like to go to Gaborone," MaMoremi said, "but Gaborone sure likes to come see him! A government official is here!"

A glossy, black car with Gaborone license plates pulled into the crossroad, parked in the field, and a well-dressed Tswana emerged to greet Rre Segatlhe. The two withdrew to the privacy of Rre Segatlhe's hut for some time, then returned to the sunlight near the kitchen shelter where Rre Segatlhe poured liquid into a basin. The man removed his shoes and socks. Rre Segatlhe spoke incantations about the blood of a sacrificed goat, and the man rolled up his trousers. Rre Segatlhe signaled, and the man stepped into the basin. They stood facing each other. The man soaked his feet in the deep red liquid. His eyes were shut; his arms hung limply at his sides; and Rre Segatlhe appealed to the gods. Rre Segatlhe spoke slowly. He framed his words with silence.

Stand still in the blood of the slaughtered goat,
It dies so you shall live.

Your heart is sick, your blood is weak,
You tire and feel pain.
Medicals cannot reach you.
What do doctors know? They are men.

I speak to Modimo.
I speak to the Badimo.

There is peace in the Great Unknown.
Your fate lives with Gods,
And so lives the fate of all mankind.

Stand still in the blood of the slaughtered goat,
It dies so you shall live.

Rre Segatlhe's voice trailed off into a whisper. He motioned in silence and bent over to pick up the man's shoes and socks. He stepped out of the basin, and with his blood-stained feet followed Rre Segatlhe through the dust back to the shade of the hut. We heard their murmurs behind the wooden door.

"He now gets his pay," said MaMoremi. "Sometimes it is food. This time it surely will be money."

Upon leaving, the visitor returned to his car, swung open the backdoor, and picked up a bundle off of the back seat. He dropped the sleepy puppy on the sand, bid Rre Segatlhe farewell, and drove out of sight. The brown, furry dog shook its body and floppy ears. Wagging its tail and yapping, it bounded toward Tsotsi. It jumped, rolled, and ran circles around his beckoning gestures.

The man had been to the doctors and the hospital in town, Rre Segatlhe explained, but they could not cure him. He was still a young man, yet he had a very bad heart. Rre Segatlhe had treated him, but his condition was poor. He would not live long.

"He is a man from town," Rre Segatlhe continued. "He paid

me well and gave me the dog. She is a fat one like the dogs in town, and she has a name—Suzy." Rre Segatlhe looked on as Tsotsi and Suzy took off with the tennis ball.

Rre Segatlhe has tolerantly left Suzy to Tsotsi's affections. Nevertheless, Hoyt and I impressed on Keith the wisdom of feeding her clandestinely. Where food and water are scarce, dogs and cats are left to find their own meals and are thrown leftovers only now and then. The cat here does quite well. He stalks about at night catching bugs and bats and keeps the lolwapa clear of lizards and snakes. Dogs, however, find little in nature to supplement their occasional feedings. They stray lifelessly between homesteads and receive a bare minimum of sustenance.

Tsotsi sneaks Suzy a dish of leftovers every night after dinner. She sleeps curled on the floor by his bed. During the day, she is full of vigor and seeks her entertainment until Tsotsi returns from school and she resumes her place at his side. Bounding toward a sleeping Tswana dog, she entices him to play. She wiggles, bows, and barks joyfully to introduce herself and is greeted by a fierce snarl in return. Not easily deterred, she tries again. Impatient with her persistence, the dog painfully raises himself; with hollow ribcage he assumes his most hostile stance, bares his teeth, and growls at her. She cowers, tail between her legs and from a distance stares bewildered at what she mistook for her own species.

The rooster is another thing. He responds to her overtures with flapping wings and a flashing beak. Like prizefighters, they face off, but since neither can appreciate the equipment and strategy of the other, their energies are wasted. Exhausted, they retreat to their corners, calling it a draw. There will be a rematch tomorrow.

Suzy has attached herself to us and follows us like a faithful pet. On days that Modise has no interviews, Tsotsi and Madala rouse him to go with them "to look at cars." Suzy bounds back and forth between Hoyt and the boys as they walk past the crossroads and disappear down the dirt road leading to the main road from Gaborone to Francistown. Besides local traffic, they watch tourists from South Africa speeding by as they head for the game parks in the north. Rre Segatlhe saw Hoyt and the boys on a recent outing and has entertained many a visitor with his fireside story.

"One of those makgoa cars sped toward Modise, Tsotsi, and Madala by the roadside. Like gold in the sun, it flashed toward them. The white, hairy arm of a fat stomach shot out of the car window as it passed, and candies flew through the air. Tsotsi and Madala knew what to do. They scrambled quickly into the grasses, grubbing around for every sweet. A confused Modise looked to the TJ Johannesburg license plate and scratched his head.

"The car screeched to a stop, backed up, and stopped again. The pink, twisted face of the white, hairy arm popped out of the window to stare at our Modise. Ha! Poor Modise is the wrong color! No more candies. The car sped away! Our Tsotsi and Madala found the Tswana santa, but Modise—Ha! He's just a starving native!"

Occasionally Rre Segatlhe leads a young woman toward me who, he explains, has never seen a white person before. I find this difficult to believe, but he insists that she has led a sheltered existence far out in the bush. She haltingly steps forward when Rre Segatlhe drops her hand, looks shyly into my eyes, and retreats quickly before I can shake her hand. She comes back to my side. We sit together, and before she leaves, she takes my hand to say good-bye. Our three-year-old and Rre Segatlhe's wise Madala concludes, "Mommy, we're a funny yellowy color, aren't we?"

For only one person has our skin color caused concern here: a woman from another village comes to buy herbs and snuff from Rre Segatlhe. After her first visit, Rre Segatlhe explained to me that for most of her life, this woman had worked as a servant on an Afrikaans farm in South Africa. She had been treated badly. Skin color alone would probably always be a significant issue for her.

On her next visit, I greeted her with special deference, but she refused my hand, calling me a *karibe* [young woman]. Insulted, I corrected her, asserting my status as mosadi mogolo. Rre Segatlhe nodded his approval. She went on to express her negative feelings about white women, and turning to me, asserted that white women were spoiled. "They do not work. Their hands are smooth and lazy!" Forcefully, she grabbed my hand and pulled it in front of Rre Segatlhe's face. She displayed my hand: a large, bony hand with knuckles heavily accented by the dirt in their crevices. The nails, broken and torn, held the grime which also outlined the rough cuticles. She turned it. Pads, soiled a soft brown, circled the lines of a light, *lekgoa* [white one's] palm. Rre Segatlhe nodded his approval. She threw down my hand, conceding nothing, while I, glad to have passed her test, decided then and there to buy hand cream on the next trip to town.

Madala toddles over to us for attention. He hugs and kisses me. He hugs and kisses Rre Segatlhe and heads for our visitor to complete his rounds.

"He cannot kiss me! He is white!" She is adamant. Rre Segatlhe sweeps up his Madala and hugs him generously.

Lekoto, Tiro's oldest brother, is one of the two children that our neighbors, Polwane and Tabo, have sent to school. It was Lekoto who took Keith to school the first day. He is in standard 7, the last grade at the elementary level, and will soon take national examinations to determine whether he will be admitted to secondary school. For the last few days he has been coming to me for extra tutoring because he, quite rightly, perceives that his chances of doing well are poor. The village school he attends has teachers who are only minimally qualified. Lekoto is determined to go to secondary school, not only to achieve earning power for himself, but also to fulfill his familial obligations. His parents are willing to sacrifice to pay his school fees, and it is understood that Lekoto, in return, will one day be able to provide school fees for the youngest children and offer financial help when the family needs it.

Lekoto failed to show up for his tutoring session after dinner tonight. Instead, Tabo came with news. His wife, Polwane, had been sick for several days. She was becoming progressively worse. It now appeared that Lekoto and his sister, Lerato, were coming down with the same sickness. This night they lay shivering in their blankets by the fire, unable to get warm.

Rre Segatlhe told Tabo that he did not have an adequate supply of medicine for treatment. It would be best if they could get to Mogoditshane to see the European doctor. We agreed that I would drive them there the following morning.

Early the next morning Tabo rushed into the lolwapa to summon help. Hoyt and Rre Segatlhe followed him home. By the time I got there, Polwane had come out of a fainting spell. The men lifted her into our car. Lekoto and Lerato climbed in beside their mother. I headed straight for the hospital in Gaborone.

A bench of bodies wound around the walls of the waiting room. Polwane, wrapped in her plaid blanket, found space between an old man holding his head and a woman breast-feeding her infant. Folding his long legs beneath him, Lekoto slumped down onto the concrete floor, rested his back and head against the wall, and closed his eyes. Lerato stood near the bench, leaning against the wall and waiting for space to sit down. A middle-aged woman untied her pink head scarf, wiped her perspiring forehead, and squirming to find comfort, shifted the weight of her heavy body on her one spot. Beside her, a boy dangled his bony bare feet from the bench. Like two pendulums in opposition marking time, they moved evenly backward and forward. Scrambling on the floor near her mother, a toddler coughed and caught the mucus from her draining nose on a dirty sleeve. Two women, who before were leaning against the entrance way in discussion, sat listlessly huddled in their blankets. These were the rural and urban sick. These were the poor. There was not one bureaucrat, not one uniform, not one white face among them. More people came in. Some, finding no place to settle, crowded near the entrance way.

I left the room to walk and found another waiting room. Here was, exclusively, the clientele not represented in the other room. They sat in chairs with magazines and crossed legs. Some chairs were empty. A nurse stopped me to ask if I had an appointment. No. Did I wish to make one now? Yes. Name? Polwane Mologwane.

"Then it is your servant who is sick?"

"No, a friend."

"She can come herself."

"Good, I'll go get her. She is waiting in the crowded room."

"Here it will cost money. These are private doctors."

"Yes, I know. I have seen this hospital before—many times, many places."

Polwane was already on her way into the doctor's office when I returned to find her. Lerato had progressed to the bench. Lekoto still sat on the floor, now holding his knees and tucking his head under his arms. We waited for Polwane to emerge, "What was wrong?" we asked her. She did not know and appeared confused. They had given her an injection, and she held out pills for us to see. She did not know what the pills were for, nor did she understand what dosage to use. I walked over to the Tswana nurse. Could she please find out and explain to this lady what the doctor had diagnosed? No. She could not. She was much too busy right now. Why—if she wanted to know—didn't she ask the doctor herself?

"Because she only speaks Setswana and the doctor couldn't

understand her." My obvious protest trailed weakly behind her white coat scurrying down the hallway.

Polwane, Lekoto, and Lerato followed me to the other waiting room. Here there were also two doors which swung open at regular intervals. I paid the fee, and we did not wait long. The diagnosis was pneumonia. Lerato was given an injection and medication and released, but Polwane and Lekoto were both to be admitted, their condition was considered to be poor.

"This way!" a voice commanded to Polwane and Lekoto before Lerato and I could take our leave. We watched them march away from us, white coat flapping behind them.

Lerato and I returned home. Friends circled the kitchen hearth sheltering themselves from the afternoon rain. They waited to hear news of Polwane and her children.

Tabo listened carefully, shook everyone's hand solmenly, put his arm around Lerato and led her home.

"Polwane and Lekoto in the hospital! Injections and pills as usual!" Molefi acridly remarked.

"No matter what the complaint—eyes, stomach, back, or head—they give the same injection!" Seipate elaborated in the same tone.

"Injection! Injection!" Ntatabo and Mariga joined the chorus. "And what are those pills? We will not swallow what we do not know; we throw them away."

"What is wrong with those white coat doctors?" Maria asked me. "They look at us from behind a desk. They refuse to touch us. They use metal, rubber, or wood; anything but their own hands! They mumble 'injection', send us out, and think they have done a great thing."

"No one tells us what is wrong, what they are doing, or why. We file in like their cattle. They do not greet. They do not talk or explain. They think we, like cattle, cannot understand," MaMoremi added.

"With witch doctors it is different," Maria went on. "They listen, they talk. They respect our bodies and our minds. They tell us what is happening, why it hurts, what we must do and why. They tell us how the medicine works."

Silent among them all, Rre Segatlhe did not respond to the outburst of discontent. It was not until I asked them why they even went to the white coat doctors that Rre Segatlhe spoke.

"No medicals are magic. No doctors know all. When a sick person comes to me, I find what is wrong and give good medicals. But it is not so simple. I do not have all medicals, and if a person is very sick, he must try everything, even the white coats! I tell this to you, but many of you refuse to go to the European doctors."

"Now often patients of the hospital are unsatisfied," he continued, "and they come to me afterwards. Injections and pills are not magic. Sometimes I can heal them when the white coat doctors have failed. Sometimes we both fail; there is no cure. Then I will use the bones and talk to the spirits. That is a powerful way to attack the sickness which the European doctors do not understand."

"*Ruri!*" [for sure], Tladi chimed in. "You, Rre Segatlhe, may know these doctors, but they do not see you. They think witch doctors are evil. I know this because I have heard them say this."

"That is their problem, not ours," Neo joined in.

"No," Rre Segatlhe disagreed. "It is our problem, too. Just as I have powers they do not understand, the white coats sit on heaps of medicals that I cannot grow or find in the bush. It is good Polwane and Lekoto will get some of their medicals, and if they return sick, I will call on the spirits and treat them also."

When Polwane was finally released from the hospital and returned home, she brought a message for Hoyt. Lekoto, still very ill in the hospital, had summoned Modise to his bedside. Hoyt left that same afternoon.

During a fitful night, Lekoto had struggled with high fever and violent headaches. He had what he described to Modise as a "powerful vision." He had seen dark clouds rolling death toward him. He ran to free himself and cried out for help. A voice broke in—to save himself, he was to offer a sacrifice. His father, brothers, and the rest of his family appeared, and he saw Modise sitting by the fire with them. "I will slaughter a goat for Modise," Lekoto promised. He repeated these words, and the darkness lifted. He opened his eyes to find himself awake, staring at bare hospital walls. He was alive; for the first time in several days, he believed he would survive. "Modise," Lekoto said, "when I am cured and on the very day that I return home, I will choose my best animal to slaughter for you." Lekoto coughed, caught his breath, and waited for Modise's response. Modise assured him that he would recover his health, even without a sacrifice.

"No," Lekoto demanded, "you are Modise, a shepherd among men, and a great friend of my father. I wish you to accept the promise that healed my sickness. It will be good for my future; this the vision has told me. I, too, must be a shepherd, a shepherd for my father's family. I must be well and pass the examinations. One day I will get a job to help my family."

Modise accepted Lekoto's promise, embraced him, and took leave of him.

It is to family, close friends, and trusted community members that a Tswana turns for support in times of crisis. Lekoto's vision, his words and intentions, have strengthened our bond of affection toward our neighbors, Tabo's family. With them, we wait for Lekoto's recovery. We share the determination that he fulfill his commitment toward himself and his family.

Still no word about Lekoto's progress. We hope he'll recover in time to take the examinations.

Yesterday, when I went to the Millers' to take a shower, I left Madala playing outside in the yard. Just before leaving, I filled up the water containers while he entertained himself rolling our spare tire in the driveway. We drove off, inadvertently leaving the tire behind.

I was away teaching when Hoyt arrived home to discover the spare tire missing. After consulting Rre Segatlhe, the two men came to the conclusion that the spare tire had been stolen. As Modise worried over the financial loss, Rre Segatlhe assured him that he would find the culprit and recover his loss. He tossed the bones onto the lolwapa floor; the thief lived in Kopong and had two wives. He would cast an evil spell on the thief to riddle him with misfortune. Thus, in order to change his circumstances, the thief would be forced to return the tire. While not entirely convinced, Modise enjoyed Rre Segatlhe's support—so much so that he looked like a true believer.

There was some chagrin when, upon my return, I announced that the spare tire was left behind in the Millers' driveway. Rre Segatlhe reminded us that all doctors make mistakes from time to time; he was no exception. We noticed that he was careful to call back the evil spirits that he had sent out to the suspect in Kopong.

The children bring mopane worms to munch on during class. Sitting near me, Gobuamang crunched and crackled her handful of worms and popped them into her mouth. I have tried to explain that I don't care to eat any, yet she continues to offer me a portion every day. To convince her, I must point to my stomach to tell her I am sick. She would not understand any other reason for turning away food. When days of hunger are remembered, accepted, and expected again, any edible morsel is savored.

The seeds of my garden have sprouted, and the rains have transformed our fields. Rre Segatlhe and Tabo wait for Mosimanegape to bring the cattle for plowing. Thorn bushes are outlined with new leaves. Ground cover vegetation has spread, thick and green. It is a feast for the goats and sheep. Manaka and Tsotsi have a difficult time corralling them at sundown.

Approaching the narrow entrance to their kraal, the goats and sheep push sideways frantically to escape capture. Spying the open fields, they bound away to settle in a patch of succulent grasses. Those jammed in close together with no space to move forward toward the kraal hop straight up into the air, landing on another goat's back. There is a protest of sound and a plaintive maaing of their discontent. Hoofs pound the dust. Horns clank against the kraal posts. The fur and bristles of their hides and swollen bellies press against each other. One by one the recalcitrant animals are squeezed out of the mêlée into their kraal for the night.

We eat *merogo* freshly picked and cooked. It is a weed now abundant in the fields and tastes like dandelion greens. It takes MaMoremi and me several hours to pick it, but our harvest amounts to a mere two tablespoons per person after the greens are boiled.

Fortunately, MaMoremi has a strong back; my two tablespoons would taste better without the back pains. Rre Segatlhe has assured me that if I had grown up in this society, my back would probably be stronger and more fit to withstand the physical strain of a Tswana woman's daily chores. As soon as they can walk, young Tswana girls exercise their backs, bending, pounding, lifting, and carrying, while doing their household chores. Women rarely speak of back problems, although they do often voice other common physical complaints: eyes, infected by flying dust and dirty hands; stomach pains and worms, often due to poor sanitation; and respiratory ailments, again probably caused by the dust.

A favorite pastime for relaxation and indulgence, other than kadi, to divert one from the aches and drudgery of difficult chores is the use of tobacco. Snuff, in particular, is coveted. A week does not go by without Maria, Seipate, or Ntatabo picking up a new supply from Rre Segatlhe. He fills their small pouches; they press a five-cent piece into the palm of his hand and move homeward, sampling sniffs.

Some nights ago, MaMoremi consulted Rre Segatlhe about stomach pains she had suffered for several weeks. Upon coming to our hut to receive his nightly dose of vinegar, Rre Segatlhe pointed to the bottle of methylated spirits which we use for our lantern. He asked if he could have a cup of it to use for his supply of medicine. "For medicine!" I exclaimed, and proceeded to explain to him that the clear, bright purple liquid was highly poisonous.

"Certainly I know what it is! Just give me a little cup," he retorted, highly offended at my lack of respect for his knowledge and judgment. I insisted that I could not give it to him because it belonged to Modise. Poor timing: Modise walked in at that very moment. Rre Segatlhe persisted, "Modise, I want a cup of methylated spirits."

"Of course," Modise replied, and passed him the bottle.

"No! Hoyt, No!" I intervened and grabbed the bottle out of Rre Segatlhe's hand. This was life and death. Both men stood shocked at the bold intrusion, unbefitting a Tswana woman, and my usurpation of masculine power.

"Rre Segatlhe, please tell Modise what you need it for," I asked.

To my relief he complied and explained to Hoyt that MaMoremi had come to him with chronic stomach pains. It was his opinion that she would be relieved of her problems if she swallowed a spoonful or two of methylated spirits. Surely we would like to help MaMoremi?

"Of course," Modise agreed, and summarily walked out. That left me clutching the bottle, and Rre Segatlhe waiting for me to turn it over to him.

"Rre Segatlhe," I pleaded, as he took it from my hand and walked off, "this is poison. It could kill MaMoremi. Please don't use it." He entered his hut.

I left mine to find MaMoremi. "Don't take it," I whispered to her in the lolwapa. "It could make things worse, even kill you. It is poison."

Rre Segatlhe approached with a spoon and the bottle. He explained to her that if she drank a spoonful of this purple liquid, it would kill the disease in her stomach. It was true that it was poison, poison powerful enough to fight what was causing her pain, and the little she would swallow, he assured her, would do her no harm.

MaMoremi swallowed it without the slightest hesitation and retired to her hut.

"Hoyt, how much does it take to be lethal?" I asked.

"I don't know," he replied.

"You don't *know*! How could you walk out that door? How could you allow this to happen?" I reprimanded him.

"Marianne, it is clear from conversations with Tabo and Molefi that Rre Segatlhe is highly regarded as a very good doctor. They speak of his many successes. No one knows of anyone who has died from his care. Did you know that some say he has an herbal cure for a mamba bite? This may or may not be true, but the rumor reveals the level of his repute."

"What's that got to do with this case? You are really going too far with . . ."

"Marianne," Hoyt interrupted me impatiently, "when you go to a doctor whom others have assured you is exceptionally good, do you fear or attempt to decipher the prescription he gives you? Do you give preference to well meaning friends who advise against medical treatment?"

"No," I had to admit.

MaMoremi had reacted no differently than I would have in my own society. Why, Hoyt asked me, did I have more confidence in knowledge acquired through medical school training than in knowledge gathered through generations of experience?

MaMoremi lay in the shade the whole of the next day. Toward sunset of the second day, Rre Segatlhe walked over to her to tell her that she was recovering. She slowly rose, wrapped a wool cloth around her middle, and joined us for a cup of tea.

Yes, it was still painful, she said, and yes, she was much better.

After dinner I went to throw the dishwater on my garden plot behind the hut. Horrors! Each seed and every sprout was uprooted and gone! While MaMoremi was resting and while all of us were out, the chickens had flown over the fence for a feast. While Rre Segatlhe could appreciate my bitter disappointment, he reminded me of his initial skepticism regarding my plans and seemed pleased that he was right.

Lekoto sent word to the crossroads that he soon would come home. We decided to make Lekoto's homecoming a great event,

149

and on a bright Monday morning, a group gathered by our truck for the ride to the hospital.

Modise was last to get into the crowded truck. He put the key into the ignition, turned it, and nothing happened. He tried again. Everyone climbed out. The hood went up, and a group of men looked knowingly at the motor. Modise fiddled with wires and moved back and forth from the hood to the driver's seat. I didn't pay much attention until it seemed clear that the truck would not start.

"We can't drive it." Hoyt admitted defeat. "It just won't turn over."

"What do you mean?" I stepped forward. "Of course it will start!" Everybody stared at me. "Modise, give me the keys. I'll do it!" He laughed. Everybody laughed. I grabbed the keys, slammed down the hood, and headed for the driver's seat. Before I shut the door, I called to Rre Segatlhe,

"Rre Segatlhe, I, the mosadi mogolo, will start this car, and you will see that I too have special powers!"

I slammed the car door shut and wriggled into a comfortable position. The thought crept in that I was providing comic relief, but I tossed it away quickly. "This car will start," I said to myself. When I turned the key and the motor started, I left the driver's seat and walked off, drinking in the exclamations, Modise's face, and Rre Segatlhe's silence. As much as Hoyt tried to rationalize the event in retrospect (the slamming hood and door must have jolted a faulty wire connection back into place), there was still no explanation for my brash intrusion. I certainly did not care to speculate on what had possessed me. Hoyt was convinced that the hot sun was getting to me, but I said to Rre Segatlhe—very transcendentally—"It's in the bones."

Lekoto arrived. He looked weak and very thin, but he was relieved and happy to be home again. When we sat with his family to celebrate his return, Lekoto revealed to us that the exams had already been administered. But, he grinned, he had not missed them. He simply left the hospital for his exams and returned to his bed when they were over. The white coats didn't know. The nurses were irritated, but it had all worked out. "Pula," we cheered his audacity.

"How were the exams?" I inquired. He shrugged. "Pula," we wished him success. While success, to his parents, seemed a foregone conclusion, Lekoto appeared worried. He left us for the kraal and returned dragging the goat he had chosen for Modise. It was a proud moment: Lekoto holding the goat, describing the distinct patterns of its fur, and remarking that "with this fur, Modise will have a fine *pathe* to sleep on."

The slaughter is scheduled for this afternoon. MaMoremi is brewing kadi again. We expect many neighbors to join us. The news of a slaughter travels fast, particularly now, just before planting, when grain supplies are low. I will join the women in song and dance and laugh at the memory of myself—months ago—closed up in the dark hut, holding my ears in protest to slaughter.

"The rear hoof follows where the front has trod."

12

Fat Kitchen and Fields

No water this morning. MaMoremi and I have used large quantities in our extra chores, repair work, and meal preparations. There is nothing to drink. Tsotsi stares blankly at the empty containers on the stoop and leaves for school, like many of his classmates, without food or drink. At least, for a time like this, we have made the right decision by allowing Keith to eat from the common midday pot of hot mealie at school. The children eat and share with dirty fingers. In contrast to other parents, we thought of the risk of disease but willed our fears away; hot mealie meal, the satisfaction to a hungry stomach, is joyful communion and a highlight of the school day.

Madala finally stopped complaining of his thirst when I sternly told him he would have to wait. Hoyt and Rre Segatlhe lifted the water drum onto the back of the truck, and Rre Segatlhe suggested I take Manaka with me to help fill it up.

By the way Manaka held onto the seat and tried to suppress the laughter on his face, it was obvious that he had never ridden in a car. As we circled around to get onto the dirt road, Tiro, who had just let the goats to pasture, waved us down.

"Ke batla lifti!" he yelled out. We swung open the door, and he jumped onto the front seat beside Manaka. He did not ask where we were going or how long we would be gone; it did not matter. For this joyride, he would abandon the herd, and if he were discovered, he would willingly pay the consequences.

So they could get a good view of the BAC housing complex, I drove slowly around the loop. Sitting forward against the front windshield, as if propped before a movie screen, they gaped at the scene: green grass and flowers, painted doors, houses for cars alone! And what was the blue water in the ground? Repeating my words, "swimming pool," they tried to imagine what it would be like to immerse their whole bodies in water. We passed a field where three children clad in splendid riding clothes of velvet and leather sat astride horses. Erect and proud, they trotted the horses to the roadside. For a moment their glances must have met the open stares and frozen wonder of the herd boys now leaning together through the open window.

The water spigot was outside. There was no reason to enter the Millers' house except to satisfy the boys' curiosity. They stroked the green-painted door and wondered what was behind it. We entered. One step inside, and they stopped to run their eyes along the smooth, straight white walls up the perfectly perpendicular corner and across the smooth white ceiling to a light fixture. Explore, I encouraged them. At their fingertips, one movement for light, and then again, no light.

Another room: a turn of the wrist for heat without flames, or were they trapped in the plate of coils? They pulled a shiny handle for cold and another for a cold they had never felt before—a stinging, hard cold.

Another room with the greatest magic of all—a room of water: water of the pool to sit over; water raining down from above; water hot, water cold, pouring out in streams as long as you wish or dripping slowly or not at all!

While we were outside filling the water drum, the woman next door rushed anxiously over to us. "Stop! What are you doing?" I missed the initial greeting.

"Hello, how are you feeling?" I translated into English.

"What do you think you are doing?" she demanded. It turns out that we have grabbed the wrong hose—not the Millers', but the garden hose for this lady's flowers. A thousand pardons.

Driving home through the BAC farmland, we spotted work crews out in the fields. We approached a pair of men working near the road. A Tswana man sat in the seat of a tractor, and in the fields, tossing debris away from its path was a field hand. I did not notice until we were closer that the field hand was white with silver hair. He paused to wave, threw another boulder to the side, and walked over to my truck.

It was Ellwyn Miller. True to Tswana tradition, he greeted. I greeted. The boys greeted. The man on the tractor greeted. I greeted him in return, and the boys greeted. We thanked Mr. Miller for the water and told him of our tour of his house. He in turn told us about their plans for the field. They were now preparing to plow by clearing the cluttered areas. We bid our Tswana farewells. *"Salang sentle,"* we called out. *"Tsamayang pila,"* they replied.

Our progress homeward was slow because we stopped to pick up every walker who hailed us down, and those we passed, we stopped to greet. Where walking is the major means of transport, it is the custom to greet everyone you meet, to chat, and then bid a formal farewell. It is true that our vehicle might give us different prerogatives, yet these, in this setting and circumstance, could not supersede the human encounter primarily important to rural life: the giving and receiving of news.

It was later that Ellwyn Miller told Hoyt and me about the complications of his position as farm manager of the BAC. Whereas he had been able to establish very good rapport with the uneducated Tswana field crew, he found it frequently difficult and at times downright impossible to communicate with some of the British administrators and educated members of the Tswana elite. It sometimes reached absurd dimensions—for instance, when last I saw him in the field.

He, as farm manager, and a young educated Tswana went to survey a particular field and plow it up. All went well until they reached a pile of debris by the roadside. Mr. Miller suggested that they get down off the tractor to remove some of the larger pieces by hand before attempting to plow up the section. The driver refused to do this, proclaiming that it was a job for the field crew. But the field crew, busy elsewhere, would not get to it for days, Mr. Miller protested, and the two of them could clear it in minutes, thereby completing the job. The driver continued to insist that this menial work was not a part of his job and refused to get off the tractor. A Vermont farmer, Mr. Miller said, was never too proud to bend to the soil, and the same, he suspected, held true for a Tswana farmer. Mr. Miller jumped off the tractor and proceeded to clear the field while the driver rode slowly behind him. Eventually, watching an elderly man stoop in labor must have humiliated the young driver after all; for the last few feet he grudgingly left the tractor to help finish the job.

Mr. Miller observed that this educated Tswana no longer modeled himself after traditional Tswana farmers, but after his British counterparts in the hierarchy of the BAC organization. He had often watched expatriate farm experts and bureaucrats orchestrating labor in the fields while remaining totally upright and unsoiled in the process. When a young Tswana obtained new status achieved by education and position, he often lost interest in the needs of the common farmer. Instead, he strove solely to improve his own situation, reinforcing a divisive class structure, and hurting the goals of agriculture. To Ellwyn Miller, it was essential for both the traditional, rural farmer and the upwardly mobile, educated, agricultural elite to understand that the labor of the hands was equal to the labor of the mind.

Hoyt agreed with Ellwyn but added that there were precedents in traditional Tswana society for social stratification. Even though many family heads preferred to control the plow, they enjoyed the unquestioned authority to order younger men to do various tasks. The irony was that once young men became educated and left their rural homes, they often continued to accept traditional ideas of social stratification while adopting Western standards for what this stratification would entail. They could, thereby, consider themselves superior to the uneducated rural elders. This stance, of course, limited what effect they, as professional agriculturalists, could have in persuading rural elders to adopt new farming practices.

Ceremoniously, Hoyt and I presented Ellwyn Miller with a gift. It was to help remedy the problem of communication he faced at the BAC. With bright magic markers, I printed out Ellwyn Miller's message on posterboard. It was an attractive poster and read as follows:

Go na le maemo, boipelo, le maikgantsho mo kitsong ya tiro ya diatla fela jaaka a morutegi wa thlaloganyo e e kwa godimo—dimo.
[There is as much status, fulfillment, and dignity in the labor of hands as in the understanding of the highly educated mind.]

Ellwyn Miller tacked the poster on the bare wall of his office, but when he returned from a day in the field, he found that his Tswana co-worker had covered it with maps.

The expatriate agriculture research team at the BAC has come up with a few very important agricultural innovations which it believes would increase the per household yield by a significant amount. Convinced of their expertise, I tried to persuade Rre Segatlhe to follow their advice to plant early.

"Are they trying to teach a monkey to climb? What can these people tell me? They come, and they go. What does it matter to them? They see one, maybe two seasons and decide the best way to plant. They say they have answers and that I do not know, yet I have been here a lifetime!" he protested.

"Certainly they say we must plant now. We have early rains. But what happens when the seeds have sprouted, and the early rains have stopped? We on the lands have no other seeds to plant; we will have nothing left. The BAC is different. It is the fat kitchen next door to poverty. It always has more seeds and can plant again. It is easy to give advice if you do not have to pay the price of failure."

"Rre Segatlhe," I urged, "your good friends Maria and Molefi are allowing their son, Tladi, to plant their field now. They decided to try these new ideas that Tladi brings home from his job at the BAC."

"I know this. For Tladi things are not the same as for me and for others. He has gotten more seeds because of his job there. He can bring home ideas from the BAC, but it is one-way traffic. What does the BAC know about our traditional ways? Tladi can plow whenever he wants to because he has arranged to use a tractor. But I must wait for my cattle. Most people cannot plow whenever they wish, they must wait for the cattle. Tladi knows these things, but truly, they do not listen to him. The BAC fat kitchen does not think of these things."

"Should each farm have a tractor, maybe?"

"Mosadi!" he exclaimed, "Where have you been? This is only for someone who does not know our life to say. If we do not have water or mealie, will we have gasoline and tools? And what is a big piece of metal to our life? Where will you find boloko to build your walls? I can say, mosadi, you are too tired just now or you would not say such a thing. A tractor here and there may be a fine thing, but our life is cattle."

"Right now my cattle are being driven home from the cattle post by Mosimanegape. On the way home he will stop at Sekaba's and Kgosana's place, where Mosimanegape is hired to help plow. Then they will plow at Tabo's place as well. Mosimanegape will earn himself many cattle by the time he grows to be a man; he is a good worker and no one can be better with cattle than Tabo's son, Mosimanegape," he said with pride.

"Mosadi mogolo, you still have much to learn. You will soon see what it is to plow the field."

I had not thought that the traditional time for planting was tied to perceived risks, reciprocal arrangements, and the inherent limitations imposed by draft power availability. Perhaps the agricultural experts had answers to Rre Segatlhe's criticisms and concerns. We would never know. The educated and the rural agriculturalists did not communicate with each other. They failed to respect each other's skills.

Because their son, Tladi, planted early, and we had consistent rain, Maria and Molefi's field sprouted rows and rows of young, healthy shoots. In contrast to everyone else's field, theirs already looked green from a distance.

Rre Segatlhe and I listened to Maria describe the new variety of beans they had planted for the first time. We rejoiced with her on the early signs of success of their crop.

Walking home together, Rre Segatlhe and I expressed different reactions to Tladi's innovative farming. Perhaps motivated by a tinge of jealousy, I compared their field to ours, and assuming their harvest would be earlier and richer, I concluded that Rre Segatlhe ought to use some of Tladi's methods next season. Rre Segatlhe made no such comparison. He was genuinely pleased that his good friends Maria and Molefi had a son who helped on their homestead and contributed to their welfare. That was as it should be. For him things were necessarily different. The routine he had for himself was right for a man living alone, with no family to help harvest or eat. There was no reason for change. If he wanted to taste the new beans, he would visit Molefi during harvest time. Given a good rainfall, his own field would be high and provide more than enough grain.

"The main thing is pula. If it continues to fall, we will all be fed; if it doesn't, we will all go hungry, no matter when, how, or what we have planted."

Walking at Rre Segatlhe's slow, steady pace, we continued homeward for several kilometers, and upon reaching the last bend, Manaka and Tiro suddenly bounded across our path. They ducked down into the high grass and bounced out again, leaping with laughter. Manaka waved his slingshot; Tiro held high the dead bird for us to see. Rre Segatlhe acknowledged their catch with a nod of approval, gave no praise, but told them to come by his place later on; he would show them another method for trapping birds.

"The rear hoof follows where the front has trod," Rre Segatlhe said to me. "Manaka hunts food, just as long ago I hunted it on my grandmother's field. An empty stomach is good for a young boy: he carves the slingshot, learns to take aim, and discovers he can satisfy himself."

"Mosadi mogolo," Rre Segatlhe called out to me affectionately, "Look there, Tabo's son, Mosimanegape, has arrived from the cattle post!" Mosimanegape approached, two cattle in front of his whip. He settled himself in the shade of the kitchen shelter. We left him to drink his tea and walked over to view the cattle. For a time they grazed in the field, but toward sunset they stationed themselves between the tall, long needled cacti directly behind our hut. They eagerly ate succulent cactus leaves. In spite of the long, sharp needles, they cracked and bit, crunched and chewed throughout the night. Was it the sounds of their lavish feast or the night itself that kept us wakeful? The night, bright with moon and heavy, confined us to our creaking bedframes. We tossed for comfort until the rising sun released us.

Piling my hair on top of my head, I stuck pins in it to keep it off my neck. Rre Segatlhe was honored and pleased that I sensed the excitement of the morning. It was the day of plowing, and I asked to participate. A few men who stood by the cattle did not know me. I felt the barriers of my white skin and sex as they looked at me and laughed when I indicated I too would plow.

The men yoked the animals and attached the plow.

Gripping the worn, wooden handles, I leaned down against them. The cattle jerked forward. The blade cut the soil and jolted the plow; I held fast. My flimsy shoes fell over clods and stubbed against rolling rocks tossed back by our movement. Stubble growth and weeds scratched my legs and fell over side to side. My knees weakened with the strain of the steady forward pull. The plow rocked; I teetered and lifted my eyes off the blade to the backsides of the cattle. There the motion was steady and smooth, the muscle machinery throbbing and bulging with strength. Tails swished with ease and hoofs beat the soil relentlessly. I tripped and faltered and fell away.

One of Rre Segatlhe's arms embraced my shoulder; the other swept out across our view. "We are children of cattle and rain," he said. *"Re lema lopetleke.* We plow our boundless fields. All you see here—as far out as the lone tree in the distance—is my land. We labor. We turn up the soil to catch the rain for seeds. When pula comes, the fields ripen, and the land gives me freedom. When a man has fields of food, he can be at peace with himself.

Here in Botswana a man's field is his greatest joy. Fields of maize and sorghum are what we Tswanas call "the Beauty of Botswana."

He looked up to the cloudless sky. "As always," he added, "we will wait for pula."

"Before the missionaries came to Botswana, there were many rainmaking rites. The rainmaker stirred medicines in rain pots and burned them to send smoke to gather clouds. Children sprinkled fields with medicines. Women danced rain dances and sang for pula. The whole tribe prayed for rain. They prayed at the chief's grave and sacrificed an animal for him; and so, too, they prayed to their living chief to make rain. The chief had power to make rain. He, as the descendant of the powerful Badimo, could ask them to approach the unapproachable, the Great One, Modimo, the provider of rain."

"Missionaries changed our ways," he continued. "Our chiefs became Christians, and we stopped making rain medicines to smoke clouds or sprinkling fields for the Badimo. We prayed with the chief and the missionaries straight to the all-powerful one, Modimo. Yet nothing has changed. We are not blessed with pula every year. Last season our crops died before they ripened. We must try everything for rain. We will sing and dance and pray for pula. The chief at the kgotla will say *"a gone pula"* [may it rain], and we will cry out, *'pula, pula, pula!'*"

Brown, freshly plowed, our field catches rain and waits for planting. It is low and straight with rows to the western sky. All around our pathways, each bush and tree bears tender shoots that push higher and grow greener day by day. Grasses bend and glisten in the dew. Their wet blades brush against our legs each morning as we walk to the kraal. The ewe with the bulging belly moves slowly toward the others at the gate. Nothing yet; we wait another day.

We gather around the kraal and peer in through the fence posts. Early sunlight streams into the kraal to spotlight the event. There the ewe alternates her attentions between her twin newborns. Still wet and wobbly, the lambs have managed to rise and now stand balanced and trembling on all fours. One after the other, their limp forelegs test the air. We wait for their first, faltering steps. A calling bird breaks the silence. It prepares to land on a nearby post, sees us, squawks, and flaps away. Aroused, the ewe maas and nudges one lamb. Jolted by the commotion, the other totters forward as well. As if to make room for new life, the other animals in the kraal crowd closer to the fence and stir restlessly by the gate to go out to pasture.

Our routines abandoned, we drink our morning tea together. Manaka boils the afterbirth for Suzy; she sniffs excitedly at his pot. We celebrate the birth in the kraal, rejoicing over the gifts of the season. Tabo and Polwane join us. Molefi, Maria, and Seipate hear the news from the children and follow to our kraal. Kgosana and Keledi cross the newly plowed field. We have not seen them since Rre Segatlhe threw bones for their infant son, Modise. When Keledi sits to join the women on the floor, she unties the baby from her back. Kgosana leaves his chair to sweep the infant from her arms. "Tabo must see that he smiles!" He passes him to Tabo who holds him high and shakes out smiles and gurgles.

With each new day, Rre Segatlhe grew increasingly worried over the health of the newborn twin lambs.

"Rre Segatlhe, why are you cutting the lamb behind the ear?"

"It is too thin. It is weak because of sickness in the blood. I am bleeding it out, but it will not be enough. Leave the washing this morning. We must go to town to find medicine."

We drove toward the main road to Gaborone, and as we approached the BAC fields, I reminded Rre Segatlhe of the veterinarian, Dr. Milne, who several months before had vaccinated our Suzy against rabies in his office at the BAC.

"The Europeans at the BAC are big stomachs."

"*Ee*, Rre Segatlhe. But Dr. Milne is not one of them."

"*Go siame.* All right. Turn onto the BAC road," he conceded.

"This white coat in the fat kitchen may not want to do anything for an old Motswana like me, but if you the *lekgoa* [white one] approach him, he just might give us medicine, and then we won't have to suffer Gaborone."

In his office driveway, Dr. Milne had just closed the back of a large pickup truck and was talking to a class of about twenty Tswana students who were settling into it.

"Rre Segatlhe, come with me. Let's go ask him together."

"Certainly not!" Stubbornly he sat in the car, commanding me to "run quickly to catch him before he escapes!" The truck was pulling out as I reached its window.

"Dr. Milne! Dr. Milne!" I waved. He stopped the motor and leaned out the window to look down at me.

"*Dumelang, borra,*" I greeted the men in the cab. "*Dumela, Rra,*" I greeted Dr. Milne. "*Dumela, mma,*" the students sang out.

Dr. Milne, confused that my frantic appeal should be followed by greetings, looked at me in a "get-on-with-it" sort of way.

"So sorry to stop you," I went on defensively. "I'm Marianne Alverson. I came to you once before with a dog . . . for a rabies vaccination."

"Yes, yes," he cut me off.

"Uuh . . ." I stammered. The pressure to dispense with Tswana etiquette, to communicate my request on the spot with no initial greeting or chitchat, left me quite speechless.

"What is it?" he smiled gently.

"So sorry . . ." I started again. He listened patiently.

Our arrival, it turned out, had been timely. Dr. Milne and his class were starting out on an all-day trip to deliver health care to animals in the rural areas. On the way, they could stop off at Rre Segatlhe's kraal. "We'll follow you out now," Dr. Milne suggested.

Dr. Milne conducted his class by our kraal. He examined the lambs and then the mother. The students asked questions, stepped forward to touch the animals, and gave suggestions. It was finally agreed that, although one lamb was by far the weaker, both were suffering from starvation because their mother was badly infected with mastitis. Dr. Milne walked over to Rre Segatlhe. He spoke to him with respect, as in consultation with another physician. He carefully explained his diagnosis and every step of the suggested treatment. Rre Segatlhe knowingly agreed with him. Students were chosen to treat the animal, and we looked on. Pus was drained out of the infected area, and a shot of penicillin was administered. Dr. Milne gave Rre Segatlhe further medication, explained the dosage, and told him that he would return for follow-up visits until the ewe was completely cured. If, he added, at any time other animals were ill, we should contact him immediately. He would guarantee a visit within two days.

"She'll come out of it all right," Dr. Milne assured us. "Good thing you came right away. So often we're only called in when it's too late, and when the animal fails to recover, our treatment is blamed. It's really extremely difficult to gain confidence among these rural people," he told me. "We've just got to train more Batswana as veterinarians. That's what the truckload of students is all about."

"*Tsamayang sentle*," I called out to them as the truck moved forward.

"Oh, . . . yes, of course," Dr. Milne responded. *"Sala sentle."*

It was talk of Dr. Milne's visit which spurred on a political discussion among the men in our lolwapa. Over gourds of *kadi*, Rre Segatlhe told the news of the day to Modise, Neo, and Tladi. While Tladi works at the BAC as a field hand, Neo, who has taken a few university level courses, has been at a desk job.

"The tall, sunburnt one is a fine doctor!" Rre Segatlhe concluded his story.

"Ee," Tladi agreed, "we know him at the BAC. He is not one of the fat stomachs—he is, like Mr. Miller, good for Botswana."

"I cannot call any white in my office a 'friend' or 'good for Botswana,'" Neo complained bitterly. "Their fat stomachs grow bigger each day, so that a Motswana like me has no room to move."

"The fat stomachs like it here too much," he went on. "They do anything just to stay longer. My English boss has just fired Kebi, the best Motswana in the office! Why? Because Kebi was too clever for him! The whites will always keep the good jobs for themselves."

"Neo," Tladi countered, "all whites are not fat stomaches, that is for sure! And all fat stomachs are not white; there are black ones too. We know who they are!"

"Yes, we know," Neo agreed, "but who put them over you? The white fat stomachs. The whites, so that they can stay on top, fire the best Motswana and promote the worst."

"Neo," Modise said, "to me, whites have complained that they try but cannot find good Tswana workers. Expatriates come here with terminal contracts . . . that means they know that they cannot stay more than two years or so. They come here to help Botswana. They would like to train Batswana to take over their positions."

"That's what they say, Modise. That's what they say. Why is it that these Europeans cry out 'good Batswana are impossible to find,' and yet they do nothing to train us better, nothing to hire and keep the best they can find?"

"Maybe it's because your idea and their idea of what's 'best' is very different."

"No, no I tell you why: the European likes to pat himself on the back. He likes to tell the world that he is the *only one* that can do anything!"

"Ee, ee." There was a chorus of agreement from men who had joined to listen. Neo continued, "Why is it, Modise, that one

European is always followed with the arrival of another European? Why? I tell you why. Sweden, Norway, U.S.A., China, Holland—many countries of the world bring money to Botswana, and they pay for their own. An Englishman takes the place of another Englishman. Where do we, Batswana, fit in?"

"*Ee, ee.*"

"Neo," Modise replied, "a European complained to me once that his Motswana worker wastes the first half-hour of every morning greeting and talking. It sometimes takes him a few hours to get down to his job. The European feels that this Motswana does not show an interest in the job but only in his friends at work. To a European, it is a man's attitude toward the job itself that determines his success."

"Rubbish!" Neo retorted. "No job is more important than the man behind it. You are a man in virtue of others. That is just what these Europeans do not understand. They are in Botswana, yet they do not try to speak one word Setswana. They are in Botswana, yet even in English they do not greet us properly at the start of each day. You are a man in virtue of others," Neo repeated.

"*Pula!*" They lifted the gourds to Neo's words, and Rre Segatlhe said, "Neo, you are very educated, and you have kept Tswana wisdom. But you are young still. When you move to the big desk, grow powerful and rich, and drink whiskey with the British, will you remember that, yes, you are a man in virtue of others, and the 'others' in Botswana must be our people, the Batswana?"

Rre Segatlhe greeted us this morning with news from the kraal. One of the lambs was found dead and mangled near the posts. Rre Segatlhe surmised that a jackal killed it but did not get away with the kill because it was scared off. Tsotsi was eager to give Suzy credit for chasing off the jackal, but Rre Segatlhe was quick to retort: "If that fat, lazy dog actually interrupted her sleep under Tsotsi's bed, she was too late!"

Just now as I write in my journal, Modise and Rre Segatlhe are digging in another row of posts around the kraal to prevent further attacks. Manaka is boiling the corpse for his midday meal. For fear that the other lamb might stray, Manaka has been instructed to keep it locked in his hut while its mother is feeding in the pasture. Madala is delighted. He has willingly confined himself with the lamb. I can hear his high, melodic voice from inside the hut calling to the lamb, "Come, come, come."

Whereas I readily accepted Madala's desire for a pet lamb, I can only express horror toward Tsotsi's fascination for snakes. With the herd boys, he has recently enjoyed killing snakes in the fields and displaying their skins on the lolwapa floor. It is certain that Rre Segatlhe has exacerbated my fears with his warm welcome toward Tsotsi's newfound prowess. "Tsotsi, Tsotsi—*oo-loo, loo, loo!*" he sings out with delight as his Tsotsi drags in his catch for the day.

Once Tsotsi returned home from school slinging a mamba. I reacted precisely as he had hoped—suppressing no emotions. It had been found and killed in his classroom; he received it as a class gift. Although deadly snakes are abundant, I must remind myself that they fear and slither away from the sounds on the path. We do have a snakebite kit, but this can hardly be a consolation, knowing that we are usually more than five minutes away from it.

With the rainy season and warm weather, all kind of insects have improved the chickens' diet. One night we spotted—crawling on the wall near the sleeping Madala—a colorful, hairy-looking spider the size of my hand. My immediate shriek woke the children, who just coming around from their world of dreams, were attacked by their father, scrambling across their beds in pursuit of the crawling beast. Madala joined my wailing chorus. So did Tsotsi with a staccato screaming plea for an immediate explanation. Undaunted, Modise in a tangle of blankets lept off the bed for his final lunge. And Rre Segatlhe stood calmly looking in on us from the doorway.

Modise, rather than kill the spider, took it upon himself to wrap it in a plastic bag and preserve it. His idea was to deliver it to an American twelve-year-old in town whose passion it was to collect and study insects and spiders. Rre Segatlhe went with him on this particular mission to town. And so did several women who wanted a lift to go shopping.

It was Rre Segatlhe who held the plastic bag as Modise drove, and it was Rre Segatlhe who came upon the idea that the spider would need air to breathe. The hole he poked in the bag was fine for this purpose, but it also allowed the colorful, hairy thing its immediate escape. Modise was to discover from his passengers, that my reaction to the spider had been culturally appropriate.

He screeched to a stop, the door flew open, and wailing women, falling over each other, made their frantic exit. That left Rre Segatlhe sitting alone in the car, holding up the torn plastic bag and trying to control his wry smile.

I am bothered by what feels like cramps in my hands. They are beginning to swell, and writing is painful. Modise has left for a morning round of interviews. MaMoremi and Madala are pounding kadi roots in the lolwapa. There are no visitors. The place is quiet, and I feel grateful that I can lie down.

I lay in bed shivering with fever when Rre Segatlhe came to sit at my bedside. He was kind and understanding. He assured me that the sickness would travel through me and be gone within a week. In the next breath, with the same smooth voice, he announced that he was about to load his rifle. I should remain calm, stay in bed to care for my sickness. What he was about to do with his rifle should not concern me, he said.

He had no choice, he explained. A patient had given him a goat's head. He had been cooling it in his special black pot. It was sitting in the kitchen shelter cooling when Suzy got to it. Suzy had committed the unpardonable crime: she had eaten the meat prepared by Rre Segatlhe. The meat of the goat's head, Rre Segatlhe reminded me, was only for the oldest of men. It was his privilege alone to divide the meat. It could only be eaten through his hands.

"How do you know it was Suzy, Rre Segatlhe? Probably it was the pig, Nixon," I told him.

"No," Rre Segatlhe insisted. "Even if it were the pig, it would be a crime. Yet with the pig, I can say, 'It is getting fatter and will land in the pot soon.'"

"No, it was Suzy. She licks her paws and lies with a fat stomach. Suzy cannot be eaten; this is a waste! She cannot do these things! I must shoot her!"

He walked out of the hut, and I, with my dizzy headache, followed him. When I reeled in the hot sun, Rre Segatlhe commanded me to go back into the hut.

At this point, Tsotsi arrived home from school. Suzy bounded toward him in her usual fashion. Rre Segatlhe felt for his rifle and started to load it. He commanded Tsoti to get into the hut.

Madala blithely told his brother, "Rre Segatlhe's gonna shoot Suzy."

Horrified, Tsotsi pleaded with Rre Segatlhe, but the old man was in no mood for protest. His reasoning was clear. Tsotsi persisted. Between them lay Suzy, oblivious to her fate, biting fleas from her paws. Tsotsi threw his arms around her and tearfully yelled out, "You can't shoot her!"

"You are a child, Tsotsi. You can tell me nothing," and Rre Segatlhe repeated his determination to shoot.

Observing the spectacle, Madala gave his solution: "If Rre Segatlhe really wants to shoot something, he can shoot Keith."

Intrigued, rather than horrified, at Madala's three-year-old logic, Tsotsi placed himself between Suzy and rifle proclaiming, "Go ahead, shoot."

Afraid of an accident, I tried to persuade Rre Segatlhe to put down the rifle. Words failed me as I struggled to keep myself balanced on two feet. I pleaded and wept while Rre Segatlhe rolled three bullets in his hand.

MaMoremi passed Rre Segatlhe a jar of kadi. He sat down, placed the rifle across his lap, and took a swig. There he was, with Tsotsi angrily defying him (something no Tswana adult will tolerate from a child), Madala, curious to see him shoot, and me, feverish and reduced to tears.

It was not Tsotsi's heroic posture nor my tears that won Suzy her reprieve. It was MaMoremi. She poured him another, and then another jar of kadi. As time passed, he began to look at me in a loving way, and I knew we had a stay of execution.

"*Go siame*. Today, because you are sick, I will not shoot," he said.

"But if she gets into any pot ever again, I will shoot her for sure. That is certain. Now get back to your bed, mosadi mogolo! And Tsotsi, go to the fields to help Manaka!"

It was time to blow out the candle. My hands hurt so much that I could not write my nightly journal. I tucked the children into their beds. Tsotsi pulled Suzy up onto his bed and fell asleep stroking her fur. Madala, with a stick wrapped into his arms, slept with his "very own rifle." The day had its impact on them.

My fever did not subside. All my glands were swollen. Modise, the boys, and I went to the hospital white coats for the diagnosis: tick fever. We were all relieved that it was nothing contagious and easily remedied with a series of pills.

We returned home from Gaborone and entered the lolwapa to find stretched across the floor, from wall to wall, a python. Rre Segatlhe sat polishing his boots while we trooped toward it, exclaiming shock, horror, and delight—it was dead.

167

"Who brought this?" We turned to him.

"I did."

"You killed it?"

"Certainly!" He was emphatic. "What else do you do when you come upon a snake? Certainly you must kill it! I was planting the seeds, and this *noga* [snake]was in my way." I imagined Rre Segatlhe, the witch doctor, wrestling single-handed with this ten-foot serpent, but he said he simply struck its head with a boulder and dragged it home.

The sheer size of the python made us shudder. We had seen similar snakes in zoo cages but had never contemplated living within the realm of actual encounter with such a beast! Tsotsi touched its scaly skin, full of admiration for Rre Segatlhe's prize. Madala peered into its round eye. Modise asked Rre Segatlhe what he would do with it. He began to explain as I turned away to lie in the shade.

Rre Segatlhe scraped snake meat to use as ingredients for his medicines. He flattened the skin, stretched it out, and pegged it down across the lolwapa floor. After picking the skeleton clean, he draped it along the edge of the kitchen shelter roof for all to see.

I sit under his decor feeling strength again. The morning sun warms my back. When it was low in the eastern sky, Tsotsi rode off to school, and we lit only a small fire to cook our tea. It is a relief to everyone that we no longer need shiver and huddle by the fire in the early morning. Madala, with the lamb trailing behind him, wanders to the field, and I marvel that I have no fears. As often as I have searched for firewood or picked merogo in the field, I have never come across a snake. It was a tick, so small that I didn't see it, which caused my only illness, and except for this recent bout, this has been our healthiest year. I write in the shade of the kitchen shelter preparing for class while Rre Segatlhe works near me pounding his medicines. We take turns breaking the silence.

"Look to the fields, mosadi mogolo; Madala is teaching the little lamb to chase down butterflies. He calls 'come-come' and the lamb runs to his feet."

"*Ee*, Rre Segatlhe, it is a sweet twosome in the field but not so when they are in the lolwapa. When Madala walks into the hut, the lamb follows him in and relieves itself. Madala and lamb walk out, and I'm left wiping the floor."

We see Seipate coming from a distance. With a bundle on her head, she is on her way to town. She stops to bring the news.

"Molema is back from the mines! Number 19, he says, is alive and well. Number 19 sends his greetings—no money—just his greetings. Like a peacock, he twirls himself about and forgets his family!"

Seipate disappears toward the sun. The blue sky is hopeful with clouds. The days and nights have been glorious, dry, and warm, with just enough brief afternoon showers to benefit Rre Segatlhe's newly planted fields. Soon we will look for sprouted seeds! Rre Segatlhe has actually been feeding the chickens to divert their attentions, and as a result, they are laying more eggs. Nixon and I continue to compete. The whole day lies before us as Rre Segatlhe and I sit together under the snake skeleton. Let the snake decorate our homestead; I simply trust this environment and have come to appreciate this outdoor life.

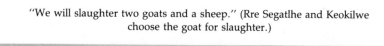
"We will slaughter two goats and a sheep." (Rre Segatlhe and Keokilwe choose the goat for slaughter.)

13

From Field to Town

Toward sundown one day, MaMoremi's oldest daughter arrived at our lolwapa.

"Morwadi!"

"*Dumela,mma. O tlhotse jang?*"

We greeted Morwadi and admired her son, Deêpe, who hung listlessly from the blanket tied to her back. Morwadi told us of the family: Grandmother's household in Old Naledi was doing well. Moremi was a real schoolboy, leaving early every morning in uniform. Sister Mpho had found work laboring on a farm. The little ones, Leraka and Elina, helped grandmother with the housework; they even went along to help her when she built walls for others. With the little money they had left last month, they planted just a few rows of cabbage outside the lolwapa walls.

"But Morwadi, what about your little family? How is it at your place in Mogoditshane? How is your husband . . . and here, your little son?" We asked her.

"That is what I have come to tell you. My husband has finally agreed to let me go. He is tired of me, and Deêpe's constant crying bothers him. It is a good thing; I do not like living with him. He stays in town too much. If he makes money at his job, I do not see it; for sure, he has lady friends in town! Grandmother will take me in, and I will find work. But first, I must find out what is wrong with Deêpe."

Together with Morwadi, MaMoremi withdrew for the whole of the afternoon. It was after the evening meal that she told Rre Segatlhe of her decision: she would leave the following morning together with Morwadi. She could not leave her mother with all of her own children. Now that Morwadi, with her child, was planning to join the old woman in Old Naledi, it would be necessary for MaMoremi to help out. Rre Segatlhe accepted her decision. MaMoremi packed her bundle, and Rre Segatlhe pretended not to care.

"You have not learned to make kadi," he complained to me. "I will make it myself, just as I wash my own clothes. You will leave too one day. I am a man living alone, and I can do everything myself!"

He got up to walk away; trailing behind was the sound of his voice, a mixture of bitterness and pride.

The following morning I drove MaMoremi, Morwadi, and Deêpe to the Princess Marina Hospital in Gaborone to have Deêpe examined. The diagnosis was malnutrition. Deêpe was admitted for a two-week stay. MaMoremi and Morwadi stood waiting for a nurse when we said our good-bye. MaMoremi and I extended our hands for a formal Tswana handshake and then broke into a hug. I pushed away through the crowd and looked back to see her again, my view blurred by tears: MaMoremi.

At noontime the parking lot in Gaborone is always crowded. A boy followed me as I tried to find my car. He held an orange to my face.

"You want orange? Only five cents!"

"Where did I park?"

"Just give me ten cents, lady, for this orange. It very, very nice, please." He put the orange into his pocket and held out his empty hand.

"Give me twenty cents, please, just twenty cents!"

"There is the car. Now, where is my key?" I rummaged through my purse. He waited, not knowing quite which way to show his face.

"Just fifty cents, please. I very, very hungry," he reminded me. The car key emerged, no coins. He flashed his winsome smile and made a last attempt. "Give me a lift! Please, give me a lift, madam."

As we drove onto the dirt road leading out of town, I asked him where he wanted to be dropped off. I was going just fine, just the right way, he assured me; he would tell me where to stop.

"What's your name?"

"Raus."

"Raus?"

"Raus. My friend give me that name. He big man, and I his garden boy for two years. Then he go back to Germany, and I have no job. He German. His friends all Herr something; I Herr Raus. I good garden boy, I your garden boy, too, please. I need job. Just give me bed. I not go in your house, please. I stay outside and fix flowers. I good boy, madam; please, give me job."

"Raus, I have no garden, no flowers. Where am I giving you a lift to?"

"Thanking you, madam. I go with you, please. I do any job at madam's house."

He was clearly confused when we passed the road leading to the BAC expatriate housing and turned down the dirt road toward Kgaphamadi.

"This is my house," I said, when finally we had arrived.

"Ow!" he exclaimed.

"*Ee, ke ntlo* [Yes, it is a hut]. *"Tla kwano,"* [Come here] I continued in Setswana, and he, looking quite betrayed, followed me toward Rre Segatlhe.

"Rre Segatlhe, this is Raus. I met him in town. He needs a job. Could we give him one?"

Raus forgot to greet Rre Segatlhe, and then the inquisition began.

Because I had to rush off to my class-under-the-tree, I left Raus before the old man. Raus shifted his weight from one sockless shoe to the other, fingered the worn lapel of his oversized jacket, and tried out his smile.

I returned to find Rre Segatlhe still on the stool in the shade and Raus leaning against the car waiting to be driven back to town. His spirit brightened when Tsotsi arrived home from school to welcome him, and I suggested he stay for supper. With the radio in the lolwapa, Tsotsi, Raus, and Madala danced to "gumba gumba" music. Manaka returned the animals to the kraal and joined them, but momentarily Rre Segatlhe's shout rang out, "Manaka!"

He rushed to his master and proceeded to the hut to get a brush. With his back to the dancers, he brushed Rre Segatlhe's shoes, and the old man told him of the trap they would set in the morning.

We ate together. Because of Raus's presence, Rre Segatlhe allowed me also to pass Manaka a plate of food. Manaka said not a word to Raus, nor did he respond to the smiles Raus tossed him; it was obvious the boy-visitor preferred to speak English with

Tsotsi. Raus and Tsotsi chattered and laughed. Manaka looked on. He inspected Raus's dusty, black leather shoes. His eyes passed over Raus's torn wool trousers, moved up to the bright red kerchief perched decoratively in the pocket of his manly jacket, and abruptly returned to his own bare feet. There they rested until a glazed look, with no focus, took hold.

"Please, can't Raus stay?" Tsotsi pleaded.

"No, Keef, I go to town," Raus responded. "I see you in town."

Why didn't you like Raus?" Tsotsi demanded.

"Because he is a tsotsi, not like you," Rre Segatlhe conceded, "but a *real* tsotsi. He is a snake. Would you put a snake under your coat? Certainly not! When it gets warm, it will bite you."

"Raus was such fun, and he spoke English too! Did you like him, Mom?"

"Yes, very much."

"Why wouldn't he stay? Was it because Rre Segatlhe didn't like him?"

"Not only. He wouldn't stay here, Keith. He likes it in town."

"Did you find out where he lives when you drove him home? Can we visit him sometime?"

"He doesn't have a place to live right now. He's looking for one."

"His family lives in Molepolole. Just like Manaka, his parents could not care for all of their children and sent him away. He was brought to an uncle who could feed him for his daily labor. He didn't stay long. He hated the work and felt he got nothing for it. He ran away to town. In town, he told me, he got something for nothing."

"Some days very bad with no food, no money, but one day I find job again." He left me with his big smile. "I see you in town. Tell Keef I see him in town," he called back.

The lolwapa without MaMoremi: Madala complains of her absence, and I share his sadness. Rre Segatlhe, rather than make his own kadi, first spent a few days with "his woman" in Mogo-ditshane and now pays regular calls to Tabo's mother who supplies him with brew. The chores MaMoremi and I had divided are now mine, but there is time enough to do them.

"MaMoremi is gone. I sorely miss her—it's lonely," I complain to Hoyt.

"Lonely! We're never left alone. There is always someone coming by. You see Seipate and Maria often," he counters.

"But only MaMoremi shared this lolwapa with me, and I miss working side by side."

"I should think you'd welcome being left alone sometimes. Besides, you can just go see Polwane more often—she's close by," he tosses out just before cycling away.

I sweep the lolwapa alone. It does not matter that it takes twice as long. We had come a long way, MaMoremi and I. At first we worked quietly together; I followed her every move. As she watched my progress, she expressed pride in me: I should teach the women of America how to sweep properly, how to smear the "shit," how to set the fire, how to find greens in the fields. Was I keeping notes? Was I writing about it for them to read? As time passed, my America receded for both of us, and our differences became remote. Together we lived the details of a day. One morning cloud gathered overhead as we walked the dry field, and we shared the hope for rain. We greeted Montsho's frequent arrivals with an unabashed and joyful chorus of exclamation at his putrid smell, "ow! ow!," nevertheless quickly paying him our respect with a bowl of food, for we knew a beautiful goatskin mat was surely in the making. While gossiping, we set each evening's fire.

"Ntatabo was clumsy again today. Did you see her drop the melon on her toe? Her feet are a battleground."

"They think Seipate's daughter is once more with child. It is the same boy she dances with in the bushes. Seipate says he wants to leave the cattle post and join Number 19 in the mines to earn bogadi, but I don't believe him. He is a lazy one, and he likes the moonlight too much!"

It is silent as I set the fire. Family comes when the food is hot. Modise mentions to Rre Segatlhe that he will drive to Mochudi tomorrow. Rre Segatlhe announces that he will come along. They talk of Mochudi. I collect the plates. Is it MaMoremi's absence that makes me aware that I am excluded from their conversation?

"I will come to Mochudi with you," I join in.

"Who will keep the Madala and the Tsotsi?" Modise inquires. "You'd better stay here," he quickly concludes.

"They can come along," I persist.

"This is not a family outing, Marianne . . . I've got work to do and errands to run. It's just a one-day trip, and it's a long drive on bad roads," Modise protests. But he can see in my grimace a determination not worth countering. I perceive the distance between us. My husband, Modise, in his concentration toward his own anthropological fieldwork, keeps well away from my emotional needs. I tell him I miss MaMoremi, I'm lonely, and he denies it. It is up to me to work my way out of possible depression. To divert myself from the emptiness I feel, I drive with them to Mochudi.

Mochudi, thirty kilometers from our place, is a town of about 12,000 inhabitants. Unlike Gaborone, it has no accommodations for an expatriate lifestyle: no paved roads, no flowers and fences, no elevators and hotels. It is a traditional Tswana village that has grown into a town. A broad, dusty road leads to a few shops where women buy their sacks of mealie or choose their favorite cloth among the blue and brown "German prints." Nearby, a smell of fat cakes! Drop coins on the counter, and in exchange, golden, greasy puffs will warm your stomach. The road narrows and branches many ways among the homesteads. One lolwapa wall leads to another, and between them, chickens scurry from children's feet.

Phutadikubo Hill is not far off. Just before it is a freshly painted concrete building with the flag of Botswana. It is pale blue with a broad, horizontal black stripe outlined in white. The melody of the national anthem comes to mind. *"Lefatshe leno la rona, ke mpho ya Modimo . . ."* [This country of ours is a gift of God . . .]. Two official cars are shining in the sun by the building, while a mule, tied to the porch post hangs his head. This is the administrative building of Mochudi, and here is the office of the chief. (His lolwapa is just over there; you can see his servant pounding grain.) But the building seems empty. The windows are open. There is no sound from within. You cross the dusty square. In the shade of a thatched shelter, people are crowded together, leaning and listening. The tree-stump fence—the sign of a traditional kgotla ground—encloses others sitting on the ground in the sun. From within the shade, you hear a voice ring out.

You climb up between the boulders of Phutadikubo Hill. Surprise! There is an elaborately built concrete residence on top. It has the facade of a once ornate, Boer Mansion, now crumbling and abandoned. British Brigade workers and American Peace Corps youths are scrubbing the interior. It is to become a museum. The crafts of Botswana will be treasured. Mochudi's adopted kinsman, Isaac Schapera, the anthropologist who recorded voluminous details of Tswana culture and history, will donate photographs, letters, and texts. Botswana's past will be remembered.

Into the sunlight again, you look down the cliffs of Phutadi-kubo Hill. The Madikwe River bed winds in the valley. Girls wring clothes out on the rocks. With buckets on their heads, women file away across the fields to return home.

"I'm going off on my own down this road to find the potter Maria told me about," I announced to Modise and Rre Segatlhe.

"Take the children with you," Modise demanded.

"No, you take the Madala," Rre Segatlhe intervened, "and we will take the Tsotsi with us for protection!"

Tsotsi, flattered by the honor to go with the men, sidled up to the old man, probably perceiving correctly that this was another of Rre Segatlhe's attempts to humor me. Without waiting for Modise's response, I skipped away from them, with Madala running to keep up.

The first person of whom I inquired directions was startled that I greeted her in Setswana. She was obviously on her way somewhere but changed her direction to take me to my goal. We walked through a thickly settled area with narrow, twisting dirt roads. Madala and I attracted attention, and children rushed toward us holding out their hands, and calling out the greeting reserved for expatriates: *"Ke batla disweets!"* [I want sweets!] *"Mpha madi!"* [give me money].

"Ga ke na sweets. Ka goreng lo seka lwa ntumedisa, bana " [I don't have sweets. Why don't you greet me properly, children], I admonished them. They were absolutely startled that the lekgoa [white one] they saw spoke like a mosadi mogola.

"Dumelang, bana," I greeted them seriously.

"Dumela, mma," they sang out, properly raising the pitch of their voices on the last syllable. Some danced their bare legs and feet in the dust while giggling; some, for shyness or shame, covered their faces; others just stared at us; but all of them together formed our curious retinue.

Madala, who has always liked parades, thought this a festive occasion. He didn't mind the girls who stroked his hair but held his hands out to walk with them. I was quite relieved, however, when my friendly guide forcefully yelled out, *"tsamayang!"* and the children scrambled away. She pointed to the lolwapa ahead of me: this was the home of a school teacher, Mrs. Kgosietsile. It was Mrs. Kgosietsile's mother who was known by all as the best potter in Mochudi. I thanked her, *"Ke a leboga, mma,"* and bade her good-bye, *"Tsamaya sentle, mma."*

Before Madala and I even entered the wall, a teenage girl rose from her sewing machine on the lolwapa floor. From out of the blue hemline of her short cotton dress, she swung her long, shapely legs, strode over to me, and sang out her school verse: "Good morning, madam. How are you today?" I returned her greeting and continued in English until it was clear from her dark, round eyes that there was not a glint of comprehension. When I switched to Setswana, she flashed a wide, white smile. Who was I? Where did I stay? In Sebele? Why?

"But stop! We must speak English. I must learn English. What is it you said—'pottery'? . . . Ah! *go bopa*! Then you must see my grandmother, and she is sleeping."

Thus I met beautiful Naledi, granddaughter of the well-known potter, whose greatest ambition at the age of fifteen is to be elected Miss Botswana in Gaborone. As I admired the dress she was sewing for the final decision, she rejoiced, "I have already won Miss Mochudi!"

"Before Mother arrives home from school and before Grandmother awakes, we must speak English—only English—together," she continued enthusiastically.

"You stay where in England?"

"I'm not English. I'm from the U.S.A."

"Ow! America! You are American!"

Her eyes rolled. Without a doubt, I had new status.

"That is a best place—America! Do you like the Supremes?"

"The Supremes?"

"*Ee*, The Supremes! They are very, very good Americans. Saturday at Mochudi functions, we are dancing American music. It is very, very good! We are drinking American Coca-Cola, American Fanta. These are very good things!"

"Look, here comes my mother," Naledi exclaimed proudly. "She is teaching the English at school."

"*Tsa, Tsa!*" she scattered chickens as she strode into the yard. Flaunting her portly stature, her bright, green dress of plaids fit snugly around her middle and flared widely past her hips. She swung through the lolwapa entrance, moved briskly toward us, and came to an abrupt halt where we sat.

"Good afternoon! I see, Naledi, that we have a visitor!" And turning to me, she introduced herself.

"I am Lydia Kgosietsile. How are you?"

"I am Marianne Alverson, Mrs. Kgosietsile, and I have come to meet you and to see your mother's pottery."

"Ah, yes. She is well known in these parts, and from time to time, Europeans stop here to buy her pots."

"*Ee, mma, ke itse sentle,*" [Yes, I know] I responded.

"*Ow! o bua Setswana! O nna kae?*" [Oh! you speak Setswana! Where do you live?]

"*Kwa go Segatlhe—mo ntlong ya gagwe, kwa masimong gaufi ga Sebele.*" [With Segatlhe—in his hut, on the lands near Sebele.]

We spoke Setswana until, at Naledi's request, we continued in English.

"She is very clever in school, and she wants to learn English," her mother said proudly.

"She is truly a very fine daughter," I agreed.

"Do you have a daughter?" she asked me.

"No," I replied, "two sons."

"Then take her with you to America," Naledi's mother suddenly pronounced. Naledi and her mother looked at me gravely. I was stunned.

"You do not have a daughter. She will make you a good daughter. She will help you in many things," she continued.

"I am sewing you dresses," Naledi added.

"But Mrs. Kgosietsile," I stammered, "I live very far away . . ."

"No, no, it does not matter," she interrupted. "I love my daughter so much that it does not matter if I ever see her again. If I know she goes to America with you, she will have good chances. Think about it. It is an idea!"

"You must stay to eat hot porridge," she continued. "It is ready! Come, you will sit by the old woman, my mother. Speak Setswana only. She has no English."

A corpulent woman sat erect near the wall. Unusual for a Tswana woman, she wore no headscarf. White-grey, tight and thick, her closely cropped hair avowed the years behind her. Her face, much like her daughter's, was dark, smooth, and plump, but her eyes, set in deep wrinkles, revealed a lifetime of squinting in the sunlight. She now held her hand up to shield them as we approached.

Children gathered around for the midday meal. Madala crowded in against my knees. Naledi passed out bowls of porridge, each with a cube of goat meat, gravy, and a piece of carrot. "*Dijo dimonate!*" [what good food!] Madala exclaimed.

"*Ruri, o mosimane wa Setswana!*" [Truly, this is a Tswana boy!] the old woman delighted.

Come to see her? Yes, the old woman was very pleased. Come to see her work? Yes, the old woman would show me her method. After the meal, we would knead the clay and build pots together.

Side by side, I sat with the artist, the old woman. The smooth, elastic clay was easy to work with, yet once my slab was attached to its base, I looked over to her for the next move. The clay wall was complying with her every stroke, her hands swiftly pushing and patting it to greater height and width. Evenly, she spread her fingers and pressed her palms around the circumference of the vessel. It took on its final shape. She dipped her fingers in the pan of water and flexed them into position as they returned to the clay. Nimbly they shaped a groove and smoothed the rim.

I dipped my hands again in water to keep the clay responsive to my redundant and inefficient attempts. With visible frustration I worked to establish an even, pleasing shape and, she called out her encouragement, *"Ee, o itse sentle! Go siame thata!"* But her pleasant manner could not deceive my eye. It was a paltry beginning.

She turned her pot while she pressed in a design with a comb just above the bulge. It was now ready to dry. She would add color in alternate shapes of the design, she explained, and then set it in her hut to wait for firing. After firing, she would polish it with a smoothing stone.

We walked to the firing pit and then to her hut where she showed me her pots, those that waited to be fired and those that were polished and ready to sell.

"They don't buy pots like in the old days," she lamented. "My neighbors go to the shop to buy plastic and enamel dishes from South African factories. It is no wonder that no one comes to learn from me! No young girls and even none of my own grandchildren are willing to sit by me to learn. When I die, so too will it be the end of my own craft."

"Of course, when I was younger, I wanted to learn my mother's trade," her daughter joined in. "I was very proud when people came from everywhere to buy her pots. It is a good thing, however, that I loved to read. For this reason I did very well in school and trained to be a teacher. Considering that my husband left me with many children to care for alone, I am fortunate to have a good profession; and certainly, I would never have the time to sit and make pots!"

"I am still proud of my mother," she quickly added. "She is an artist. Sometimes Europeans like you come to buy her things but not often enough! It is not just because of her age that she does not work so much anymore; it is also because there are still many pots waiting to be sold. As she says, no one chooses to learn her trade. When she is gone, there will be no one to haul clay from the river and grind rocks for color."

"My fingers are still good," said the old woman. "It is my back that brings trouble—*go botlhoko!*" [how it hurts!]

"How old are you?" I asked her.

"I have traveled far—I am 84 years! All my life, I have lived right here in Mochudi."

"*Ee, mma.*"

"What is it like where you stay in America?"

"There are many artists like you where I live. They build pots with clay—sometimes using their hands the way you do, sometimes using a wheel."

"A wheel? . . . what do you mean a wheel?"

Motioning with my arms, drawing the object in the air, and pushing my foot across the lolwapa floor, I tried to demonstrate the potter's wheel.

"Such a wheel I would like to have! This very thing may help me with my backpains!"

"How do you live in America?" she asked, growing increasingly curious. When she heard about the long winter season with a snow ground cover that lasts for three to four months, she looked horrified and immediately tried to console me. Did I have to return to such hardship? "Why not stay in Botswana," she suggested. She had, of course, imagined a one-room hut and lolwapa in the snow. I tried to mollify her concerns by drawing a picture of our house, with stairs, many rooms, a kitchen, a bath, and central heating. Even if houses provided necessary facilities and were big enough to walk around in, it would still be extremely difficult to remain confined for three months, she said. How did a person get food?

My Setswana vocabulary was not up to this conversation. Mrs. Kgosietsile interpreted as I gave an elaborate description of trucks unloading at grocery stores; sidewalks, streets, and snow plows; the family car with snow tires; down jackets and boots. From the look on her face, I might as well have described adaptations for living on the moon.

Determined to convince her that I actually enjoyed my life at home and failing adequate Setswana vocabulary, I sketched a picture of a mountainside with a pond at its base. I drew in all the winter sports I could think of—skiing, sledding, toboganning, ice skating, snowshoeing, even a snow sculpture. She shook her head and only repeated that she would never want to put her toes down into cold snow. But you would be wearing thick, warm boots, I reminded her.

"Why should my feet be weighted down? I like to feel the ground on the soles of my feet!" she insisted. "Where you live is a terrible place. I have an idea!" She brightened. "You bring over from your place that wheel you told me about—the one to make pots on—and then you must stay here with us. We will work together, and you will make pots when I am gone. We will add another hut for your family. Botswana is, after all, the best place to live!"

"Grandmother does not understand America," Naledi concluded. "It is because she stays only here in the lolwapa. On the school holidays, I will come to visit you at your place." Naledi continued, "Segatlhe . . . I know of his place. I am coming there, and I am bringing you a blouse that I am sewing just for you!"

"*Go siame. Ke itumetsi,*" I thanked her. It was time to leave. Rre Segatlhe, Modise, and Tsotsi would surely be waiting at the car.

Madala dawdled along every lolwapa wall, contentedly drawing attention to us. They stared. We greeted. They greeted and stared some more. I finally picked him up and took him on my back to speed our way along the crowded roadway. We returned to a starving threesome at the car.

"Where were you? We've been waiting for you so we can get going again!" Modise exclaimed impatiently.

"We'd better pick up some lunch before we leave," he added.

"Not for us, thank you. We've eaten!" I replied.

Modise sent Tsotsi off to buy fat cakes, and meanwhile, I regaled Rre Segatlhe with our experience.

Sensing an estrangement between Modise and myself, Rre Segatlhe warned, "Behave yourself, Modise, women are slippery things. From the old pottery woman MaoKeef has a very good job offer!"

We arrived home at sundown.

"My field swallows the sun. The seeds are warm and well. "*Oo-loo-loo!* It's good to be back on the lands!"

"*Ee*, Rre Segatlhe, *Ee!*"

Maria sat with her back to our approaching car. She did not

turn at the sound of the motor nor at the slamming car doors. Rre Segatlhe and Modise went straight to her.

I did not hear the news until I put the sleeping Madala to bed and kissed Tsotsi good-night. Molefi was admitted to the tuberculosis hospital.

"The coughing was part of Molefi's speech for years," Maria continued. "We had gotten so used to it that we did not notice it getting worse. He never said much about it. Sometimes he walked away to cough alone in the field. What bothered him lately was that he was feeling tired and weak for most of the day. He was determined to dig the dam wider but just could not work; he fell over yesterday. This morning he told me we should go to town. That is all he said."

"How long do you think they'll keep him?" she asked me.

"It depends on how bad his case is. It could be a very long time, Maria. Tuberculosis is a very serious illness. It is good that you have Tladi and Mariga with you. Have you told Seipate?"

"*Ee*, she knows, but now I must go to tell Ntatabo."

"*Sala sentle*," she said as she turned away.

"*Ee, mma, tsamaya sentle*," I replied, watching her walk to the path toward Ntatabo's place.

Tuberculosis. When, where was I warned of this hazard? Yes, it comes back to me now. At the start of our voyage many months ago—the ship, *H.S. Oranje*, sailing away from England toward South Africa.

In the laundry room an American voice had greeted me, "There aren't many Americans aboard. Where're you from?"

"New Hampshire. And you?"

"Oklahoma. We're goin' te start a mission church. You been t' Africa before?"

"Yes, once, to the Republic of South Africa."

"That's a beautiful place! Where're you off to now?"

"Botswana."

"Botswana! That's a really nice place. We lived there fer four years. Jes came back fifteen months ago. What church you with?"

"None. My husband's an anthropologist."

"What? Well, you'll like it there. Where you been assigned housin'?"

"We're not going to live in town. We hope to live out on the land in a traditional hut with rural Tswanas,"

"You hope WHAT? Now you wouldn' wanna do THAT! You'd have t' live in a mud hut and eat nothin' but corn mush.

You'd get very little water. There's a lot of wind and dust in the air. You'd be surrounded by filth and tuberculosis!"

"Say, you are the first person I've met who has been to Botswana! I'm trying to learn Setswana from a book. Could you help me with the pronunciation?"

"Setswana. I don't know any o' that. You don' need that! Jes live in town. It'll be hard for you te find a place if you're not with a mission or a government agency, but believe me, you'd better try! I tell you, you'd better drop your idea o' livin' with the natives; you'd just be exposin' yourself and your children to tuberculosis!"

We visited Molefi at the TB hospital. He came out into the yard, looking thin and small in the large, regulation pajamas. He asked about the field, the dam, and the animals. We passed him the forbidden indulgence: tobacco. The nurse came by, commanded him to return inside, and told us to leave. It felt like a prison, he told us, pulling on his billowing cotton pants. And no one knew how long he would have to stay.

At sundown Tabo cycles by and calls out a greeting on his way home from work. Since Molefi has left, he is sure to stop in. Rre Segatlhe pulls up chairs, and the two of them sit together, facing the field and passing the gourd. They speak of many things. Tabo tells Segatlhe of the man at work who has two tongues and succeeds only at milking the dry cow. Rre Segatlhe gets up to pour more kadi. Tladi cycles from the BAC farm. He too knows the one with two tongues and tells his own story. There is laughter. An empty chair, Molefi's chair, is among them—there is silence. They follow the sun. It sinks low into the field and slips away.

Just as he is the first to rise in the morning, Rre Segatlhe is the first to bed down. He finishes his evening meal, comes for his vinegar, and while we hear the rhythm of his heavy boots returning across the lolwapa floor, he calls out: *"Robalang sentle, bana."*

"Yes, father, and may you also sleep well," we reply. The door to his hut bangs shut. There is a faint light at his window, but only for a short time; soon darkness returns to the hut. It does not matter which darkness. He will not linger by a winter fire, nor will he try the freedom of a warm summer's night. Rre Segatlhe beds down early, the same time, the same way, regardless of the season. He is consistent, regular, predictable; he is, like the sun, a clock to us.

There is, on a summer's night, another life. Hoyt and I have walked on the edge of it to look in. While the elders are asleep, so are the rules they govern. Asleep are the infants and toddlers. Youth is out to play. Either the day's work is done, or it waits until sunrise.

"Who has kadi tonight?"

"Mariga has brewed. We will drink there."

"Did you hear Letele? She told Kalo she would go to the grass!"

"Ow!"

"Sh! We know nothing. Her husband comes home next month."

We drink and talk and wend our way home. Tiro and Sekaba pass by as they walk the path to Sejaro's place. We hear "gumba gumba" from across the field. They will dance all night to the battery-operated player, to the "gumba gumba" jive from Johannesburg.

"Modise, I'm tired. My back aches."

"Yes, the day was long," he agrees.

A group of young girls is dancing by the roadside. Their short skirts flap to stomping feet. Clap! Clap! left, Clap! Clap! right. We walk closer still. Linked by their shadows, they face the moon. In its pale light their skin shines blue-brown, and we recognize Tabo and Polwane's daughters, Lerato, Gomolemo, and Gobuamang; Seipate's Lesego; Maria and Keorapetse from my class. They sing in close harmony, and their voices ring out a chorus.

Tula Baby robala, robala
Tula Baby robala . . .

Lesego steps forward and she sings in a high, clear voice. Meanwhile the others, in swaying unison, repeat the rhythm, singing down the scale in soft, deep tones.

Skumba kwa toropong
Skumba kwa toropong
Skumba kwa toropong
Skumba kwa toropong.

Modise and I find our beds. Tsotsi has left with Manaka, probably to cross the field for "gumba gumba." Before his empty bed, Suzy snorts and flicks her paw in a dreamworld. Madala sleeps, and we are falling asleep to "Tula Baby robala, robala" and children clapping in the light of the moon.

But there are nights which are not so peaceful. I cannot continue to ignore the tensions that have built up between us.

"We should talk to each other more. Sure, we take walks sometimes, but we never *say* anything to each other," I complain.

"When are we ever alone together? And when we are . . . we're both too tired . . ." Hoyt rationalizes as his voice fades and his arm flops over the pillow on his face, his transition into sleep.

I nudge him. He is asleep, or pretending to be. Once before I cried myself to sleep, but now my frustration gives way to anger. I try pounding him awake. No response. I pull off his pillow and shine the flashlight into his face.

"Cut it out, Marianne! I'm tired."

Nevertheless, he is aroused. He sits up suddenly. The flashlight falls off the bed to spotlight the mud wall and leave us in the dark. I grab my say.

"You go your own merry way, Hoyt. You leave me here to do all the work. You arrive at sundown, grub down the food, talk to men, and collapse into bed. Hell! What do I get out of this relationship? I have to nag you to take the kids down the road. You never think of them yourself. You have plenty of time for your informants but precious little for me. You're not a father. You're not a husband. You're a bloody roommate!"

"I took you to Mochudi just the other day!" Hoyt exclaims. "Did you stay with me? No, you went *your* merry way!" His voice grew harsh.

He shook with anger. "I can't take your holier-than-thou shit, Marianne. You're always telling me what I don't do for you. What support have you given me?"

"Support!" I yelled. "You're telling *me* about support!" I was flabbergasted. "What am I doing here? You just dumped me here with the children and took off down the road every morning. I begged you to somehow include me in your work. You rejected me outright!"

"That was in the very beginning," Hoyt explains. "By the time I could have used you, you weren't even around."

"You never asked me!" I assert.

"You never listened . . ." he tries to counter.

"Support!" I repeat, "You dump me here and ignore me. I cope on my own, survive off my own interests, and *then* you criticize me for . . ."

"There you go again," Hoyt interrupts.

"Damn it, listen!"

186

"Sure, I came here with a project. Marianne, you just assume: 'That's great. He's an anthropologist. He knows what he's doing—off he goes, leaving me to smear floors!' How often have I envied your freedom, Marianne! I've had all kinds of pressures that you don't have a clue about." His fury burst forth, "Not *one* clue!" There was a long pause, and then his voice softened.

"Sure, I came here with an interest and a method, but I had a lot of real problems. Fieldwork for me does not draw on 'natural' personality traits. Unlike you, Marianne, I am not basically gregarious by nature. Fundamentally, I do not *like* the bulk of fieldwork. I do not *like* making contacts. I do not *like* the small talk that I have to go through to set up interviews. Until I painfully established rapport here, until at last I found a few reflective, philosophical informants who for me were intrinsically satisfying, I was not enjoying myself—I was working, collecting data and not knowing where I would end."

"You don't know, Marianne, that there was a time toward the beginning of our stay that I went absolutely berserk. I mean crazy! You don't know because, above all, I had to appear competent to you. You have always had expectations not just for my performance but for my success. Yet there were times that I felt totally inadequate—times when I feared I lacked the ability to see this through."

"Truly, Hoyt, I had no idea about your feelings. Your competent appearance convinces me, and I cannot deny that I expect you to succeed because . . . you always have . . . and I want you to . . . but I want you to *share* difficulties with me. I have them, too. We could have helped each other."

"Ethnographies, you know, are written as if you don't exist as an ethnographer," Hoyt went on as we snuggled closer together. "Anthropologists write up their thing but rarely present the basic problem: how does the anthropologist's presence in the field affect what he learns? Personal presence is a big factor in determining what knowledge you receive. Should you—can you even *try* to bracket your own identity away from your attempts to understand the culture?

"It gets very complicated because you react to the culture as you speak its language, as you live within its rules. For a time, as I said, I went crazy. I lived between two worlds. I did nothing. I left this lolwapa, walked out of sight, and sat under a tree. I experienced for the first time in my life the sensation that I could not communicate my feelings. I can't even tell you now what they were. Looking back, I can't understand myself. I was nowhere, I suppose, and I just withdrew.

"Then, one day, I remembered Malinowski's diary. His wife published it after his death. It revealed his personal conflicts during fieldwork. In all honesty, I had to accept that the knowledge, the reality, I sought could not be independent from my standpoint as the observer. Anthropology could provide principles and methods for informing experience, yet the experience itself necessarily had to include who I am. I would read the culture like a book. I would translate the culture from my training and experience, and my results would be but one of an infinite set of interpretations. When I accepted this perspective, I finally came out of my box and dared commit myself to this work."

"How's it now?" I asked.

"I have reams of data. It looks good—very interesting."

He picked up the flashlight. "I know it's been hard on you," he admitted. "We're living on top of each other in this hut, yet we're in separate worlds. Haven't you noticed? We've become a Tswana couple. The men talk to men. The women talk to women. Sometimes they mix, but usually just in private, usually just in the still of the night."

"*Ee*, Modise. But Hoyt, this is not my idea of marriage."

"*Ee*, MaoKeef, good-night," he agreed.

"Listen to my last interview with Montsho," Hoyt said. He was beginning, more and more, to share his work. He turned on the tape recorder, and we listened.

Modise: Montsho, if you think of a ladder with ten rungs, where each rung represents success in your life, the bottom rung being the least successful and the top rung being the most successful level, where are you now? Where were you five years ago? Where will you be in five years?

Montsho: Modise, I am overcome. [There was a long pause.] Modise, that is a heavy question which I must think about. I cannot answer it now.

"Montsho did not answer me until this morning," Hoyt said. "He ran into the lolwapa just as I was shaving."

"Modise," Montsho said, "I must talk to you. I had a terrible dream. I was climbing your ladder . . . but I fell off . . . and died.

Modise, I cannot answer your question. It is impossible. I am afraid to climb your ladder."

"The rural sample is nearly completed," Hoyt said. 'I've got to establish rapport with town dwellers next. I'll have to go to town, sit in *shebeens* and drink."

"With your gregarious nature, you'll use your social skills," I quipped.

"I still don't like this part of fieldwork, and I'm going to give you a chance to be supportive," Hoyt countered. "I want you near me, and I promise I'll play with the boys, and I'll kiss you good-night."

"You want me to sit in shebeens? What're you leading up to, Hoyt?

"If I'm going to understand the effects of town life, I cannot commute the eighteen miles to town everyday. I've got to stay in town."

"Surely you don't mean we're leaving here?"

"At first, I had thought we would leave in about a month, but now this offer has come up," Hoyt continued.

"What offer?"

"We have been offered a house in town. An expatriate couple, leaving for England for the Christmas holidays, will let us their house for a minimal fee. It's actually more like a house-sitting arrangement. The only stipulation is that we move in by December 10, feed their dog, and pay the maid."

"December 10! That's in ten days! Impossible!"

I tried to find someone to continue the school. Perhaps just one of the women working at the BAC might like teaching a couple of hours a day. Mrs. Miller, working full-time for the Tswana youths' 4-B Club, gave me a few names to try, and I went knocking on doors. There was only one that seemed mildly interested.

"Oh, yes, I am very interested in primary education. I plan to get a degree when I go back to Holland."

"Teaching my class will give you a first-rate opportunity to learn to teach," I told her. "The class is highly motivated, and their response is supremely rewarding to a teacher's efforts. They appreciate *any* effort on the teacher's behalf; they absolutely love school!" I emphasized.

"But I don't speak Setswana."

"That doesn't matter at this point. You could start with English conversations. I'll introduce you and explain to them that you have not spoken Setswana. I can get you started. Tswana reading is quite phonetic. You'd easily catch on. The children will be patient, understanding, and very grateful."

"No. No. I just can't do it! I will get my degree in Holland and teach over there."

The personal approach having failed, I tried a bureaucratic one. Because my concern did not deal with an established school, the Ministry of Education referred me to the UN Youth Advisor for Botswana.

Across the concrete square to another building, up the elevator, past the receptionist, and into another room. A big, grandfatherly man with a shock of grey hair rose from his desk and extended his hand to me with an Irish lilt of a greeting. He listened to my request; he, very regretfully, could be of no help. He was kind and had the best of intentions. Personally he was frustrated with his own job. He had come here from England determined to make a creative and useful contribution in his new post as "Youth Advisor." Along with two Tswana co-workers, he had worked out a program for the local development of potential for children bypassed by the school system. They had written a lengthy report outlining specific proposals, but the report had never been circulated. It had been sitting on someone's desk for the last six months. There was confusion as to who should read and authorize the report. As yet, no department had considered it germane to their interest. The "UN Youth Advisor" requested by the Botswana Government had done his job: he wrote a report; he advised. Who should listen to, authorize, or implement the advice had not yet been determined, nor did it seem high priority that such decisions be reached.

Thus ended the search for my replacement. Dazed and empty-headed I walked across the fields to my teaching-tree. Sejaro, playing soccer, picked up the worn tennis ball, threw it high, and his voice, my school bell, announced my arrival. The boys scattered back to their books. The girls stuffed playing stones in their pockets and pulled pencils and books out from under their legs.

No easy words came to mind. Resigned, I knew there were none. Trying hard to avoid the look on individual faces, I gazed at the group—like in a dream—and said something.

"Modise and I . . . and Tsotsi and Madala . . . must move to town because Modise has to work there. . . . Yes, in just six more days. . . . No . . . we probably will only come back for visits. This will be our last day of school. But in two days I will take you to town for a special good-bye. We will all pile into the truck, drive to town, and go to the cinema."

Some cheered. Others still sat staring blankly.

"And after the cinema, Modise and I will have a grand mokete—a mokete for our farewell to you. Everyone will come. We will slaughter two goats and a sheep. There will be food for all and plenty of beer for your parents. We will all dance together."

They cheered.

"You have learned a great deal. Every one of you can be very proud. . . . Yes, Sejaro? When will I come back?"

"For a month or so, we will live in town, and I'll come back for visits, but after that we will get on an airplane and fly back to America. . . . When will I come back? I don't know. Maybe never."

Thus I abandoned them, and they, one by one, drifted away.

"Don't forget—in two days, the cinema!" I called out.

"*Ee, mma,*" Sejaro replied in a serious voice.

Maria Maloma still sat there with book in hand. Tears filled her dark, round eyes. She had read every book three times over. To all my questions, Maria's hand had eagerly waved to respond. Now I spoke to her: "Maria, it is true, you are the best reader. You are a perfect student! It is very hard for me to leave you."

"*Ee, mma,*" she replied softly. We sat in silence, she in her sadness, I in my guilt.

In the principal's office of the Boitumelo School, Maria Maloma stood by the wooden chair, and facing his desk, she read the primer in a loud, clear voice.

"She reads very well, Mrs. Alverson. Of course, she could do the work in standard 2, but . . ."

"Oh, let me assure you," I interrupted, "the Ministry of Education has accepted my school as transfer credit before, sir. Another one of my students by the name of Moremi has transferred into standard 2 at Bontleng Primary School in Gaborone. You can call the principal, Mr. Molefi. He will tell you."

Maria sat down again. He dialed the phone several times.

"Hallo, David? *Ke tsogile. Wena o kae? Ee. Ee.* Now, David, do you have a student by the name of Moremi who transferred this year into standard 2? Yes, he came with that woman. I am with that very same woman *now*." He laughs. "I see. *Ee. Ee.* Yes, the very same thing is happening over here right now. *Ee.*" He laughs. "I see. Very well. Thank you. Good-bye."

"Who will pay her fees, Mrs. Alverson?"

Her parents have agreed to pay, sir. And the Millers (as you know, he is manager of the BAC farms), they would like to buy her uniform and shoes, sir. We all wish to help Maria Maloma because she is really a very special student."

We filled out the form. Maria was extremely serious throughout the procedure, but when we drove home, she kept trying to cover her mouth with her hand. It embarrassed her that she could not stop smiling.

"You promised to take them *all* to the movies?!"

"*Ee.*"

"How're you going to fit them in the truck?"

"They'll have to squeeze in," I shrugged.

They squeezed into the open back of our truck one on top of the other—bare legs, bare feet, and whatever clothes were on their backs: Sekaba's same red shirt and torn shorts; Nkabo's bare chest and patched trousers; Gobuamang's short, blue dress, high at the waist, two sizes too small. Hoyt watched with disapproval as I threw caution to the wind, rearranging legs to shut the back panel of our mini-truck. Rre Segatlhe relented; he submitted at the last minute to Manaka's sad face. "*Go siame—Tsamaya!*" [All right—go!] One more in the front cab; that makes four. "Manaka, get up on Tiro's lap. *Go siame! A re ye!*" [Very good! Let's go!]

"Take it slowly over the potholes," Hoyt warned me, "and for God's sake, watch what you're doing!"

Rumbling through the crossroad, bumping slowly down and up each rut, we headed for the main road. "*Tabo! Le kae!*" Tabo saw them, smiled, and waved them on. "*Montsho! Montsho!*" they sang out. Montsho, by the side of the road, flagged us down. "Children! Man was built with legs for moving. Why do you ride your fat bottoms with feet in the air?" We laughed and left him pondering in the dust. Waving wildly, the children continued to yell their greetings to every figure in the distant field.

We passed the gate and turned off toward Gaborone. Their territory behind them, the children sang and laughed in the wind. Some had been to town before; they told the others. But the cinema! No, this they had never seen!

We hit the paved road, passed the government buildings, and turned left into the shopping mall. Gaborone, at last! The road felt smooth, the car luxurious; and the children, every last one of them, fell silent and watched.

En masse, we crossed the parking lot. I approached the theater with some anxiety. What was playing? Foolishly, I had made a commitment without checking the theater schedule. I looked up at the lettering across the front: Capitol Theater—Red River, Starring John Wayne. Relief—not bad—in fact, it would be perfect.

Walking across the pavement littered with candy wrappers was not like thorns and sand to their bare feet. My purchase at the ticket window sounded impressive. "Twenty three children and one adult, please." They filed past the stunned ticket man, through the glass doors, and walked up the carpeted stairs to their balcony seats. Before sitting down, Sekaba stood rubbing his hand back and forth across the soft nap of his seat. Gobuamang gripped the arm rests and bounced up and down. Maria and Keorapetse dangled their legs, while next to them Tiro sat erectly, with his long legs crossed and his hands neatly folded in his lap.

I passed out candy. "Sweets, sweets," jolted my memory and my guilt. The lights went out. Down three rows of faces, I watched their wonder and delight as the screen lit up. Enraptured throughout, it did not seem to matter that they could not follow the words. They cheered for the good and hooted down the villains. I sucked candies and missed the whole thing. Confined, as if strapped into my airplane seat, I was an expatriate, abandoning them.

We filed out of the theater into the late afternoon sunlight. Chattering and laughing, they followed town rules as they perceived them: throw candy wrappers on the pavement and kick them along. So captivated were they by John Wayne's presence that upon returning to our truck, they tried out his swagger. Sejaro was particularly good at it and gave a grandiose performance in the parking lot.

"Rre Segatlhe will be pleased," I comforted myself. "The herd boys will be back in time to corral the animals before sundown."

". . . collect all your school children to help you fetch wood."

14

Mokete, Our Farewell

Manaka and Tiro tied a white cloth to the tip of a straight branch, our flagpole. The flag flew at the entrance of our kraal as the news spread: a mokete on Saturday, a mokete all day with food and plenty of beer. Rre Segatlhe, in generous spirit, directed our preparations. Kadi would not be enough; for this event, we would have to get sorghum to make real bojalwa. Modise was to fetch MaMoremi and her family out of Gaborone. We would need their help to brew, and, after all, they would not want to be left out.

"Mosadi mogolo," he commanded me. "How do you think we can cook the mealies and meat?"

"As usual."

"Mosadi mogolo! What do you think? We will slaughter three animals! We will feed over a hundred people! My pots aren't big enough, and your little pile of wood won't cook a pig's tail! Go to your sisters, Ntatabo, Maria, and Seipate. Tell them you need their biggest pots. And collect all your school children to help you fetch wood. Your pile must be as high as the roof of the kitchen shelter!"

Across the fields we dragged tree trunks, two by two. We cleared the underbrush from the Moshu Forest and scattered into the field beyond to gather up the dead wood. The girls moved down the path, one behind the other, each with a bundle of sticks perched on her head. I reshifted the pile in my arms, feeling clumsy in contrast to my graceful entourage.

One after the other we ducked the branch of the thorn tree on the curve. In front of me, Seipate hesitated, picked a thorn, and continued while scraping her teeth clean. We climbed the hard,

195

red surface of the sandhill, and when I reached its crest, I looked out past the termite hill to the kraals in the distance. That I should leave this familiar foraging ground: first, for the pavement of Gaborone, and then for the interior of a jet plane—to streak across the sky above, look down, and see nothing below!

I lagged behind the women and girls and watched them descend the hillside. No one looked back, and I stood still. Their faded clothes blended into the matte colors of the pale morning sky and grey-green fields. They moved with gentle rhythm like the breeze rustling grasses. It was no longer possible to distinguish Gomolemo from Lerato or Maria from Seipate. Their succession was a dance, and I vaguely recalled, once before, distancing myself from them. Now I was as far removed from the sensations of being a strange newcomer as I was from the realization that I would leave this place to become an outsider.

I held onto this view—the women walking through the valley in the early morning light—as if to force it into memory. What would I remember? Rre Segatlhe's voice? The warm lolwapa walls? What control did I have on the focus of my recollections, and how would the memories themselves shape the meaning of this experience?

Or was it the other way around: would the meaning, which I had created out of this experience but could not yet articulate, determine my memory and its significance? Had I in my daily life in this "other" place acquired new values or ideas that would change me? I tried to step away from my identity as mosadi mogolo—MaoKeef: who *was* I right now? But it was impossible to extricate this moment from my vision of the past or perception of the future. I lived a Tswana sense of time. As months ago I worked to take on the role of mosadi mogolo, I would with equal difficulty leave it behind.

It is not important that Tswana time mark past, present, and future. A Tswana moves through life with continual ancestral time; the origins and the future (which itself leads back to the origins) move along with the rising and setting of every sun and moon: ". . . like the shadow of this hut given by the moon, life is round. We travel in a circle from the Badimo back to the Badimo."

Time is ubiquitous, its breakdown of no concern. People arrive and events occur. There are no words to express "on time" or "late." It is the event, not its time, that has meaning. We meet to gather wood when all have arrived. We return when all have

196

collected. We look to each other, not a clock, to participate together in the event.

The priority of the human encounter over the precision of the hour changed my perception of every day, week, and month. Stepping back from the women, my sisters, and girls, my children, I prepared myself for separation. I would leave behind a part of myself—this place and its people, its rhythm and time.

Old Maria returned to my side. *"Ke eng?"* [What's the matter?"]

"I was just thinking, Maria, that soon I must leave."

"Yes, and when you return, Molefi will be home from the hospital, our dam will be twice as big . . ."

"No, no," I interrupted. "We will never be back. We live much too far, much too far away."

"You will be here again. . . . You are here now . . . but still you cannot carry wood properly!"

She picked up my pile of wood and carried it on her head, while I, protesting, ran to keep up with the old woman.

Rre Segatlhe set a bowl of mealie and meat and a full gourd of bojalwa on the lolwapa floor. The old woman from Kopong sat down near the bowl to begin the ceremony to bless the food. Circling her, the rest of us sat farther back to look on and listen. All the while, on the periphery, more people silently entered to join us. It was still early in the afternoon, yet already over seventy people had come from the lands. Men and women that Modise had met in town arrived wearing their finest attire: women with scarves, hats, or beads; men with polished shoes. Naledi caught a ride from Mochudi and brought her battery-operated record player. MaMoremi, who had come several days in advance to brew beer, wore all her clothes for the occasion: two dresses, one on top of the other, and her red sweater.

A group of women gathered behind the old woman from Kopong. They sang a hymn in Setswana, one they had probably learned in church. She closed her benediction with words to Modimo, thanking him for food and rain. She praised Botswana. She praised America. She praised Rre Segatlhe and Modise. She praised the bowlful of food.

"Pula!" everyone shouted. The solemn air was broken, and people turned to greet each other. Rre Segatlhe grabbed my arm. It was my job to pour bojalwa; a line was already forming by the kitchen area. MaMoremi and I dipped and poured, greeting each person. *"Go monate! Ke itumetse thata, mma!"* was the response. When finally we left the shaded shelter to join the party, the children were lined up for their share of meat and the adults were eating and drinking. Seipate dipped her hand into the soft mound of mealie, while next to her Naledi balanced a portion on her fork. At a quick glance, it was easy to spot the rural folk, not just by their bare feet and dress, but by their manner of eating. As Tsotsi, carrying his plate of food, passed his father, Modise swooped his fingers into Tsotsi's food. "Just a taste!" he pleaded, as Tsotsi ran off to join the boys.

Between the three barrels of bojalwa and kadi, there flowed at least one hundred gallons of beer. I had insisted it would be too much, but when all had arrived, Hoyt estimated that we had close to two hundred guests. By the time the sun was hot, no one was in a condition to be bothered by it. They set down their gourds, grabbed hands, and danced. *"Opela le bina!"* Ntatabo pulled me into her dancing group; we linked hands once again. A chorus of rhythm swept us into a whirl of dust. Our feet stomped and hands clapped, and with my sisters, I heard myself ululate a shrill trill. I broke away to look around. Several groups were dancing simultaneously, and between them, individuals with gourds in hand sang, twirled, and shuffled to express their joy.

"Ke itumetse thata, thata, mma!" They shook my hand as I walked through.

"Ee, le nna, ke itumetse, thata!"

I walked past the lolwapa wall. Near the flag, Tsotsi and the herd boys joined a group of townies to dance gumba gumba around Naledi's player. Gumba gumba rang out to the contrapuntal sounds of the herd boy's cymbal—tin plates, licked clean, slapping flat hand and thigh. Elbows and knees pounded the air, vibrant with their singing voices, high, low, and cracking in between.

It was Montsho's arrival that changed the ambience. Montsho, the hero, walked in bare-chested with his one-stringed *nkonkokwane* slung over his shoulder. Supporting the instrument on a battered can, he sat proudly waiting for the dances to end. He waited for his moment of silence. To all, Montsho, the nonconformist, was known as the entertainer. Montsho had left his family to live in the rusty hull of an abandoned 1948 Bedford truck. He had his own way of doing things. He shunned the traditional role as resident head of his family to live a solitary life, yet in doing so, he cared for his family as he cared for the entire community. He worked at his skill, sewing hides, and when he profited, he distributed his gains. When South African tourists bought his impala rugs, he took half the money to his wife and children and gave the rest away. What use did he have for paper and coins? For himself, he kept little. He lived simply, moving from place to place to hunt game. No one had ever seen him cook for himself, nor did he fetch water; thus, in hunger, he passed no homestead without asking for mealies, nor did he cross a river or puddle without bending to drink.

Everyone knew Montsho by his craft and his way of life. They could see him by his walk as he crossed their fields. They could smell him as he approached. Never did he (nor would he ever) bathe! What was there to wash away? Water was for drinking. They knew him by his ideas. Montsho was a free spirit who moved among them, who took and gave what he could; and this, he knew, they treasured.

"Ow! Montsho! You stink, as always!" The crowd gathered. His moment of silence came. Montsho played his *nkonkokwane*. He played, and he sang; and then he rose to dance. As the crowd moved in around him, he pushed it back for room. He filled his chest and shouted, then threw himself on the ground. Rigidly he lay on his back with his arms stiffly held together and stretched out straight past his head. Pulling his knees up, he jerked his body forward. He arched his neck and wriggled his shoulders to scrape his back along the sand. He was a chungalooloo, a long, fat centipede, writhing on the lolwapa floor; this was his Chungalooloo Dance. Children clapped, men shouted, women ululated. We danced a circle around Montsho's Chungalooloo Dance.

Montsho got up again, his back covered with dust. No one wiped it off as he mingled through the crowd shaking hands.

I went looking for Hoyt. "Have you seen Modise?"

"Over there!"

Toward the fields, away from the dancers, Modise sat with an elder. Between them the tape recorder reeled on, while the old man played his *serankure* and sang praises. Deep in his music, he seemed oblivious to all around him. Modise switched the "play-back" button. The old man listened intently. Suddenly he shook his head, took up his instrument and repeated the section, determined to improve himself.

"Modise," Rre Segatlhe commanded, "it is now the time for

you to say some words." Modise followed Rre Segatlhe to the water drum.

"Climb on top of the water drum and speak."

In Setswana, for himself and his family, Modise said good-bye. He told them of the book he would write. He promised that he would remember their words. He thanked Rre Segatlhe. He thanked the community, and everyone cheered. Next to me, Maria's rolling tongue rang out a piercing trill above all the others. One after the other, men climbed the water drum to sing out praise poems—to America, to Modise, to me, to our children.

We sat on the warm, rosy lolwapa wall facing the sunset. "MaoKeef, *tsamaya sentle*," they said. "Go well." They disappeared down the paths as it grew darker, and the moon, like a heavy melon, lay low in the nighttime sky.

We celebrate Modise's birthday with Rre Segatlhe.

15

On The Expatriate Calendar

Granadillas ripen each day on the terrace vine. We pick one with a brown, shriveled shell, put it in an egg cup, cut the top off, and eat its pulp for breakfast. What exquisite sweetness! Picking granadillas is our only link to the environment; all else is bought and paid for.

The walls are white and straight; the chairs soft; the beds big enough to roll over in twice. We hold our hands under the faucet and watch the water spill away. We read under lamps at night and don't know the shape of the nightly moon.

We revel in the privacy. Doors to rooms close; they even lock. Every drawer and cabinet has a key.

No one comes to greet or share the news. Bella, the maid, arrives at 7:30 A.M. to serve us coffee. We are to pay Bella her fee for this month: 18 pula (about $25). That for expatriate, Gaborone standards is a "high" wage for a domestic servant. In return, she is to maintain the household daily according to norms which I could never set for myself: fix tea or coffee for the "master" and "madam"; make beds; wash dishes; scrub kitchen floor; do laundry; clean bathroom. Then after an afternoon break in her servant's quarters, she is to return to wax and polish all floors; wash walls and windows; and fix tea or coffee for "madam." She returns to her quarters again to prepare and eat her own evening meal but is expected to return to wash dinner dishes and perhaps take down the laundry, fold it, and put it away, or sprinkle it to be ironed the next day. When there is no laundry, she is to clean the oven, stove, or refrigerater; wash drawers, cupboards, and windows, inside and out; and iron. There is always something to be done, says Bella.

To wash clothes, she folds a towel for her knees and bends over the bathtub for two hours, scrubbing fabric across her calloused knuckles. She sweeps loose dust with broom and dustpan and scrubs, waxes, and polishes floors, moving swiftly on all fours while sliding with her pail or paste wax, brush and cloth. There are no household conveniences for cleaning, no vacuum cleaner, no washing machine, and the iron, although it plugs in, reflects the weight of its name. "Modern" household devices are difficult to obtain and expensive; labor is plentiful and cheap.

Four o'clock: Bella arrives with tray, porcelain tea cups, silver cream pitcher, a petite glass bowl with sugar cubes, and a platter of biscuits. Madam, it is tea time."

"Madam, it is tea time," she repeats.

"Thank you, Bella. Very nice, Bella, but . . . uuh, from now on, I'll make my own tea when I want it, O.K?"

She looks confused.

"And, uh, I'm sitting here right now. Could you forget about the floors today? They're still clean. I just don't think they need to be done everyday. In fact, I really think that you could just do them once a week."

"Just one time in the week, Madam!"

"Yes, one time. And my name is not *madam, Mma,*" I continue in Setswana, "Modise and I cannot live here like this. Just for this month—while we stay here—you can wash clothes in the bathtub and do the floors once a week, but forget the rest; I'll do it."

"*Ee, mma,*" she replies sullenly and turns to walk away.

I call her back to join me for the tea. She stands next to an empty chair and looks at me. I pass her the biscuit plate; she takes the plate and puts it on the table.

"*Nna fatshe.*" I beckon her to sit down. But she refuses. I stand up as well, pass her a tea cup, and sip my tea standing next to her. She giggles lightly and sits down.

"What is your Tswana name?"

"Modiane." Her voice is sad. She looks down to the rug and continues in a soft monotone. She tells me of her family in Mochudi and that they depend on her monthly wages. Because I have reduced her labor, she now thinks that her wages will be cut. I apologize to her that I have not made it clear: she will, of course, earn her usual salary. We will pay her 25 pula at the end of the month. Thereafter, we will return to our home in America, and her "master" and "madam" will return to this house to resume their routine.

"Modiane," I ask. "Why are you looking at me like that?"

"You are American?" she smiles.

"Yes," I reply. "But *nna, kwa masimong, ke mosadi mogolo* [on the lands I am the old woman]. *Ke itse go dila* [I know how to smear the dung floor]," I add playfully.

"Ow!" she laughs in disbelief.

"*Ee, mma. Ke go itse sentle!*" [Yes, and I am good at it] I say proudly.

Concerning the Tswana identity which I have tried to express, Modiane says nothing. In English, Bella repeats with delight: "So . . . you are an American!

Bella comes by to introduce her good friend, the maid next door. "My madam likes to know the Tswana names," Bella turns to her friend.

"Leepi . . . but here they call me Hilda," the young woman explains to me.

"I was MaoKeef or just mosadi mogolo on the lands, but my English name is Marianne," I reciprocate.

"Bella tells me that you are leaving Botswana in just one month, madam. Please, madam, if you have anything to sell, anything you will leave here, please tell us first," Hilda pleads.

"We have very little here. Most of our things were given away at the lands," I tell her. "But come sit down. Let's have some tea."

Bella and Hilda speak of their jobs. For now, they feel lucky to work for people who pay them good wages. Other friends receive less for the same work. In two years, however, their expatriate families will return overseas. New people, with different English, different ways and different wages, will move in. Probably they would have a good chance at keeping their jobs if they observed carefully and learned quickly. If their pay was reduced and the job circumstances too humiliating, they would do what they had done before: risk looking for another job. The search for a new job is always difficult.

"Why not try to find a job with a Setswana family?" I ask.

"Never!" they reply adamantly. "These Tswanas in town, they are rich! But they pay as little as they can get away with, and they work us twice as hard—just like the Boers in South Africa!"

"That is why I was first frightened when you spoke Setswana; you could have been like a Boer," Bella admits. "But you are one of those whites who like us, and that is why you speak Setswana. It is good for me you are American. Many Americans can pay a few more pula. Some even have machines to wash clothes!"

"But jobs with Americans are hard to find," Hilda adds. "My aunt works in a compound with four flats for American Embassy officials. If there is a job, she will tell me, and I will run!"

The doorbell rings. "No, Bella, I will get it." While the dog barks wildly at his feet, a young boy calls out to me, "Madam, please, madam, I need a job." He fires out, staccato, each word again, pausing between them for further emphasis. It is probably an English sentence he has memorized, because he does not understand my English response, but simply turns away when I shake my head and say, "No."

The maids are gone when I return to my cold cup of tea. I sit alone, bite into a biscuit, and stare out of the window into the garden. The "garden boy" is squatted by the walkway edge, trimming grass with scissors. His back glistens in the sun. His shirt hangs from his pants pocket, and he pulls it out, now and then, to wipe his forehead.

. . . *Saturday* . . .

This final one-month stay in Gaborone is perhaps a good transition for us. We are still among the Tswana but live a town life which is closer to our life-style at home. We have not bothered with precisions of the clock yet, but our time is measured. We are aware of weekdays again.

This is Saturday: Hoyt comes home at midday. He leaves behind shebeens and town houses to come home alone. He enters our gate, *Tsaba Ntsha!"* [Beware of Dog!], and latches it behind him. There is no one to greet in the garden. He opens the door and closes it. He drops his papers and equipment on a table and sinks into a chair. News is there if he wants it. He can also take off his shoes, slowly sip an ice-cold beer, and—if he wants it—he can withdraw into his own silence, into the privilege of privacy.

But isolated moments are still within the Tswana life-world, and when it enters our doors we embrace it.

"Look who's here!" Hoyt called out from the doorway.

"Lekoto!" the children shouted.

Lekoto greeted everyone. Bella and Hilda stared at his worn, khaki jacket, mumbled a greeting, and withdrew with a brief *"salang sentle."*

I had not noticed until now how tall Lekoto had grown. His

body was so thin that he could button his jacket, but the sleeves fell far short of his bony wrists. Similarly, his legs had grown too long for his trousers so that he appeared—as he was—a grown-up schoolboy in last year's uniform.

Shortly after we sat down to exchange the news, Lekoto told us of his problem. He had passed his examination but only with a class 3, a passing C grade. His attempts to apply at various secondary schools had repeatedly failed for the same reason: only class 1 and 2 passes would be accepted into secondary school; a grade C pass was not good enough this year.

He had just tried the night school in Gaborone and received the usual rejection. There was only one place left to try: Lobatse. If Lobatse turned him down, he did not know what he would do.

We asked Lekoto if he had told the schools that he had been hospitalized with pneumonia before the examinations, that he came from a small, village school where children were only minimally prepared for the national examinations. No, he had not mentioned these considerations. Hoyt offered to write a letter of recommendation to the secondary school in Lobatse in which he would present Lekoto's case. If the last school turned him down, I suggested we request that Lekoto repeat the examination, and I could help him to prepare for it.

"Yes. Yes," Lekoto replied.

"Good. Then you must come here everyday. We must get started. We'll prepare for your reexamination," I repeated.

"Yes. Yes," Lekoto responded.

We drank hot tea.

"I have seen Rra Segatlhe. He has found the answer to my problem," Lekoto said. "At my birth, it was decided that I should live with my father's elder brother—for he is the keeper of the family cattle and has no sons. As you know, Modise, my father's brother, because he is the eldest, is also my own father. I, as my father's eldest son, was the first son of the family, and I, as inheritor, was to keep the cattle. But when the time came for me to go to my father's brother's place, my father and mother could not let me go. They did not fulfill the agreement between my father and my father's oldest brother. Instead, my father found work at the BAC and sent me to school.

"Rra Segatlhe has said that my father's older brother felt badly treated. While he would be happy for me to go to school and get a job, he must have some promise from me that he will not be left out when I bring home the rewards of my schooling. After all, he too has sacrificed for my schooling.

"It is clear: there is a spell on me to halt my success. Rra Segatlhe read it in the bones. Tomorrow morning I will do what Rra Segatlhe has told me to do: I will go to my father's older brother, stay with him, and promise him that I will always know my duty to the family. I will promise him that I know that he, as the eldest brother, is the keeper of our wealth, and that I, as the inheritor, will add to the wealth of the family through my success.

"Rra Segatlhe is sure that I can break the spell of envy. He threw the bones again. They say I *will* get into school; I *will* get a job and earn money one day!"

I brought Lekoto a blanket and pillow. "Sleep on the couch tonight. It's too late to go home."

Hoyt shut the bedroom door. We fell into bed, and I whispered, "Hoyt, be sure to write Lobatse in the morning . . . and mention that you teach at Dartmouth in the U.S.A. That might help. The letter's got to be there before he is . . ."

"Uh-huh."

"If he doesn't get in, he'll just have to come here everyday for tutoring . . ." I rambled on.

"He won't."

"He said he would," I countered.

"He couldn't say 'no'; his 'yes' was polite."

"I've got to convince him."

"You can't argue against witchcraft. It's more powerful than the rules of the educational bureaucracy."

"Hoyt! That's ridiculous. What're you trying to say? . . . Hoyt, you don't believe that ?!"

The pillow was over his head.

Early the next morning, we had bid Lekoto good-bye and hardly closed the door when Bella, dressed in her Sunday finery, rushed toward us.

"Ow! Master! Ow! Madam!" she cried out as she carried the blanket and pillow from the couch. "You let that Tswana boy sleep here! . . . You forgot to lock the cabinet and drawers! If he helps himself, I will be blamed!"

Keys, a ring full of keys; what were my instructions? . . . After Bella polishes the silver, count the pieces before locking the drawer. Whenever leaving the kitchen, keep the food pantry locked. After the linen has been ironed and put away, it should be counted. . . .

. . . Sunday . . .

Bella dresses for church. She and Hilda are devout Christian Zionists.

Bella joined the church after leaving Mochudi and coming to Gaborone. I asked her why she left Mochudi, and she explained that she had been the victim of witchcraft. When her husband died, she had refused to go to his brother's place. Instead, she packed her belongings and moved in with her own parents with her two children. She refused her brother-in-law's request to send her children to live with her husband's family, and for this reason, Bella explained, her husband's family had consulted a witch doctor. A spell was cast. She became very ill. When she finally recovered, she found no job. Her only choice was to flee the area.

Two times last year she returned to Mochudi to visit her children at her parent's home, but she will never go back to Mochudi to live. "This is because of the power of witchcraft," she explains.

"But, Bella, what about the God of your church here in Gaborone—doesn't He protect you!"

"No, no, Madam, you do not understand. That is something altogether different. That has nothing to do with Tswana witchcraft. The God in my church is what I sing and pray to; it is so I can be a good Christian!"

She walks off in her new Sunday hat.

. . . Monday . . .

A new week comes up like a sunrise, and there is a sense of beginning again. On the lands, we have that feeling at the time of the new moon. The night is clear, the moon an eyebrow. Darkness soothes and brings on sleep. But what is there to a Monday? A groggy face, a cup of coffee, and a scraping chair.

Between Mondays, there is less time than from moon to moon. The narrower I define my own space of time, the faster it seems to go by. The faster I perceive time to be passing, the more of it has escaped my consciousness. I want to shout, "Hold!"

The boys look with horror as I pick the ticking egg timer off the kitchen counter and smash it to the floor. The eggs are hard—so what, and "Momma's goin' crazy," says our Madala.

Today I am invited to an afternoon tea at three o'clock. My invitation is engraved:

You are cordially invited to attend a tea to welcome
Mrs. Etienne Fournier
to Gaborone, Botswana, . . .

I do not know the hostess. Am I invited because I live next door, or am I invited because I should provide "quaint backdrop"? It must be the latter, because I am introduced upon arrival as "a woman who actually lived in the bush" and "speaks Setswana." That announcement provokes some "ahs," but proves quite meaningless to the guest of honor, Madame Jacqueline Fournier, who for a few minutes struggles valiantly to express herself in anything but French.

"C'est difficile parler en anglais. Le 'a,' pour moi, c'est très difficile à prononcer."

"*Ee!*" I reply enthusiastically.

"Exactement! C'est ça—le 'a.'" She repeats my tone of voice.

"No, no, I didn't say 'a.' I only meant to agree with you by saying "*ee.*" You see, in Setswana *ee* means 'yes,' but, of course, I meant to say 'oui' instead of *ee.*"

Who am I talking to? She sips her martini, and I try to continue in French.

"Oui, c'est *thata* difficile—*ga ke itse* pourquois. . ."

What am I saying? I have no control; Tswana words slip in.

She goes on in French without a hint of confusion, and what she says does not relate to anything I have tried to say, nor to anything around us. She speaks of the airport officials who let her keep her blue bag, and then of her garden in the Ivory Coast, where I presume she and her husband have spent the last few years as expatriates. She says they "hopscotch around bleeding the world" and lists the countries they have "blessed": Algeria, Mauritius, Senegal, and the Ivory Coast. Her image—or is it candor?—leaves me speechless.

The martini in her hand cannot alone be responsible for the fact that she reeks of alcohol. Sunk in her chair, she sways from side to side. She smiles loosely. Her red lips quiver like cherry jello as she tells me of the parrot she left behind in the Paris apartment. Madame Jacqueline has obviously arrived tipsy at the party in her honor. She has settled in, blissfully crocked.

While this realization initially strikes me as pathetic and somewhat humorous, by the end of "teatime," I have to consider that

Madame Jacqueline's party strategy has distinct advantages. What can her fuzzy vision distort?

I move to a sober conversation on the veranda and find a seat near a glass table with tea and cakes. Around me are flowery dresses and sunglass smiles.

"Did you know Botswana is no longer an *underdeveloped* country? The government has done *so* much in the last six years!"

"Yes, just last year it was among the bottom twenty-five countries, and now it's not. The gross national product has increased because of the new mines, I suppose."

"Isn't that wonderful!" everyone agrees.

"We should all go tell Seipate," I suggest.

. . . Tuesday . . .

"Hey, Maokeef! Hey, Raokeef! Good evening! Good evening!" His smiling teeth shine in the dark. He steps out from among his companions, and we recognize Raus.

"Keef is where?"

"At home in bed."

"You go to cinema tonight? Good. Very good!"

He smiles again. It seems to genuinely please him to see us in this context: in line with Tswana bourgeoisie and European expatriates, in line with ironed dresses and fashionable shirts.

"Did you find a job yet, Raus?"

"No, but I find one, Maokeef. I find one tomorrow."

Hoyt puts twenty cents in Raus' pocket, and we wait in line to buy tickets to see *Gone with the Wind*.

The Capitol Theater combats expatriate boredom; it draws full capacity audiences for decade-old reruns. On weekends, town youths may scrounge for matinee tickets to see their favorite American westerns or Hong Kong "Kung Fu" films, but on weekday nights like this, they hang around waiting for pennies to drop.

"*Ke kopa* twenty cent, please," a young boy pokes at Hoyt's sleeve.

"*Ke kopa* twenty cent, please, Raokeef," he begs again.

"*Mosimane* [boy], you do not greet me!" Hoyt scolds. "Do I look like a bank?" Modise continues in Setswana. "Have you tossed away your Tswana law?"

Mosimane! You must greet people before you do your business," Hoyt rebukes him.

The boy, confused at this white Tswana elder, looks down to

the pavement and shuffles to the shadows, but only for a moment is he put off track. He emerges once again. "Please, twenty cent," he whispers to a man behind us. The man reaches into his trouser pocket while the boy waits frozen, shoulders curled, head bowed. Respectfully, one hand holds the elbow of his taking hand. It closes in on the coins, and he quickly retreats to his colleagues waiting in the darkness for his sign. The next boy rushes forward into the light. But our line moves faster. We are behind the glass door, moving up the carpeted stairs while Raus and friends pool their earnings for the night.

. . . Wednesday . . .

The bulletin board, posted in the shopping mall of Gaborone, is a favorite expatriate stopping place, and I too cannot leave town without stopping there. Bureau of drawers and bicycles—like new—are advertised on three-by-five cards; so are the announcements of events of the week. I could join a tennis club, play a symphony with the Gaborone Music Society, or sail on weekends with the Sailing Club at the Gaborone Dam. I could fill every night of the week: Monday's stamp club, Tuesday's bridge game, Wednesday's museum lecture. Gaborone may be 100 kilometers east of the Kalahari Desert, but it does not lack any club or society for which there is expatriate fervor.

I stood in front of the bulletin board, thinking out loud one day, "I wonder if there's a Humane Society?"

"Oh, yes, in fact, there is!" my neighbor enlightened me. She proceeded to give me details, but I stopped her short. "Thank you. No, I don't want to join up. I was just curious, given Tswana culture, whether. . . ." My voice trailed away, and she noticed, above all, that I was American.

"I haven't seen you around before, and I guess I could say I know most of the Americans here."

"We used to live in a rural area and moved to town only a few weeks ago."

"Peace Corps," she grinned knowingly. "I suppose you're quite relieved to be in Gaborone. Say! I'm having a tea for a few of the American wives this afternoon. Why don't you bring your children and get acquainted?"

One invitation leads to another. We are getting to know the American community. Today our family has been invited to an afternoon barbeque at the home of the First Attaché of the American Embassy. Hoyt refuses to go. There is some of Rre Segatlhe in him. But the children and I, thinking predominantly of the good food, grass lawn, and swimming pool, close the door on Modise and head down the road for the "best" part of town.

The residence is impressive. Keith points out the high walls, the wrought-iron gate, and the bars on the windows and concludes that it is a fortress. Brian and I, immediately attracted to a pair of peacocks strutting on the lawn, wait in hopes of seeing a tail spread out. One peacock pokes at a rose bush; the other turns proudly away from us and ambles around the corner.

Our hostess, Annette Bishop, greets us at the door. She is outgoing and very friendly.

"Actually we just moved in last month. What a relief! We just couldn't manage in the other place. I have to do so much entertaining, and it was terribly small. We always need at least four bedrooms and then, of course, a rec room, pool, and courts. Why, otherwise, I'd go mad driving the kids around! Come, I'll give you a tour of the house and then you can join everyone on the patio."

The children run to a ball game on the lawn. I sit among Americans: a diplomat, a Fulbright scholar, a Red Cross nurse, and an AID research worker.

"She met him at the Riding Club. They're having quite an affair, and everyone knows about it except Roger!" I think of the Riding Club and Roger and smile with everyone's laughter. Ice cubes tinkle against my glass.

"Anyone for a swim before the steak's on?"

Mine is the only chair to scrape away from the hors d'oeuvres. Perhaps the other guests prefer to preserve their coiffures, because Mr. Bishop, who abandons his ball game with the children, and I are the only adults in the water. It is elegant swimming in a kidney-shaped pool with a mosaic tile floor.

"Just call me Brad. . . . Annette tells me you lived in the bush!"

"Yes."

"No pools there, I guess," he remarks, laughing.

"No pools. Definitely no pools. We got water from rain puddles. But we *did* have a peacock. We called him Number 19."

After eating, we sit in the shade on lacy white lawn chairs. In his tennis whites, Brad Bishop appears, racquet in hand. The tennis court lies abandoned in the hot sun.

"Anyone gonna bat the ball around awhile? No takers, huh?"

Keith takes his last swim, and we get up to leave. We pass through the arched doorway. "Come anytime," Annette calls out, as she clutches the ring of keys to her fortress. "The doors are wide open." American hospitality, a casual place in the sun, only eighteen kilometers from Rre Segatlhe's place.

. . . Thursday . . .

We Alversons, as expatriates, do our share of entertaining.
A letter written by our Canadian neighbor, John Hunter,
to his daughter

Dear Peggy,

Julie and I enjoyed talking to you on Sunday. It was a mistake, I'm afraid, to promise to write you a long letter. You heard all the news from Gaborone, fit to print, on the phone. We did receive a telegram from Mom announcing that she would be returning from Dar Es Salaam on Saturday. Your sister and I have been living on scrambled eggs since she left. Well not quite. We did dine on chili beans on one occasion. Come to think of it, I could tell you about that evening. It turned out to be a bit of an event.

It was last Thursday, and Julie and I were invited to dinner at the Alversons. (Alverson is a professor of Anthropology at Dartmouth College on sabbatical and is living with his family in Osborne's old house, behind us.) We had finished off a seafood entrée and were halfway into a bowl of hot chili beans when there was a knock on the door. Marianne (Alverson) answers it. It is the kid from next door. He announces, rather calmly, that their maid is choking and that his parents are out. Marianne excuses herself and disappears with the kid. About fifteen seconds later she appears at the door and screams for her husband to come quickly. Alverson exits. Your sister, the two Alverson boys, and I continue to munch away on our chili. Sixty seconds later, Marianne reappears and yells at me to go and get my car. (The Alversons, preparing to leave the country, had sold theirs.) Galvanized into action (but carting about three pounds of chili beans in my stomach), I run three blocks to our house, jump in the car, and roar back to Alversons' neighbor.

The kid is out in front and directs me to drive across the lawn to the kitchen door. I hop out of the car and spring into the kitchen. The scene is something like this. Marianne and two Batswana girls are standing in a corner, clutching each other, and wailing mysterious female sounds. Alverson is on his knees with his index finger in the mouth of the maid. The maid is flopping about on the floor like a recently caught trout, eyes rolled back, frothing at the mouth, and making a variety of ghastly sounds. Her face

214

has been painted with four or five bright red solid circles about 1½" in diameter. My inclination is to retreat and deposit my chili beans in a quiet corner of the garden. Alverson, however, pleads with me to help him get her into the car. The girl is not light. It is something like trying to gather up 150 lbs. of writhing jello. We finally get her into the back seat. The two Batswana girls pile in as well. I take off at high speed, Alverson beside me, for the Princess Marina Hospital. No sooner do we get going than one of the girls in the back announces, above the gurgling din, that she wants us to pick up her mother, her grandfather, and her aunt and take them along to the hospital as well. (In Botswana, an impending death is regarded as a social event to which relatives are invited—not unlike a Bar Mitzvah.) As the Peugeot is designed for four passengers and as we are already one 150 lb. trout over the limit—not to mention that the trout is about two minutes removed from that great trout pond in the sky—I demur and continue on with maximum dispatch for the hospital.

Tires shrieking we make the last turn into the hospital drive and jam on the brakes. (The gurgling is getting ominously quieter.) Two nurses are walking by. Alverson jumps out of the car and asks them where the emergency ward is. "There is no emergency ward." "Where do we take an emergency case?" He gets some vague directions. We take off again, meandering around the dark hospital grounds—and after about five minutes, away at the back of the hospital, we see a light and head for it. I hop out of the car (Alverson is beginning to gurgle a bit, himself!) and run into a ward full of suffering humanity. Wending my way through a labyrinth of beds replete with moaning freight, I locate a doctor and nurse making rounds. I tell them I have an emergency. They tell me to bring it in. No one offers to help. I grab a wheelchair that some poor soul has momentarily deserted and go roaring back through the labyrinth and out the door.

If getting 150 lbs. of writhing jello into the backseat of a Peugeot is difficult—getting it out and into a wheelchair (not to mention keeping it in a wheelchair) is a feat which makes threading a camel through the eye of a needle seem devoid of challenge. We manage, however, and wheel her back past the beds to the doctor and nurse who are standing where I left them with their finger in their ear.

The sight of our flopping, frothing charge moves the nurse to go and get a wheeled stretcher. The doctor tells Alverson and me to put the girl on the stretcher. He stands back like Christian

Barnard while Alverson and I go into our act again. Alverson grabs her legs and gets kicked about for his trouble. I grab her arms and get frothed on for mine. Half the moaners have struggled from their beds of pain and are gathered about to watch this unusual athletic event. Half wrestling, half weight lifting; two men vs. one girl. We finally make it—but our job isn't over. We have to hold her on the stretcher while the doctor and nurse go about taking blood pressure and diverse and sundry other things. Alverson and I are looking frantically at each other while all this is going on. We seem to have, unwittingly, become unpaid employees of the hospital. Finally an injection seems to calm the patient. No one dismisses us. I half expect to be ordered to go and clean bed pans. When no one is looking, we sneak out and drive away. Alverson says that we should get back and finish dinner. I take the position that God gave men alcohol for just such nights as this. Alverson, "though not a devout man," agrees. We repair to our house and demolish a bottle of brandy.

The sequel to this harrowing tale: Alverson contacted the hospital the next day. The girl was recovering. They believe she was having boyfriend trouble and had been working up a little magic routine in order to get him to come around and see her that night. In the process they think she swallowed some of the paint she was using—and that it contained some powerful toxicant.

Thus concludes my tale of an evening out at the Alversons'. Their dinner may be simple fare—but I must admit they provide one hell of a floor show.

Tons of love,
Dad

. . . Friday . . .

It is December. The day is hot and dry. I watch the "garden boy" connect the hose and wonder about Rre Segatlhe's field. In Gaborone it is time for expatriates to recreate their Christmas rituals. At the shopping mall, they buy cards, plastic trees, and felt stockings. A cardboard Santa with fur trim and beard smiles through the store window into a sweltering heat. People party by their pools, and children shine, pedaling bright cycles down the back roads. In our yard, Keith and Brian trim a thorn tree. Content to forget about Santa (there's no snow for his sleigh), we feast on Christmas Day.

Tomorrow we leave. Packed bags in the hallway, we have one place to go on this, our last day in Botswana. John Hunter has lent us his Peugeot. We drive out of Gaborone, turn off the main road to Mochudi, and swing open the creaky cattle gate. Heading straight for the setting sun, we bounce along the rutted, dusty road.

He sits motionless as we approach. The air is still. Not even a calling bird breaks the silence. We enter the lolwapa. The walls are crumbling. The floor is broken up. I want to reach for the broom.

He rises to greet us, and we listen to his heavy boots thud across the floor to get us chairs. Suzy wags her tail with recognition, sniffs and licks at our legs, and settles her skeletal self at Keith's feet.

"Christmas for you!" Hoyt hands him a bottle of brandy.

"*Oo-loo-loo! Oo-loo-loo! Ke metse a kgosi!* [It is the water for kings!]

"You are living alone?"

"*Ee*," he responds. "Look at the field. Rain will come. There will be a good harvest!"

We turn toward the beauty of Botswana: his field, rows and rows of straight, green cornstalks. Behind it, the sun slips away, and against a red sky the lonely mountain turns black. "I will throw the bones," he says.

They spill out of his pouch onto the lolwapa floor. He bends over to read them.

"It is good," he simply says.

"What is good?" I venture to ask.

"We can be happy. This moment will come again. You will sit in this lolwapa, on this chair, and look into my eyes again. I will be still an old man, a madala . . . and some years closer to the Badimo. It will be another time, but the same place and the same moment.

As the bones told it.

16

Return: As the Bones Told It

"Did I live under this big sky?"

"Yes, Brian. Once upon a time."

"I remember," says Keith. "My name was *Tsotsi*."

"What was my name?"

"What was Brian's name, Mom?" his older brother asks.

"Madala."

"Mom, what's Madala mean?" they both demand.

"Mom?"

"Dad?"

Hoyt and I, lost in memories as the train travels through Botswana, look out to thorny bushes, grassy plains, and desert sand; an occasional tree lends meager shade to a herd boy and his goats.

"Do you remember Moremi?" I ask Keith.

Low hills, like rugged mountains, rise suddenly from the utterly flat terrain. Huts and kraals repeat in miniature the mountain shape. Footpaths wind between bushes from hut to hut, to the lands, to town. Shadows grow long. We shield our eyes from a blinding sun as the iron snake turns toward Gaborone.

After six years our family returns to Botswana, the place of Rre Segatlhe's lolwapa.

Botswana is not a mystery. It's not just anywhere, tucked into the African continent. Botswana appears on the TV screen every-time there is a news release on one of its neighbors in Southern Africa; and landlocked, as it is, between political "hot spots"— South Africa, Namibia, The Caprivi Strip, Zambia, and Zim-babwe—this occurs fairly often. Occasionally we will pick up a newspaper and see its familiar outline, like the size and shape of

Texas on display. Editorials have described Botswana as an "ideal African democracy," as "an African country coping with drought." International organizations cite Botswana as a model to solve problems of world food production, for despite its drought, cattle production has increased and agricultural research still hopes for goals of self-reliance. Botswana has been described on financial pages as a country of "tremendous mineral wealth and beneficial investment potential."

The capital town of Gaborone thrives. It has expanded to city proportions. There are new highrise office buildings, new banks, new churches. The road from Gaborone to Francistown is being paved! There is talk of a new airport. Where will they build it? Perhaps out Khaphamadi way, in a place called Sebele. Take the paved road to the BAC and there is a new medical clinic. Even rural schools, like Boitumelo School, have new additions: flush toilets. Construction work abounds in and around Gaborone.

We walk on streets in search of names and faces we remember and cross on broken pavement; we cover our ears to seal out clangs of crashing metal. "Look down!" Hoyt alerts us through the clatter. Around the foundation site, tossed in the rubble of urban waste, are the remnants of another time. As rubbish, Stone Age rock cores and shavings lie scattered in the dust. Cast off are the hand axe, the spearhead, and cleaver, strewn like chunks of concrete among the twists of rusted wire. Crumpled papers fly in fine, powdered dust. We shield our eyes and walk on gingerly.

"You see, Modise, we have made quite some progress!" Neo proclaims at the steps of his government office.

"I am living in Gaborone now—in my own home! And you know that I have married. My wife also has a good job. One child is in school already! . . . Yes, it is truly regrettable that my children do not know the lands. Of course, I truly believe they must also learn the rural wisdom, and it is for this reason that I have made a decision: when they are older, they will visit their grandparents every other weekend. My father, Keokilwe, will teach my son to slaughter the goat. Truly, this is what I have decided."

"And where is your brother, Sejaro?" I ask.

Perhaps he does not hear my voice over the noise of construction. Neo does not reply, but turns to me, "You must go to the lands . . . my mother, Ntatabo, will dance with joy to see you again!"

The expatriates we once knew have been replaced by others, all, that is, except Dr. Milne, whom we bump into in front of the town public library. He continues to teach veterinary medicine.

"Your Segatlhe never did seek me out," he complains. "Too bad. Heard—indirectly and too late—of the fate of his goat herd: every one of them was lost to sudden disease. Too bad, really," he shakes his head.

"Modise! Modise! You are back to Botswana!" Kebi exclaims. "*Ke a leboga.* I am well. I am at Technical School. It is because of the good Mr. and Mrs. Miller. They send money. Their church in Vermont sends Christmas to the village. Please, when you see them, tell them we dream they will come back."

Memories can linger, and they can haunt the walls of a fortress. There is one attaché that the American Embassy in Gaborone cannot forget. His picture flashed across the world press, *Time* and *Newsweek*. Like Tswana oral tradition, the story of Brad Bishop is passed on to each succeeding American representative. Brad Bishop left his suburban U.S.A. home, taking with him the corpses of his wife, Annette, his mother, and his three sons. The bodies, brutally bludgeoned to death, were found in a sandpit, but Brad Bishop, whose car was found in the Tennessee woods, disappeared. Speculations as to his fate and whereabouts continue.

"I never made it to the contest," Naledi laments. "I was ill in hospital when they chose Miss Botswana." She is with her husband and infant son. They live in Mochudi, not far from her mother's place. Her husband is a school teacher, and they are just starting a family. Her grandmother, the potter? She died. There is a museum on Phutadikabo Hill. Her pot is in a showcase.

"MaoKeef! MaoKeef!" Except for his broad smile of shining, white teeth, we would not recognize him. His voice is deep, his chest broad; Raus has grown to manhood. He is between jobs, he says, and will find a job tomorrow. No, he has not yet married. He has a friend; they live together on a back road in town. He walks the street, wearing a fine tweed jacket, and bids us a cheerful good-bye.

We follow the dirt road to Old Naledi and the squatters' section of town. The dirt road narrows. We are pressed between hovels, cluttered with garbage. The air is foul. A woman is crying. A drunkard staggers into our path. Children scavenge the ditch for soda cans. Green bushes grow near a lolwapa wall. It is MaMoremi's place. The lolwapa looks lovely: the walls are hard and smooth, the floor is smeared with style; rows of cabbage grow nearby. I see her coming out of the hut. We stare at one another one brief moment before recognition. *"Ow! Ow!"* All is for the better: there is a regular family income. Moremi left school after standard 3 to work for a construction crew in Gaborone. He likes to build. Morwadi and her sister, now also with child, work on a nearby farm. The little ones, Leraka and Elina, go to school! Yes, the old mother is still with us—see the walls, see the floor! We are, by now, surrounded by MaMoremi's curious neighbors, and MaMoremi fetches kadi to sell for this occasion.

His English name is Richard, MaMoremi has told us. We will find him in the Office of Government Statistics. We enter the complex of new government buildings and ask the guard: "We are looking for a young Tswana man named Richard. Can you please help us?" The Tswana guard thinks carefully, but only repeats the name, "Richard?" We cross the walkway toward the adjacent building and find another guard. "Richard. Yes! You must go that way, over there. Take those stairs to the second floor. He is with the computers." Lekoto sits behind a large wooden desk in a computer room. *Oo-loo-loo!"* Yes, he finished school successfully in Lobatse. We tour his office, meet his colleagues, admire his work.

"No, I do not live here in town," says Lekoto. "I have my own little room in a two-room concrete house on the grounds of the BAC. I share this place with a friend. I cycle to work every day. I cannot live in town because it is too expensive. True, my salary is good, but it is not for me alone. Do you know two of my sisters are now in school?! And have you heard the news? My parents had another baby—last year—a boy! Yes, truly! Modise, MaoKeef, you must go to the lands to see them!"

The main road north of Gaborone is paved all the way to Sebele, but leave the paved road and head west, and the gate creaks as ever and still does not swing shut. The ruts in the road are deeper, wider. All else is the same. Except for Maria and Molefi's place, every path, every household, every kraal and field looks just as it was.

Maria Malomo is pounding grain in her lolwapa. She proudly tells us that she is completing her sixth year at school. Soon she will take the exams for high school. She intends to do well, but where will she find the money to pay the high tuition? Have we heard from poor Joseph Pulanka who used to ride Tsotsi to school on his bicycle? He was caught breaking into the expatriate home at BAC where his mother washed clothes. They sent him to prison for six years. They locked him up with criminals. He is so ashamed of what he did. The worst of it is that he cannot finish school . . . and there is nothing for him to return to at home.

Tabo and Polwane show us their one-year-old son.

"Mosimanegape, our fine cattle herder of a son, died . . . it was three years ago. He is buried there." They point to the field. Gomolemo calls to her child to greet us. Still there is no husband; she continues to live with her parents. It is a help. The little ones, Gobuamang and Leta, can now go to school! Lekoto has a fine job in town and sends money home. And Tiro has just come home from the South African mines. He wears shoes. Sejaro went with him. They both say it is rough, but they will go again one more time. The mines are money for cattle. Did we hear of Number 19?

Seipate stares with the toothpick hanging from her mouth. She squints to focus better. She sees us. We hug; she backs away; we hug again. "All is as it was," she says. "You missed the wedding—that boy, Moses, finally married Lesego! They live at his place. My mother died just before the wedding . . . and the peacock, he never came home: he died in the mine."

With Seipate, we walk to Maria and Molefi's place. Maria ululates as we approach. It is marvelously high and shrill. She runs to me. We cry as we embrace. She pulls me around the lolwapa. "See here, Mariga holds my new grandson! . . . This way, come . . . Tladi has built a concrete-block house!" Incredible. Molefi crosses the field. He is old. He is a madala, like his friend Segatlhe. Segatlhe lives alone. Manaka left him five years ago to become a Tsotsi in town.

Rre Segatlhe sees us coming, waits motionless for our approach. It was as he expected. He knows his bones. He holds his Madala, grown twice as tall. "Tsotsi, it is as it had to be," he gently tries to explain. "I had to shoot your Suzy. She just could not live like a Tswana dog."

Postscript

John Hunter, our Canadian friend, is back in Botswana for a second term, this time as director of the Institute for Development Management. He writes to us:

Dear Marianne and Hoyt,

Unanswered letters are piling up around me. But I have my priorities. You shall have an immediate (well almost immediate) answer to yours despite its lack of seniority. . . .

As for your request to find your Rre Segatlhe and let you know how he's doing. I'm sorry, but I cannot help you. As you may or may not know, Gaborone has a new, very fancy airport (which it doesn't need). It was built smack on old Segatlhe's lands. The government relocated all the villagers thirty kilometers or so to the north. Segatlhe is not there. His friends say he is still alive but do not know where he is. The new airport and its little used runways have swallowed up all of Segatlhe's lands and, in some mysterious fashion, seem to have swallowed up Segatlhe as well. The old man is gone, and the village you loved is no more.

Write. And give my best to Keith and Brian.

Love,
John

Glossary

Apartheid   South African term for its system of racial segregation and domination by whites.

Badimo   Spirits or ancestors.

Bakgalagadi (plural); **Mokgalagadi** (sing.)   Member(s) of a Tswana tribal group, known for subordinate status, now living in or near the Kalahari Desert

Basarwa   Setswana term for "Bushmen" of the Kalahari Desert, known as "San" in anthropological literature.

Biltong   Afrikaans term for jerky or dried meat.

Boers   (Afrikaans word for "farmers") Among Tswana, a generic term for all whites in South Africa; Boers here refers to Afrikaners and English who collaborate in any way to support apartheid.

Bogadi   "Bride price"; wealth transferred from groom's family to that of bride upon marriage.

Bojalwa   Beer made from sorghum.

Boloko   Cow manure.

Bomma (plural)   Mothers, women.

Chungalooloo   Zulu word for millipede; Rre Segatlhe preferred, and we adopted, this Zulu term rather than the Setswana word for millipede, Sebokolodi.

Dumela, Rra (to man); **Dumela, Mma** (to woman); **Dumelang, Bomma** (to women); **Dumelang, Borra** (to men); **Dumelang, Bana** (to children)   General greeting equivalent to "hello" or "greetings" used any time of day.

Dumela, Rra, o tlhotse jang?   Hello, father (Sir). How are you this afternoon?

Ee   Yes [pronounced "ay" as in "say"].

E kae?   Where is it?

Ee, le nna, ke ithumetse thata   Yes, I, too, am very happy.

Ee, o itse sentle   Yes, he/she knows it well, (understands).

Ga e yo   There is none.

Ga ke na kadi   I don't have any kadi.

Ga re itse sentle gore o batla eng   We do not know exactly what (it is) you want.

Go dila boloko   To smear a floor or build a wall with a mixture of dung, earth, and water.

Go monate   Delightful; It's nice, sweet, delicious. To give pleasure (generically, or for food).

Go siame   It's all right, fine.

(Ka) Goreng?   Why?

Kadi   Homebrewed beer made from the kadi root.

Ke   Pronoun, first person singular; also used with a different tone to express: "It is."

Ke a leboga   I praise you; I am thankful; thank you.

Ke batla lifti   ("Lifti" from English) I want a lift.

Ke eng?   What is it? What's the matter?

Ke itumetse   I am happy; also used to express thankfulness.

Ke itumetse, thata   I'm very happy.

Ke kopa   I ask/beg for.

Ke mosadi mogolo   I am an old woman.

Ke tsogile. Wena o kae?   Response to a morning greeting: I'm fine (literally, "I rose well"). How are you?

Kgalagadi   Kalahari Desert

Kgotla   Tribal governing assembly convened often to try legal cases.

Kraal   Corral, enclosure for keeping goats, sheep, cattle.

Le kae?   How's it going? How are you all?

Lekgoa (singular)   White one.

Lolwapa   Courtyard enclosed by wall and huts of the family compound.

Madala   Zulu term for the oldest of men.

Makgoa (plural)   White ones.

Merogo   Edible greens.

Mma (sing.)   Mother, woman.

Mmereko   Wage-paying work.

Modimo   God.

Mokete   Celebration, as in a feast and party.

Monna mogolo   Old man.

Mosadi (sing.); **Basadi** (plural)   Woman; women.

Mosadi mogolo   Old woman.

Mosimane   Boy.

Motse, Kika   Large, wooden mortar and pestal used to pound grain.

Mpha   To give, as in "mpha Kadi" [give me beer], pronounced "mpa."

Mpho   Gift, Pronounced "mpo."

Nna fatshe   Take a seat, sit down.

O tlhotse jang?   How have you been spending time? How have you been? (Greeting used in the afternoon.)

O tsogile jang? (sing.); **le/lo tsogile jang?** (plural)   How have you arisen? How are you? (Greeting used in the morning.)

Opela le bina   Sing and dance.

Pathe   Goatskin mat.

Pula   Rain.

Re batla se ga metse   We want (something) to draw water.

Robalang sentle, bana   Sleep well, children.

Rre   My father (contraction of "rra," father and "wame," my).

Rra, ntshwarele, Rra, ga ke na madi   Sir, excuse me, Sir, I don't have any money.

Rondavel   Round hut with thatched roof (from Afrikaans).

Ruri   Truly, for sure.

Sala sentle (sing.); **Salang sentle** (plural)   Good-bye, stay well.

Sarankure   Stringed instrument made of flattened tin can and attached fingerboard with string(s) which is bowed or plucked.

Shebeens   A public place to drink liquor. (Gaelic term used in Southern Africa).

Skumba kwa toropong   Shuffle to town.

Tiro   Work, deed in traditional culture. No implication of wage labor.

Tsaba Ntsha   Beware of dog.

Tsamayang!   (You all) Go! Get out of here!

Tsamayang pila   Go well, Good-bye.

Tsamaya sentle (sing.); **Tsamayang sentle** (plural)   Go well, Good-bye.

Tsotsi   Street kid; brash, ill-mannered, cunning, urban hustler.

Tula baby robala   Hush baby, go to sleep.

A Note on the Setswana Language

The Setswana language has nine "classes" of nouns, unlike most Indo-European languages where there are two or three classes: masculine, feminine, and sometimes neuter. In Setswana the class of a noun and whether it is singular or plural is indicated by a prefix before the noun. The word, Tswana, for example, can be placed in several different classes by the prefix that is added to it:

Setswana means language or culture, tradition, ideas of Tswana;
Botswana means the place of the Tswana, i.e. the country;
Motswana means a Tswana person;
Batswana means Tswana persons.

The word for woman is mosadi, for women, basadi. Man is monna, men, banna.

While the characters for representing written Setswana are taken from the Latin alphabet, many Tswana speech-sounds have no close counterparts in English or any other Indo-European language. Below is an attempt to give a rough guide to pronouncing Setswana words that the reader will encounter in this text.

Vowels	Example of Similar English Sound
a	"a" as in father or ah
e	"i" as in bin, or "e" as in bet or eh
ee	"ay" as in hay
i	"ee" as in beet
o	"u" as in put, or "o" as in boat
u	"oo" as in boot

Consonants

g	"ch" as in Scottish word for lake, lo*ch* or German expression a*ch*
kg	similar to "ch" as in lo*ch* or a*ch*, but with greater force and expulsion of air
h	a silent consonant, indicating only that the preceding consonant be articulated with a distinct puff of air
kh	"c" as in *c*ub
ph	"p" as in *p*ub
sh	"s" as in *s*ip
th	"t" as in *t*ub
r	trilled "r" as in Spanish pe*rr*o
tl or tlh	"tl" as in bo*ttl*e
ts	"ts" as in hi*ts*
tsh	"ts" as in min*ts* or "tch" as in hi*tch*

The stress in pronunciation is almost always on the second to the last syllable of words with two or more syllables.

Pronunciations of Some Words Used in the Text

ee	"AY"
kadi	"KAH-dee"
lolwapa	"lo-LWAH-pah"
Madala	"mah-DAH-lah"
makgoa	"mah-KGO-ah" ("KG" as indicated, like a*ch* or lo*ch*).
Mariga	"mah-REE-gah" ("g" as indicated, like a*ch* or lo*ch*).
Modise	"mo-DEE-seh"
mogolo	"mo-GO-lo" ("g" as indicated above)
Montsho	"MOO-nn-tsoo"
Mosadi	"mo-SAH-dee"
pula	"POO-lah"
Segatlhe	"seh-GAH-tlee" ("G" as indicated above, like "ch" in lo*ch*)
Seipati	"seh-ee-PAH-tee"
Tladi	"TLAH-dee"
Tiro	"TEE-ro"
dumela	"doo-MEH-lah"
mpho; mpha	"MM-po"; "MM-pa"